DENUCLEARIZATION AND PEACE ON THE KOREAN PENINSULA

Edited by Peter Hayes and Chung-in Moon

YONSEI UNIVERSITY PRESS

Denuclearization and
Peace on the Korean Peninsula
Edited by Peter Hayes and Chung-in Moon

Published in the Republic of Korea
by Yonsei University Press
50 Yonsei-ro, Seodemun-gu, Seoul 120-749. Korea
Tel: +82 2 2123-3380~2 Fax: +82 2 2123 8673

ISBN 978-89-6850-136-4 (93340)

YONSEI UNIVERSITY PRESS

CONTENTS

INTRODUCTION

Peter Hayes and Chung-in Moon

In 2014, the situation on the Korean Peninsula looked bleak. North Korea had conducted 3 nuclear tests, completed long-range rocket tests, and initiated major conventional overt and covert military incidents between North and South Korea.The DPRK's new leader, Kim Jong-Un, unleashed an extraordinary campaign of nuclear threats in the February-April 2013 period, matched by major military exercises and deployment of nuclear-capable bombers by the United States and the ROK.

Such a cycle of escalation and lethal threats is not new in the Korean Peninsula. Indeed, the two Koreas entered on just such a cycle in the late nineties. In response to his willingness to engage in dialogue with the DPRK's leader Kim Jong-Il, President Kim Dae-Jung participated in the June 2000 Summit in Pyongyang, signing a number of historic agreements with the North. For his efforts to reverse the cycle of nuclear threat and to overcome the division of the two Koreas by seeking peace and reconciliation with the DPRK, the Nobel Committee awarded him the Nobel Peace Prize.

In 2014, nearly a decade and a half later, democracy and human rights in the ROK itself are challenged again by polarization and social conflict while the rift between Seoul and Pyongyang is widening, not closing. Given this situation, the Kim Dae Jung Presidential Library with the support of many senior political and intellectual leaders in the ROK convened a conference on denuclearization and peace on the Korean Peninsula. This volume contains the contributions to this workshop by leading experts on these subjects from the ROK and abroad and sheds light on what must be done to realize a nuclear-free and peaceful Korea and Northeast Asian region.

****

The book is organized in three sections. The first sets out to understand the nuclear quagmire in Korea and the region. The second enquires and outlines ways out of this quagmire and to solve the nuclear problem peacefully in Korea and the region. The third examines the extraordinary contribution to this agenda by President Kim Dae-Jung, and how his approach should inform future diplomacy to resolve peacefully the nuclear issue in Korea and beyond while promoting reconciliation between the two Koreas.

The starting point for any examination of the risk of war and nuclear war today in the region is Korea, specifically, North Korea. In chapter one, Choon-geun Lee assesses the DPRK's nuclear weapons capability. Lee traces the origins of this capability back to the nineteen fifties when Kim Il-Sung ordered the creation of a basic nuclear research and education at Kim Il Sung University in 1955 and training of many North Koreans in the Soviet Union and East Europe in fundamental physics. By the seventies, the DPRK had begun to establish a self-reliant nuclear fuel cycle and began to develop its uranium resources while deepening its skill base by creating a college of nuclear physics at Kim Chaek University. By the mid-eighties, the DPRK began to explore a dual track, the construction of a power reactor, and the acquisition of nuclear weapons capabilities. By 1987, it was evident that it was constructing a reactor that could produce plutonium suitable for weapons and in the early nineties, was also conducting fundamental research into developing an enrichment capability—again, a dual-use item. After a slow-motion, incremental process of operating, freezing, disabling, restoring, and expanding all these capabilities in the period of the US-DPRK Agreed Framework, from 1994-2002, the DPRK obtained all the necessary elements of a nuclear weapon, now tested three times.Although its nuclear weapons may be affected by shortages of various components and materials, as is typically the case with the North, it found ways to improvise and work around these deficits to produce working nuclear devices. In the same manner, we can anticipate that it will miniaturize warheads sufficiently to fit onto short, medium, and (when available) long-range missiles and bombers. Lee concludes that the DPRK's nuclear weapons momentum based on self-reliance faces no insuperable technical obstacles, given time.

Given the dire implications of the DPRK proceeding to deepen and expand its nuclear weapons, in chapter two Peter Hayes and Chung-in Moon examine whether South Korea should therefore itself acquire nuclear weapons. They note that all policies and strategies of the United States and the ROK have failed to stop North Korean nuclear armament, and that unsurprisingly, voices in the South are now calling for the ROK to develop and deploy its own nuclear weapons or for the United States to re-deploy tactical nuclear weapons withdrawn in 1992 back to South Korea. They note that public opinion favors an independent nuclear force, but not when it puts the US-ROK alliance at threat. In light of the calls by various politicians and security intellectuals in Seoul to pursue one of these two options, they examine in detail the political and military impacts that implementing them would have on the ROK, inter-Korean political and military relations, and on regional security. A careful examination of the pros and cons of each option leads them to conclude, in contrast to voices in favor of South Korean nuclear armament, that the nuclear weapons option, be it by domestic development or by re-deployment of US tactical nuclear weapons, is neither feasible nor desirable for South Korea. This is due above all to severe political, legal, and institutional obstacles that would block Seoul from making nuclear weapons. But is also follows from the considerable military disadvantages of relying on nuclear weapons both for symbolic threat and for military deterrence or defensive purposes.Moreover, they find that conventional weapons can fulfill all conceivable military contingencies that face the ROK in a war with the

DPRK, and that residual nuclear deterrence derived from US home-based nuclear weapons suffices to offset DPRK nuclear threat projection against the ROK and other parties. They conclude that the ROK should instead stick with the alliance, place primary emphasis on conventional deterrence with a measured upgrade of specific capabilities to offset DPRK asymmetric strategic options; and reinforce and deepen the ROK's non-nuclear national narrative when it comes to nuclear weapons in order to contrast it with the DPRK's crude nuclear threat projection that reveals its strategic weakness.

Their argument leads naturally to the question of China's role in reigning in and reversing the DPRK's nuclear breakout. In chapter 3, Hua Han examines the potential nuclear proliferation effects of continued North Korea nuclear testing and armament. Han points out that some of the alarmist arguments that the DPRK's proliferation will drive Japanese and/or South Korean nuclear proliferation are over-stated and derive from domestic politics in these two US allied states, or from a US desire to exploit the DPRK nuclear threat to justify deployments that may in fact be aimed at China more than the DPRK. Given that American nuclear deterrence and its extension to US allies remain strong, she is skeptical that the North's proliferation will have dire consequences for regional security. However, in a tantalizing brief reference, she suggests that a regional mechanism and dialogue to solve the nuclear problems of this region and to maintain regional stability is badly needed.

The underlying capacity for nuclear proliferation is acquisition of a nuclear fuel cycle. In chapter 4, Won-young Yang Lee reviews the impact of the March 11, 2011 Fukushima catastrophe on the future prospects for nuclear power in Northeast Asia. Until this accident, Japan was a global leader in development and expansion of nuclear power. The fact that such an accident can occur in Japan led China, South Korea, and many other states to review their nuclear power commitment, to suspend pending licensing and construction, and to reconsider their overall mix of fuel supply technologies for realization of energy security. Although China plans to expand its nuclear power reactor fleet very quickly, under any scenario, nuclear power will be a relatively small contributor to its total generating capacity, and an accident in China could easily disrupt this program. South Korea faces siting and other constraints to further expansion of nuclear power, and only slow growth can be anticipated. Japan itself will likely restart a fraction of its power plants, but energy conservation and renewables may displace much of its nuclear power over the coming decades. In short, according to Yang Lee, the momentum for rapid nuclear power growth has been setback severely in Northeast Asia, and may never recover fully.

Given these apparently unstoppable trends, what can be done to solve these complex problems?

In chapter five, Hiromichi Umebayashi outlines the origins and conceptual basis of a Northeast Asia Nuclear Weapons-Free Zone (NEA-NWFZ). This zone would aim to reverse the DPRK's on-going nuclear armament as the countervailing military response by Japan, the ROK, and the United States, especially via US nuclear extended deterrence; prevent a nuclear arms race between all these states; and establish the institutional foundations for a NEA-NWFZ, including verification and possible side agreements on energy security as a first step towards building cooperative security in the region. Umebayashi reviews the various forms that a NEA-NWFZ could take, but favors the three plus three formulation whereby the two Koreas and Japan form the non-nuclear core; and the nuclear weapons state guarantee their non-nuclear status and freedom from the risk of nuclear attack. He proposes that it is time to begin drafting a regional comprehensive security agreement that would include this zone plus other necessary conditions, to start a regional dialogue between states that would move it from concept to action.

In chapter six, Peter Hayes outlines how a regional NEA-NWFZ could bring about an end to nuclear threat projected by nuclear-armed states in the region, including North Korea. He explains how the DPRK might participate in such a zone from the outset. He also addresses the thorny issue of nuclear extended deterrence in the region, and suggests that it is possible to end nuclear threats by nuclear weapons states in the region against non-nuclear weapons states by creating the zone—but maintaining strategic deterrence between the nuclear weapons states should one of them threaten to use or attack a non-nuclear weapons state party to the zone, or should one of the latter party to the treaty break out and proliferate nuclear weapons. Hayes concludes that such a zone is the only way to manage, reduce, and eventually abolish nuclear threat in Northeast Asia, including those aimed at and coming from the DPRK.

In chapter seven, Yoon-won Park describes the possible regional cooperation agenda to strengthen nuclear safety in Northeast Asia in the aftermath of the 2011 Fukushima disaster. Park admits that post-Fukushima cooperation between Japan, the ROK, and China remains at a rudimentary level. However, it is possible that the trilateral Top Regulators' Meeting (TRM) launched in 2008 could become a substantive communication and coordination mechanism. Since Fukushima, each country has strengthened its nuclear safety management and regulatory framework, but transparency is still insufficient in all countries, but especially in China, to secure the trust and confidence public given the impact of the Fukushima event. He proposes a variety of ways that the TRM could play a more productive role as a consultative body including setting common safety standards and developing emergency coordination and assistance action plans in the event of another nuclear power safety crisis.

In chapter eight, Wooksik Cheong explains forthrightly that the US and ROK governments have failed completely to arrest the DPRK nuclear weapons program. He argues that the allies must adopt a new approach that would show the DPRK that it would gain much more by abandoning nuclear weapons than by keeping them. This approach entails addressing the core conflict issues that drive North Korean threat perceptions, and converting the armistice regime in Korea into a peace regime, based on trust-building and institutionalized cooperation that embeds their interests into interdependence with the DPRK.

In chapter nine, Taeho Kang revisits the sorry story of the Six-Party Talks. Kang argues that because increased military pressure and sanctions have done nothing but accelerate the DPRK's nuclear weapons program, it is essential to adopt a new approach that addresses the North's core security concerns directly, not just the nuclear issue. Direct dialogue with the DPRK's leaders is the only way to re-introduce them into international society and diplomatic negotiations to realize peace and end their nuclear weapons program. Many years of talks have led nowhere, but it is critical to reactivate dialogue in search of an end-game that is actually implemented by all parties.

In chapter ten, Gareth Evans considers the lessons learned from Kim Dae-Jung's contributions to overcoming apparently insurmountable obstacles to avoiding war, reducing and abolishing dependence on nuclear threat, and constructing peace, starting with Korea. Evans calls this "being on the right side of history in North East Asia generally and on the Korean Peninsula in particular." He suggests that first and foremost, leaders must adopt a cooperative security approach to the general geopolitics of North East Asia; second, make achieving nuclear disarmament a vital national security interest; and third, achieve a nuclear free and sustainably peaceful Korean Peninsula. For Koreans, he avers, this approach means not acquiring nuclear weapons. Rather, Koreans must figure out how to achieve a nuclear free and sustainably peaceful Korean Peninsula.This imperative demands that Koreans must avoid conflict between North and South, and create the conditions for peaceful unification; reverse North Korea's nuclear weapons program and denuclearize the peninsula; and redress the atrocious crimes and other indefensible human rights violations occurring in the North.

To effect these policy goals requires a comprehensive approach such as that proposed by Morton Halperin, which involves a new Treaty on Peace and Security in North East Asia with the following elements: termination of the state of war in Korea; a permanent monitoring council; mutual declaration of no hostile intent; provisions of assistance for nuclear and other energy; and, most ambitiously, establishment of a North East Asia Nuclear Weapons-Free Zone, embracing both Koreas and Japan, which all the NPT nuclear-weapon states would agree to abide by. Protection would be given to South Korea and Japan by their having the right within a certain period to withdraw from the Treaty if its denuclearization provisions were not being effectively implemented. Such an approach accords with the vision that drove Kim Dae-Jung's great initiatives, including ensuring massive South Korean investment in China that endows it with substantial influence in China's policy toward the DPRK; the Kaesong industrial zone, which is the first arms control measure to affect territory controlled by the North Korean military—an unspoken strategic achievement far more important than the economic benefits to both Koreas of the zone's operations; and the political breakthrough and agreements struck at his June 2000 summit with Kim Jong-Il.

"He was," concludes Evans, "a man who in everything he said and did was on the right side of history."

****

These ten chapters provide the reader with an excellent introduction to the deep structure of the nuclear and security issues that divide the region and make the inter-Korean conflict so intractable and dangerous. As the authors on the practical agendas for conflict resolution and constructive peace-building argue in section II, it is possible to envision pathways out of the quagmires and gridlocks that have brought dialogue and diplomacy to a near stand-still. However, as Gareth Evans argues in the concluding chapter, it will require leadership that is currently missing in all states party to the Korean and nuclear conflict in Northeast Asia.

We hope that this book will help these leaders, their advisors, and policy makers in all realms of state, market, and civil society, to find their own pathways whereby they may contribute to the realization of cooperative security in this region, to inter-Korean reconciliation, and to reducing and eventually abolishing nuclear threat. The publication of this book would have not been possible without devotion and hard work of staffs of the Kim Dae-jung Library. We would like to express our cordial thanks to its entire staff. Our special gratitude goes to Won-Tae Koh who handled most of administrative and editorial works in turning a conference proceeding into an elegant book. We also acknowledge contribution of Shin-ki Chang and Ju-jin Park in organizing the conference. Finally, we are thankful to Wooksik Cheong who volunteered to translate Korean manuscripts into English.

PART I

UNDERSTANDING THE NUCLEAR QUAGMIRE IN KOREA AND NORTHEAST ASIA

CHAPTER 1

ASSESSING NORTH KOREA'S NUCLEAR WEAPONS CAPABILITY[1]

Choon-geun Lee

North Korea's nuclear power has grown consistently by conducting three nuclear experiments, and the country has announced that it has tested small and light-weight nuclear warhead during its latest experiment. This experience suggests that the North is in possession of a small nuclear warhead that can be mounted on missiles. The country, by revealing its large-scale uranium enrichment facility, boasted that it can raise its nuclear storage capacity by vast amounts. Now it is declaring, by mentioning a "new type of atomic experiment, its development of a much more advanced nuclear weaponry."

But the reading of this display of nuclear weapons capacity by neighboring countries are varies according to their key interests and understanding of North Korea. The US interest in international security and nonproliferation is deep and South Korea sees denuclearization, inter-Korean cooperation and unification as key policy issues. China puts emphasis on border security, raising regional influence, North Korea's regime stability and economic recovery and resolving of its energy crisis. Regional players sometimes misunderstand the North's true intentions and stumble in drawing up measures.

[1] A version of this essay in English containing graphics is found at Choon-geun Lee, "Assessing North Korea's Nuclear Weapons Capability," NAPSNet Special Reports, May 11, 2015, http://nautilus.org/napsnet/napsnet-special-reports/assessing-north-koreas-nuclear-weap ons-capability/

A closer and more intricate examination into North Korea is needed to avoid these pitfalls. The history and assessment of the North's nuclear program is revisited by examining the history of the country's science technology and education, as well as its national research development plan and foreign cooperation in areas of science and technology. This review should eliminate any unnecessary debate and provide a detailed forecast of future developments. Even though the results do not drastically differ from the current on-going ones, a more objective observation can be made from inductive analysis.

HISTORY OF NORTH KOREA'S NUCLEAR PROGRAM AND THE COMPLETION OF NUCLEAR FUEL PERIOD

Japanese and Soviet influence

The history of North Korea's nuclear weapons program reaches way back to the Japanese colonial period. Japan's Institute of Natural Science and Chemistry, Riken, discovered a rare earth resource mineral in the current North Korean region. Analysis revealed that about 4-5% of the content was of uranium oxide. When World War II ended, Japan had produced several tons of the mineral and was about to deliver it out of Korea through Incheon. The US military government confiscated the minerals, questioned those concerned and wrote up a top-secret report on the trend of Japan's nuclear research. This paper was declassified a few years ago and made public.[2]

The graphite electrode plant built by a Japanese company in the Hamgyong province during the colonial age also influenced North Korea's nuclear development. The Noguchi business group grew successful by developing and excavating quality graphite mines, and by manufacturing

[2] Jong Hyeok Lim, "The Investigation for radioactive mineral in North Korea by Japanese research institutes at Japanese colonial era," KAST Symposium, July 2007.

goods out of them through state-of-the art production plants. The groundwork for development of graphite moderated reactor using North Korea's natural uranium and graphite was laid during this period.

The Soviet Union, which was in competition with the United States during the Cold War, also showed keen interest in North Korean uranium. Aircraft-based uranium resource exploration, its development and exports was a key area in the Soviet's technical cooperation with North Korea. Kim Il-sung had also emphasized many times on the importance of earning foreign exchange by resource development and its shipments to the Soviet Union. This experience served as momentum for North Korea to send scientists to the Soviet-led bloc for training and the nation's interest in building nuclear related research and facilities.

1950-1960s: Forming the groundwork

Building up the groundwork for North Korea's nuclear development accelerated in the mid-1950s. Kim Il-sung in 1952, in the midst of war, constructed the country's Institute of Science. In the mid-1950s, some three years after post-war recovery, Kim ordered for the initiation of basic nuclear research and manpower cultivation. In 1955, nuclear physics course was set up at the Kim Il Sung University's department of physics and a year later a nuclear physics lab opened up in the Institute of Science's mathematical physics institute. North Korea, around this time, sent an extensive number of researchers to the Soviet Union and East Europe for overseas studies.[3]

Nuclear technology surfaced as one of the core tasks in the state's overall science technology blueprint. This emphasis was due to the fact that nuclear power was recognized as being critical both for military and energy issues. North Korea's first 10-year science development plan in 1957 included research and development of the nation-wide underground resources, including uranium. As ties with the Soviet Union withered in

---

[3] Ho-won Suh, *The Great Leader Kim Il-sung Comrade's Science Technology Guidance*. National Science Institute, 2002.

the 1960s, the plan ended up not being properly fulfilled. But a vast research of the country's resources was executed as planned.

This period was also when the country's first nuclear reactor was built. The IRT-2000, which used enriched uranium as fuel, was constructed in Yongbyon through cooperation with the Soviet Union. The reactor entered operation in 1965, thus allowing a balanced development of the country's nuclear research, personnel training and applied uses. As the Korean peninsula's security situation turned for the worse, Pyongyang established its Military Science Research Institute to embark on high-powered weaponry.

1970s: Establishing the self-reliant nuclear fuel cycle

In the 1970s the world was hit hard by a global oil crisis. North Korea, the energy policy of which centered around coal, further strengthened its domestic-based energy initiatives. Kim Il-sung pushed for a stronger domestic-based energy supply and procurement policy. The country also started examining ways to use its uranium and graphite buried in its land.

The North's science and technology circles in the 1970s, like other fields, also entered a 'test of ideology' phase amid the country's establishment of the 'Monolithic Ideology System of Kim Il Sung' and the 'August 18 Axe murder' incident in 1976. Many scholars and professors in the state research labs and universities were demoted and exiled to regional labor sites. The supreme leader's commands were the ultimate goal that had to be carried out and executed without question. The North then formed the 'Juche Science Technology Revolution Theory' and refocused the country's core research projects from that of basic studies a more production-based applied ones.

Around this time the country began educating highly-skilled scientists to initiate full-scale nuclear development. The newly established Kim Il Sung University's department of physics offered majors in nuclear physics, chemistry and radiation chemistry. In the Kimchaek University of Technology, a college of nuclear physics was set up, housing majors in nuclear materials, nuclear engineering, nuclear reactor design, physical engineering and applied mathematics. The number of graduates in nuclear studies soared.

This time was also when a plethora of nuclear-related books were published. Most were translated works of existing foreign works, but the government's effort to acquire a massive number of books to strengthen its level of nuclear academia and researchers is worth noting. The country joined the IAEA in 1974 to enter a more systematic growth and research of its nuclear program, and hosted many technical assistance missions in uranium and other nuclear development topics.

Early-mid 1980s: From research to production

In the 1980s, North Korea's national economy was paralyzed due in part to a domestic energy crisis. The economic gap between the two Koreas also widened substantially. The fallout from the reform of socialist countries led Kim Il-sung to seriously consider the future path of the country. Apparently, it was around this time when the country began exploring seriously nuclear power not only to power the country but to develop nuclear weaponry. The North, at the 1981 national scientists convention, stressed the importance of nuclear power using home-grown resources. It greatly strengthened research and manpower cultivation.

The country, around this time separated its nuclear development program into basic and applied divisions. Most of the applied branch was moved to Yongbyon. Nuclear-related curriculum at Kimchaek University of Technology was revamped extensively. Within the college of nuclear studies, majors in nuclear material and nuclear physics were retained while other majors — applied mathematics, nuclear engineering — were relocated to basic undergraduate studies. Overseas studies programs were also expanded.

Nuclear research was also divided into to basic and applied branches. Yongbyon was further geared towards applied studies. Noteworthy of the country's two '3-year science technology development plans' were the inclusions of developments of uranium enrichment and fast-breeder reactors using lasers and chemical exchange processes, the reprocessing of used nuclear fuel and processing/handling of nuclear waste.

Uranium enrichment research using lasers seems to have been conducted in a college of sciences under the Academy of sciences in Pyongsong. This particular college housed a laser instrument that was provided by the Chinese scientific community. North Korea seems to have been unsuccessful in reproducing this laser equipment. From the late eighties, nuclear studies continued to appear in the country's state research and development plans. This emphasis, as will be mentioned later, appears to be due to the Yongbyon region as a whole being realigned as part of the military's munitions division. All studies most likely prioritized military use. Related studies became classified as the country's nuclear weapons research pushed further forward.

Mid, late1980s: From energy to weapons

Following this national mobilization, North Korea succeeded in developing the UF6 production process, which is the pre-enrichment phase. In 1986, it began operations of the 5 MWe nuclear reactor and later conducted partial operations of the radiochemistry lab, a reprocessing facility.

Following the construction of reactor in Yongbyon in 1987, full-fledged nuclear arms development began. The command agency was first realigned. The nuclear research institute, which was later reorganized into the nuclear committee, was again expanded into the ministry of nuclear industry, becoming a government body overseeing part of the country's nuclear industry. It was later brought under the ruling party's military munitions division, which oversaw the Yongbyon area's arms research and development.

Related education and agencies were also expanded. The Physics Institution, which was established in 1980 for the education of researchers' reeducation and their children's schooling, was enlarged in the Yongbyon Physics Junior College in late eighties that included a doctoral program. Information pertinent to the college, being a part of the military, was shrouded in secrecy and those from other regions did not know the existence of this place nor were eligible for entry.

The college housed three undergraduate schools, with a total of ten majors. Among these, three were dubbed the 'elite course' dedicated to the gifted students, while the reactor engineering major was a 3.5-year vocational course. Another consisted of a 4.5-year program that included six months of military training. All students received on-the-job training at Yongbyon's production and research facilities. Most of the final semester was spent in the field.

Weapons research was also conducted in and out of Yongybyon. According the ROK Defense Ministry, some 70 high explosive tests were conducted in the area to the west of Yongbyon in hilly areas. Tests on finalized detonation device were also carried out between 1993 and 1998. The country ended up testing its first atomic explosion in the Mantop Mountain regions on October 9, 2006. It was the first pre-announced nuclear test that included the timing and the power of the experiment. Chinese researchers saw this as the manifestation of the North's confidence.

Halt in disablement

We can reexamine the North's disablement process following the agreement sealed on February 13, 2007. Related parties saw the suspension of plutonium production as the most pressing matter. Through negotiation, the parties achieved suspension of fuel processing, reactor and reprocessing facilities. Added to this was the suspension of uranium enrichment using centrifuge and exports to Syria and other rogue nations.

Prioritizing the halt of plutonium was then the most rational choice and the process for some time went fairly smoothly. Following the disablement process, the parties negotiated additional steps, such as the extracting plutonium stocks and used nuclear fuel, dismantling of nuclear arms and test facilities and the termination of the IRT-2000 reactor.

The good start, however, proved not to be sufficient. Six months after the North announced that it had disabled its nuclear facilities, it restarted the 5 MWe reactor. Despite the facility being worn down, it was possible to produce additional weapons-grade plutonium. Signs were detected recently of a possible reopening of the North's radiochemistry laboratory. This signals the additional reprocessing of reactor-produced plutonium.

Uranium enrichment

The North Korean nuclear crisis entered a new phase when the country's foreign ministry issued a statement on April 2009 hinting that it was enriching uranium, with the state officially confirming it in June. The issue, which first surfaced during US special envoy Kelly's visit to Pyongyang on 2002, became a critical development.

Uranium enrichment on North Korean documentation first appeared around the late eighties. The country included the completion of a nuclear fuel cycle in the 1st and 2nd '3-year science technology development plan' and embarked on developing core technologies through enrichment using lasers, reprocessing of used nuclear fuel and disposal of nuclear wastes.

The state science technology development plan is treated as the immutable legal requirement for North Korean officials. Therefore, agencies and responsible scientists must carry out the plan and report on the results. The undisclosed, military area within the blueprint is suspected to have included development of applied nuclear weaponry.

This trend is also seen within the annals of the North's overseas science cooperation. In the nineties, the Chinese Science Institute and the North Korean Science Institute's mechanical engineering lab conducted a joint research into a high-speed centrifuge for biologic use. The lab was North Korea's finest research facility but had received a Chinese centrifuge sample due to a lack of domestic resources. The joint study was suspended after an explosion accident during an experiment.

Pakistan also reportedly provided 20 P-1 centrifuges and schematics for the P2, as well as a tour of their facilities. North Korea reportedly imported 150 tons of high-strength aluminum, enough to build 2,600 centrifuges. Many experts back then, however, saw the aluminum imports as parts for the outer casing of the P-2 centrifuge. Experts believed that the North was not capable of producing the maraging steel used in the rotor. North Korea was seen as having faced an obstacle in its centrifuge development. The country, however, showed American scientist Dr. Hecker in November of 2010 its massive uranium enrichment facility housing 2,000 centrifuges.

NORTH KOREA'S NUCLEAR CAPABILITY

Completion of self-reliant nuclear fuel cycle

North Korea's nuclear weapons development capability currently stands as follows. First, the country, using its own raw materials, succeeded in completing a closed and self-reliant nuclear fuel cycle. It possesses over 20 million tons of uranium resources and is capable of producing 2.9 million tons worth of yellow cake using the refining facility.

The yellow cake is transferred to the Yongbyon nuclear fuel production plan and is converted to uranium metal. It is later turned into aluminum alloy then inserted into the magnox jacket crown to be used as the reactor's nuclear fuel rod. The Yongbyon facility is reported to have a capacity to produce 100 tons of uranium fuel rods annually, which is equivalent to two 5 megawatt-electric(MWe) reactors.

There are currently 2 reactors operating in Yongbyon. The 50 MWe and 200 MWe reactors were suspended since the Geneva Agreed Framework and is currently unsalvageable. The IRT-2000, provided by the Soviet Union, began operations in 1965. It had an initial output of 2 megawatt-thermal(MWt) but the North upgraded it up to 8 MWt. The country uses it for isotope production and research. It uses a small amount of highly-concentrated uranium for fuel.

The graphite moderated reactor, central to the weapons-grade plutonium production, was built in 1986. It was operational until April of 1994 and later went through several shutdowns and re-openings over international sanctions. The cooling tower was blasted as part of its disablement procedure. The North, however, has resumed low-output operations. When equipped with 8,000 nuclear fuel rods, it can proceed about 6-7 kg of weapons-grade plutonium in about a year. This is close to that needed for a single nuclear weapon. The country has reportedly produced about 44-50 kg plutonium at the most. This is equivalent to that needed for some 6-10 nuclear arms.

Spent nuclear fuels are sent to a plant known as a radiation chemical lab. There they are reprocessed and plutonium is extracted for nuclear weapons. The plant is reportedly capable of processing spent fuel produced by the 5 MWe reactor in about 100 days. This plant houses a production line for metallic plutonium.

Construction of a new reactor

Unlike previous graphite moderated reactors, there are new light-water reactors being built. In November 2010, the North showed Dr. Siegfried Hecker its uranium enrichment facilities and its light-water reactor then under construction. The country shows off these facilities as proof of its possession of uranium enrichment facilities.

The North said that the reactor was designed with a 100 MWt heat output and a 30 percent heat efficient. Dr. Hecker estimated that its power output stood at around 25-30 MWe. The reactor is reportedly made via home-grown technology, with self-produced low-enriched uranium to be used as nuclear fuel.

There remain facilities and technology that the North must procure given its lack of international support and use of a different type of reactor. The country is known to have developed a uranium oxide-type nuclear fuel and use cover material made using zirconium alloy or stainless steel. Operational details are yet unknown. A reactor must have facilities and manpower that can tailor and support high temperature and high pressure. It remains to be seen whether the North can successfully build and operate such technology and facility.

David Albright of the ISIS asserted that the reactor can be used in producing weapons-grade plutonium. He believed that with full optimization, the reactor can produce 20 kg of weapons-grade plutonium a year. This amounts to about 3 nuclear weapons worth. The North has begun production of enriched uranium and is capable of reforming the reprocessing plant to also process spend nuclear fuel.

Massive manpower cultivation

North Korea is believed to have produced 7,000 expert-level nuclear personnel and 3,000 nuclear researchers. This can be deduced from the following. The Kim Il Sung University, since the 1950s produced 10 experts a year for 20 years. Since 1973, it has produced 60 a year for over 40 years. This adds up to a total of 2,600. Given the Kim Chaek university ran 5 graduate major courses, it likely produced about 2,800 experts.

We can deduce about 3,000 additional manpower from other educational agencies. The total rises to 8,000. But we must consider the retirees. The mostly highly-trained staff that spent time overseas probably stands at around 250-300. The number of real core personnel involved in nuclear arms is estimated to stand at around 300.

Table 1-1 shows the majors at the Yongbyon Physics Junior College. There are 10 majors or courses within the schools of nuclear material, nuclear electricity and nuclear energy. Among these, three are known as the 'elite course.' The reactor engineering course is a 3.5-year technical college course. Other majors are 4.5-years long and include six months of military training.

<table>
<tr><th>College</th><th>Major</th><th>College</th><th>Major</th></tr>
<tr><td rowspan="4">Nuclear material</td><td>Nuclear material</td><td rowspan="7">Nuclear energy</td><td rowspan="2">Reactor (3.5 years)</td></tr>
<tr><td rowspan="2">Nuclear material (elite course)</td></tr>
<tr><td rowspan="2">Reactor</td></tr>
<tr><td>Nuclear chemistry</td></tr>
<tr><td rowspan="3">Nuclear electricity</td><td>Nuclear measurement</td><td rowspan="2">Reactor (elite course)</td></tr>
<tr><td>Nuclear process</td></tr>
<tr><td>Nuclear process (elite course)</td><td>Molecular physics</td></tr>
</table>

Table 1-1: Yongbyon Physics Junior College's education program

Those enrolling in the elite course go straight to college, without entering the military, after graduating from high school. Having elite courses in all three colleges show how much the North puts emphasis in Yongbyon. All education bodies here utilize the entire Yongbyon region as a training facility. The final semesters are on-the-job training. The country is basically self-cultivating its nuclear related manpower in Yongbyon.

Centrifuge production, uranium enrichment

The North's uranium enrichment capability has gained some attention amid the revelation of its enrichment facility to Hecker. The North, in fact, has accumulated much experience and technical facility relating to uranium enrichment since the 1980s. The Navier-Stokes Equation and other formulaic research projects can be found in its 5-year state science technology plan in the early 2000s and other projects run by state-run research agencies.

The country in May 2009 revealed its P-2 centrifuge during Kim Jong-il's field guidance at a machinery plant in Heechon. A flow-forming machine was later revealed as well. In November 2010, the North showed American scientist Hecker its massive uranium enrichment plant housing 2,000 centrifuges.

This plant consists of two zones and six cascades, with a reported capacity of an annual 8,000 kg SWU or separative work units. The plant enables the North to produce about 40 kgs of enriched uranium, sufficient to build about two nuclear weapons.

A Chinese expert with experience in centrifuge production once noted that North Korea can produce probably up to 1,000 to 1,500 P-2 centrifuges by now. If correct, this asset means that the country can drastically speed up nuclear weapons production when it succeeds in producing weapons-grade highly-enriched uranium.

Existence of a fully-operational uranium plan means that the country probably possesses smaller enrichment technology laboratories and production plants for large-scale centrifuges. It is possible that other enrichment facilities could exist in other places besides Yongbyon. Uranium enrichment facilities use low power levels and can be operated in underground tunnels or sealed buildings, making it hard to find them due to the lack of thermal and other signatures. Assuming the North has additional enriching plants in other regions, David Albright has forecasted that the

North may have 90-220 kgs of weapons-grade enriched uranium. This is equivalent to 4-11 nuclear weapons. Some experts argued that the North used some of these for its third atomic test in 2013. The possibility can't be ruled out given the North's persistent venture into nuclear arms.

Development of weapons-grade nuclear arms

North Korea reportedly produced weapons grade plutonium using a 5 MWe reactor. It is also alleged to have developed and tested an implosive-type nuclear weapon. The level of success can be deduced from the results of the country's three nuclear weapons. Dr. Jungmin Kang, calculated the detonation force based on the readings from the CTBTO and USGS (see Table 1-2).[4]

	CTBTO magnitude (Mb)	USGD magnitude (Mb)	CTBTO blast force (kt)	USGS blast force (kt)
1st (2006)	4.0	4.2	0.5	0.8
2nd (2009)	4.5	4.7	1.8	2.8
3rd (2013)	4.9	5.1	4.5	7.3

Table 1-2: Seismic force, explosion power from the North Korea's underground nuclear tests

But there are many possible sources of error when applying equal seismic force and interaction formula in every situation. This uncertainty arises because the results vary drastically over the type and state of the terrain. Normally the shockwave tend to be bigger when the rocks surrounding the test are harder. It is also larger when the rock has a lower porosity from moisture. The size of the earthquake can be reduced drastically by creating a large vacuum hole in the detonation room

[4] Jungmin Kang, "Denuclearization of North Korea," (paper presented at CSIS-EAI Conference on Korean Unification, Washington DC, December 10, 2014, unpublished.)

The results in Table 1-2 are all based on the assumption that the rocks are hard with lots of moisture. The Korea Institute of Geoscience and Mineral Resources assessed the North's third nuclear test as having a power of 6-7 kilotons also under such assumption. But this calculation is based on a very conservative estimation.

Although the Punggye-ri test site is formed largely of granite, the area may also have large amounts of cracks and soil deposits. Its moisture levels could also be low, leading to high porosity. A measurement of 10-12 kilotons for the third nuclear test would not be far-fetched. This yield would be considered a 'normal' nuclear explosion. The North could be seen as having succeeded in developing weapons-grade nuclear weapons.

The situation may have taken a serious turn if the North used highly-enriched uranium in its third test. Just like China's first atomic test in 1964, if the North uses highly-enriched uranium with an implosive detonative device, the blast force could rise much higher even with a smaller amount of nuclear material. If North Korea uses such method, the North can drastically boost its nuclear arms stockpile and speed up development of its high-capacity nuclear weapon.

Nuclear arms miniaturization

After a successful detonation test, the next step would lead to the development of a miniaturized nuclear warhead. Many experts for the past several years estimated that it would take North Korea several years to develop a miniaturized nuclear warhead. But the US and South Korean military officials have suggested the possibility of the North already having developed miniaturized nuclear warheads. In my view, the North has probably succeeded in this challenge, based on the five following reasons.

First, the North, in terms of nuclear development, fully took advantage of the so-called latecomer's advantage. Decades have passed since the appearance of the first nuclear weapon. The country took note of the developmental path of its predecessors and was able to acquire data from the Soviet Union and China. Its attempt to miniaturize nuclear arms was preceded by a long nuclear weapons development project. Its Scud missiles are designed by the Soviet Union to load nuclear warheads. It is natural for country with a small nuclear production capacity to try to miniaturize its nuclear arms and load it onto its ballistic missile.

Second, the North notified China in 2006 after its first nuclear test that its blast force was 4 kilotons. Its nuclear material use was reportedly 2 kg. Most experts then said that it was impossible for the North to make a small high-capacity nuclear weapon in such short period. The North, against all doubters, set its goal towards developing a miniaturized nuclear weapon, keeping in mind the imperative of loading it onto a missile.

Third, when Pakistan's Abdul Qadeer Kahn visited North Korea in 1999, he was quoted as having witnessed 3 nuclear warheads with a 24 inch diameter and 64 detonators in an underground facility some 2 hours away from Pyongyang. The dimensions are small enough for the weapons to be loaded on missiles. Jang-yop Hwang, the late former North Korean politician who defected to South Korea, also said that the North succeeded in developing small nuclear arms.

Fourth, the country has a history of developing alternative material through the policy of self-reliance. Many experts predicted that the North was incapable of producing cutting-edge material, such as heat-enduring ceramic. But they fail to note that the North's research and development based on the philosophy of self-reliance is quite different from other advanced states abundant with technology and material.

China, two years after its maiden atomic test in 1964, conducted another test using missile warheads made of fiber-glass and other self-made material. North Korea may also have taken such route. In an age when technological progress has skyrocketed and international borders becomng more diluted, many alternatives and secondary options exist.

Lastly, the North may have taken full advantage of its horizontal tunnel labs. Normally, nuclear tests are analyzed by measuring the blast force and nuclear material analysis from air sampling. But in underground lab testing, various equipment can be put in place intricately to individually measure implosion effect, neutrons, gamma ray, and amount of x-rays. This method is referred as a proximity physical measurement.

Testing in sealed underground horizontal labs can produce pure measurements without external interferences. It also allows long-term results from periodical sample readings from test labs. The X-Ray thermodynamic effects that require vacuous settings can only be measured properly in an underground horizontal laboratory.

North Korea is believed to have acquired sufficient measurements and data to overcome and improve upon its three previous nuclear tests in its underground facility. Other nuclear nations have also moved its overground atomic research into more underground settings in order to conduct proximity physical measurements to push the envelope in nuclear technology.

Boosted nuclear arms development

After the third nuclear test, suggestions were made on North Korea possibly testing much more advanced nuclear weapons. One of those was made by the South Korea Defense Ministry. While examining the research trends of the North's science technology field in the early 2000, I also have raised the possibility of the North developing a reinforced nuclear weapon in the near future.[5]

Included in the second '5-year science and technology development plan' were studies on "D(heavy hydrogen) - T(tritium) nuclear fusion," "Separation of Li^6 from natural Li(Lithiun) deposits." Included in three short-term research from the 2010 plan was enriching heavy hydrogen from hydrogen sulfide and water.

State of the art equipment, along with nuclear fusion material such as heavy hydrogen, are required to realize D-T nuclear fusion. Given the situation, it is most unlikely for the North to have these at its disposal. Handling of tritium is especially difficult, as its form is gas and require a reactor for production. It also has a short half life of 12 years.

---

[5] Choon-geun Lee and Jong-seon Kim, "North Korea's Nuclear and Rocket Technology Development and Outlook," (in Korean) *STEPI Insight 22* (2009), http://www.stepi.re.kr/ app/publish/view.jsp?cmsCd=CM0018&categCd=A0501&ntNo=22

The North, therefore, will refer to China's pathway in its way forward, while focusing its energy on its limited resources. One of such efforts may be the development of reinforced nuclear weapons from a D-T atomic fusion, by amalgamating Li and heavy hydrogen into tritium.

Test of such advanced atomic weapon can be done in a lab without an actual nuclear explosion. It is possible by combining high temperature, high pressure plasma and concentrating the explosion on a single point using reflective mirrors to produce an environment of several thousands of degrees in temperature.

China provided North Korea with laser nuclear fusion equipment in the eighties. The North placed this hardware in the facility in Pyongsong and expanded its capacity to boost its test conditions.

The country's scientists in May 2010 announced that they succeeded in nuclear fusion via the *Rodong Sinmun*. Many skeptics said that without highly-sophisticated equipment, such as a Tokamak, a nuclear fusion would be impossible for North Korea. But they failed to notice that there were many ways to achieve nuclear fusion.

The Chinese press blasted North Korea in harsh rhetoric. This is probably from the fact that they knew the North used the China-provided laser nuclear fusion equipment. Further development of nuclear fusion technology would lead to development of reinforced nuclear weapons arms and even hydrogen bombs.

NORTH KOREA'S ENERGY CRISIS AND CASE FOR NUCLEAR DEVELOPMENT

For quite some time, the North has asserted its right to pursue nuclear development for peaceful use. Recently, it has been arguing that its enriched uranium was for use in its self-made light-water reactor. The United States, under the Geneva US-DPRK Agreed Framework, agreed to provide a light-water reactor in Sinpo, North Korea in return for the North giving up nuclear weapons.

The country is, in fact, in a state of national economic crisis, with the energy problem bearing the brunt. This reality can be seen in the country's effort to compensate for its energy deficit by highlighting its need for nuclear power.

The eastern, mountainous regions tend to house a large number of hydro plants, while the industrial, southwestern plain regions have a higher number of thermal plants. The problem of hydro plants, accounting for 40 percent of the country's energy source, is that rainfall drops substantially in winter. The country has established a high-powered electric grid along the boundary dividing the east and west. According to the North's plan, the nuclear power plant in Sinpo, was supposed to provide stable electric power through transmission lines.

But the plan fell through amid the Sinpo reactor construction debacle. The country's thermal energy production also fell after the United States suspended provision of heavy oil (although this was more due to lack of coal and hydro than the scarcity of heavy fuel oil). The North's backlash was fierce, given the economy was hit hard. It was virtually impossible for the North to sustain its regime relying only on domestic thermal and hydro power without international support.

The overall state of the North's energy problem can be characterized as a lack of natural resources and technical supply. This is why the cost of energy production per unit capacity is two to ten times higher on average than advanced states and even higher than the international average. This phenomenon was also common among other former socialist countries.

North Korea, therefore, in tackling its energy crisis, is looking to implement a rational alternative. The country is making technical and economic analysis of its overall energy system, energy flow as well as cost balance calculations. To this end, the North is trying to adopt global energy models and create a rational energy supply plan. Points of consideration are 1) minimum cost, 2) energy efficiency, 3) stability, 4) safety, and 5) cost sharing. The energy supply scenario based such points is shown in Table 1-3. This table shows a long-term blueprint consisting of measures to overcome the immediate crisis and further steps towards sustainability.

A recovery from the immediate energy crisis would take more than ten years. This phase focuses on the state's planned energy consumption and strengthening of control and supervision. The country's energy supply demand policy will be under a much more stricter leash. It will also probably be more interconnected with the nuclear arms development program.

Classification	Recovery Phase	Activation Phase	Sustainability Phase
Applying principle	Safety, National assurance	Minimum cost, stability,cost sharing	Modernization, stability,efficiency
Energy production	Coal mine development, modernization, plant restoration, nuclear introduction	Production based on demand, dispersed generating, small-sized heavy oil generation	Co-development of foreign resource, super critical coal power, compound circulation generation
Energy supply	Planned supply, limited imports	Energy commercialization, energy service company	Energy trade, energy market service
Energy consumption	Planned consumption, Order-based saving, supervision and control	Consumer-based consumption, policy and saving	Consumer consumption, minimal energy and output standardization

Table 1-3: North Korea's energy supply/demand scenario

FORECAST AND IMPLICATIONS

After decades of effort in its nuclear endeavor, North Korea has completed developing its nuclear cycle using homegrown resources. Its nuclear industry has grown substantially. It has developed nuclear armsment which it is strengtheng in size and quality. If the North succeeds in developing weapons-grade enriched uranium and reinforced nuclear arms, it will reach a point where the international community can no longer ignore nor tolerate the North's nuclear capacity and capability.

Success of miniaturization and loading of nuclear warheads onto missiles would be another flash point issue. Many experts until recently could not conceive the notion of the North successfully loading a small-sized nuclear weapon on its missile. They believed the weight and mass was too big, while the means of firing, accuracy and re-entry capability were also insufficient.

In truth, as revealed during the 2010 Yonpyeong shelling, much of the North's conventional weapons have become quite old. Its nuclear weapons also probably lacks in many respects from a lack of parts, resources and technology to support it.

But various signs that appeared recently allow us to see that the country, based on its philosophy of self-reliance, overcame a large part of the obstacles. As South Korea's defense capability isn't sufficient to bear such threat, it is imperative to reassess the North's overall nuclear capability and draw up countermeasures.

South Korea must initiate a much deeper level of study on the North's nuclear-related technology and draw up contingency plans. This strategy should cover not only direct nuclear weapons development but also the country's long-term science and technology blueprint as well. The North's National Science Institute is deeply involved in military research. Basic and mid-to-long-term studies are mostly conducted by the institute and universities.

Also needed are technical interpretation, case studies and policy research into the concept of peaceful nuclear use on the Korean Peninsula. The two Koreas in the early 1990s agreed to make the peninsula free of uranium enrichment and reprocessing facilities. The South kept this promise but the North did not. We need to review our own nuclear policy as well as examine what the implications are for the South arising from theNorth's argument for a peaceful use of nuclear power. The North's nuclear capability and infrastructure must be a key factor in preparations for unification as well contingency measures towards a possible North Korean state of emergency. The Presidential Preparatory Committee for Unification can deliberate on the nuclear cycle assuming a post-unification scenario. The nuclear issue has wider-ranging implications than any other matter and requires a much more comprehensive approach in drawing up countermeasures.

CHAPTER 2

SHOULD SOUTH KOREA GO NUCLEAR?[1]

Peter Hayes and Chung-in Moon

Introduction

Pessimism looms large in South Korea because twenty years of negotiations with the North resulted only in disastrous outcomes. The Six-Party Talks are regarded as a futile enterprise. Military options have long been considered unrealistic, while the Bush administration pursued a hostile neglect strategy that ended as a failure. The strategic patience strategy of the Obama administration has not worked either. Consequently, hard-line military options are favored. Attention is paid to missile defense (MD), especially the architecture of 'kill chain,' which has two important components. One is active defense such as the acquisition of intercept missiles including advanced version of Patriot missiles. The other is offensive defense that is predicated on preemptive surgical strikes even at the risk of conflict escalation. But it would be extremely difficult to reply on preemptive strikes since unlike 1994, targets in North Korea are now concealed. Subsequent escalation and insurmountable collateral damages could be another obstacle to this option. Geopolitics also matters. North Korea is different from Iraq. China, Russia, and even South Korea

[1] Prepared for presentation at an international conference on "Denuclearization and Peace on the Korean Peninsula," organized by the Kim Dae-jung Presidential Library on December 10, 2014. A shorter version appeared as an EAF Policy Brief (July 28th, 2014). Sections of this chapter first appeared in Peter Hayes, and Chung-in Moon. 2015. "Korea: Will South Korea's Non-Nuclear Narrative Defeat North Korea's Nuclear Breakout?" in *The War That Must Never Be Fought: Dilemmas of Nuclear Deterrence*, ed. George P. Shultz and James E. Goodby (Stanford: Hoover Institution Press), 377–435. and is published here with permission; and in Peter Hayes, Chung-in Moon, "Should South Korea Go Nuclear?" *NAPSNet Policy Forum*, July 28, 2014, http://nautilus.org/napsnet/napsnet-policy-forum/should-south-korea-go-nuclear/

would strongly oppose such military actions. Catastrophic consequences of military actions would make the majority of South Koreans opposed to military actions. consequently, a growing number of hardliners in South Korea are raising nuclear deterrence as alternative. The pros and cons of South Korea going nuclear is an important policy question.

Some South Koreans Favor Nuclear Weapons

After North Korea tested a third nuclear device on February 12, 2013, many South Koreans felt helpless, frustrated, even outraged. Their reaction has become quite worrisome. An opinion poll conducted by the Asan Institute for Policy Studies immediately before the test revealed that 66 percent of respondents supported South Korean development of its own nuclear weapons. After the test, over 70 percent of respondents favored nuclear weapons development. If the North undertakes the fourth nuclear test, as it proclaimed, national sentiments in South Korea will only grow. It is precisely because Pyongyang continues to build up its nuclear armory while the Six-Party Talks aimed at dismantling that weapons program are suspended that South Koreans are upset.

Such pro-nuclear attitude is not confined only to the general public. Some political leaders and intellectuals also openly advocate the nuclear option. Mong-joon Chung, seven-term National Assembly member of the ruling Saenuri Party, conservative candidate for Mayor of Seoul, and a front-runner in South Korea's next presidential election, has been one of the most vocal advocates of "go nuclear." *Chosun Ilbo*, the most influential conservative daily newspaper in South Korea, has also campaigned for the nuclear cause. A large number of conservatives and nationalists alike have aligned with nuclear armament. In short, there is growing support for this radical shift in the ROK's political and military posture at popular and elite levels.[2]

---

[2] See D.J. Kim, "S. Korea needs to consider acquiring nuclear weapons," *Chosun Ilbo*, July 10, 2012; G.J. Cho, "South Korea's Nuclear Armament for Self-Defense: Secret Story of Israel's Clandestine Nuclear Weapons Development," *Monthly Chosun*, February 2011; refer also to Mong-joon Chung's remarks: "The nuclear deterrence can be the only answer. We have to have nuclear capability," in K. J. Kwon, "Under

US Nuclear Analysts Examining Implications of South Korean Nuclear Proliferation

A recent debate in the United States has further complicated the dialogue in Korea. In the February 2014 issue of *The National Interest*, David Santoro, a nonproliferation specialist, wrote an article, "Will America's Asian allies go nuclear?"[3] Santoro notes that there are powerful voices in South Korea and Japan that call for deployment of their own nuclear weapons rather than relying on US nuclear extended deterrence. He attributes this trend to North Korea's provocative behavior, China's aggressive rise, and the general perception that defense budget cuts in the United States represent a weakening of US security commitments in the region. Given their technology and financial resources, he worries that South Korea and Japan could develop nuclear weapons. He observes that their nuclear breakout would effectively end of the global non-proliferation regime and collide with US efforts to reduce the role of nuclear weapons in international affairs. Thus, he argues that the United States must threaten to end alliances with South Korea and Japan if they go nuclear.

Elbridge Colby, a fellow at the Center for a New American Security, rebuts Santoro's argument in the March issue of *The National Interest* arguing that the United States should "Choose Geopolitics Over Nonproliferation."[4] Colby contends that the ultimate goal of US foreign policy is not nonproliferation but "protecting Americans' security, liberty and prosperity through moral means." He argues nuclear nonproliferation should not be regarded as *summun bonum*, and that the scenarios regarding nuclear-armed South Korea and Japan must be evaluated coolly, based on strategic gain and loss, opportunity and risk to US national interests

---

Threat, South Koreans mull nuclear weapons," CNN, March 18, 2013, http://www.cnn.com/2013/03/18/world/asia/south-korea-nuclear/ On redeployment of US tactical nuclear weapons, see "'Unwanted Decision' should be made for the protection of the country and people," Editorial, *Chosun Ilbo*, February 13, 2013; *Chosun Ilbo*, February 20, 2013.

[3] David Santoro, "Will America's Asian Allies Go Nuclear?" *The National Interest*, January 30, 2014, http://nationalinterest.org/commentary/will-americas-asian-allies-go-nuclear-9794

[4] Elbridge Colby, "Choose Geopolitics Over Nonproliferation," *The National Interest*, February 28, 2014, http://nationalinterest.org/commentary/choose-geopolitics-over-nonproli feration-9969?page=6

before deciding whether it would support either country going nuclear. Although he argues that there might well be situations in which South Korean or Japanese pursuit of nuclear weapons would justify Washington cutting them off, Colby holds that under a number of plausible circumstances it would be unreasonable to scrap these alliances, which are ultimately instruments of geopolitics, solely based on the standards of nonproliferation. He maintains that, under certain conditions, for instance if the threat from China grows materially worse, adjusting existing extended nuclear deterrence arrangements or even tolerating some form of proliferation among Washington's Northeast Asian allies might better suit US interests than simply terminating the alliance with them. Colby further notes that if the United States were to follow Santoro's advice, it would, because it would not necessarily enjoy sufficient leverage over Tokyo or Seoul, run the risk of losing both the proliferation game and its allies.

Perceived Advantages of Nuclear Weapons to South Korea

Colby's view gave new hope to South Korea's conservative pundits by hinting that, under certain conditions, alliance and nuclear weapons' possession are not necessarily incompatible and that they could go in tandem, as they have in Europe. Fear of losing alliance with the United States is one reason why they were hesitant in pushing for domestic nuclear weapons development in the past. Why are these South Koreans so obsessed with nuclear weapons now? They offer several rationales.

First, they argue that North Korea has already become a nuclear weapons state, profoundly altering balance of power on the Korean Peninsula. The only way to cope with nuclear North Korea is to secure a credible nuclear deterrence capability. Their logic is based on *lex talionis*, the legal notion of an "eye for an eye," only updated to a 21st century notion of a "nuke for a nuke," a strategy termed "symmetric deterrence."

Second, some pundits suggest that nuclear weapons would endow South Korea with a bargaining chip to compel North Korea to abandon its nuclear weapons. In this case, Seoul would go nuclear only when and if Pyongyang adheres to its nuclear weapons path, implying that this decision would not be irreversible, even if taken. A variant on this argument that one hears in Seoul is that South Korea's threat to go nuclear will push China to put much more pressure on North Korea out of fear that South Korean proliferation would result in Japanese nuclear weapons—a nightmarish outcome for China that could add three more nuclear-armed countries in its region.

Third, doubt about the credibility of American extended deterrence has played a role in precipitating this line of thinking. Some South Koreans are skeptical that the United States would use nuclear weapons when and if the North posed an existential or lesser nuclear threat, particularly if the North attains the ability to threaten the US homeland. This is the fear that was described as "decoupling" during the Cold War, in which US nuclear deterrence would recede in its utility for extended deterrence as its allies' adversary could increasingly threaten the United States itself. Thus, they argue that South Korea should have its own nuclear deterrent capability to substitute for dwindling or ineffective US nuclear deterrence. We address this issue at the end of this section as it bears close examination once the DPRK is able to strike the US homeland.

Finally, enduring distrust of China, Russia, and Japan serves as another catalyst for pro-nuclear South Korean sentiment. China, Russia, and North Korea already have nuclear weapons. And recent strategic moves by the Abe government suggest to many South Koreans that it is simply a matter of time before Japan is armed with nuclear weapons. Should this come to pass, then South Korea would be the only non-nuclear state in the region, leaving it dependent and insecure in South Korean minds. Because American disengagement from South Korea and the region cannot be ruled out, this fear of abandonment is grounded in the real world, even if there is no immediate prospect of American withdrawal from the Asia-Pacific region or indeed, of a nuclear-armed Japan.

Disadvantages of Independent South Korean Nuclear Weapons

In contrast to these voices in favor of South Korean nuclear armament, we argue that the nuclear weapons option, be it by domestic development or by re-deployment of US tactical nuclear weapons, is neither feasible nor desirable for South Korea.

Above all, we see its feasibility is very low because of severe political, legal, and institutional obstacles. There is no doubt that South Korea has the technological and financial capability to develop nuclear weapons. But it has never been easy, and won't be so at any time, for South Korea to arm itself with nuclear weapons, let alone with a submarine or bomber-based nuclear retaliatory capacity that is immune from pre-emption and needed for a secure second strike—the basis of stable nuclear deterrence. While it develops its own nuclear weapons force-and assuming that doing so leads to rupture of the US-ROK alliance-South Korea would be highly vulnerable to a pre-emptive first-strike by Russia and China who would certainly target it, without a countervailing ability to strike back after suffering a nuclear attack. This may not be of concern in peacetime; but in wartime, these two nuclear weapons states would be obliged to treat a South Korean nuclear force as a potential threat (and likely already regard North Korea's nascent nuclear force in exactly this manner.) Where would South Korea test and deploy the weapons under such circumstances? In whose backyard?

John On-fat Wong argued decades ago that two small states armed with nuclear weapons in a military standoff are engaged in an unstable relationship that is best described as "mutual probable destruction" because of their incentive to use first their nuclear weapons rather than lose them.[5] That is, given the time it would take each side to strike, an independent South Korean force facing off against the North Korean nuclear force would be characterized by escalation imperatives that would make the peninsula highly unstable, with potentially catastrophic consequences. Far from reinforcing South Korea's already overwhelming offensive military

[5] John On-fat Wong, "Security Requirements In Northeast Asia" (PhD diss., University of Wisconsin, 1982) 77, available from Proquest dissertations, and John On-fat Wong, "Security Requirements in Northeast Asia," NAPSNet Special Reports, May 13, 2014, http://nautilus.org/napsnet/napsnet-special-reports/security-requirements-in-northeast-asia/, See also Peter Hayes, ""Mutual Probable Destruction": Nuclear Next-Use in a Nuclear-Armed East Asia?," NAPSNet Policy Forum, May 14, 2014, http://nautilus.org/napsnet/napsnet-policy-forum/ mutual-probable-destruction-nuclear-next-use-in-a-nuclear-armed-east-asia/

capabilities—including in almost every dimension where North Korea has developed offsetting "asymmetric" capabilities—South Korean nuclear weapons would undermine deterrence based on conventional forces, and even reduce South Korea's ability to use its conventional forces in response to a North Korean attack (see below.)

Put in more theoretical terms, both Koreas would be faced with a nuclear-armed adversary with a mutual incentive to strike first and therefore, to remain in a state of constant nuclear alert in case the other side intends to attack immediately (in contrast to general deterrence, where nuclear weapons cast a long shadow that makes commanders very cautious but there is no immediate intention to attack and therefore no reason to stay on constant high alert.)[6] This state of constant immediate threat of pre-emptive nuclear attack would push both Koreas to invest heavily in improved surveillance and intelligence capabilities needed to pinpoint nuclear targets for successful pre-emption, especially given the potential for deception in location and deployment of nuclear weapons. It would be difficult for either Korea to achieve sufficient confidence that such intelligence were reliable enough to launch a pre-emptive strike, at least as soon as either gains more than a few warheads and disperses them. Indeed, for South Korea, going-it-alone without US support and possibly losing the United States altogether as senior ally implies reduced confidence in its intelligence, surveillance, and reconnaissance information provided today mostly by US extra-peninsular assets, implying that the South's ability to identify targets to attack pre-emptively may be lacking.[7] However, it is also possible that in a crisis, intelligence that suggests a pending attack combined with partial but reliable data as to location of a substantial fraction of the other's nuclear forces could lead either Korea to mount a damage-limiting pre-emptive strike.[8]

---

[6] The distinction between immediate and general nuclear deterrence was made by Patrick Morgan, *Deterrence:a conceptual analysis*(Sage Publications, 1977).

[7] The authors thank Chris Twomey for this point.

[8] We are indebted to Christopher Twomey for making this point in his review of an earlier draft of this essay.

The complications that independent South Korean nuclear weapons capability would cause for UN Command and Combined Forces Command would be enormous. Put simply, no US Commander-in-Chief is going to put American forces in harm's way in Korea if South Korea wields nuclear weapons outside of US political and military command-and-control. In the European context, only the United Kingdom with its "special relationship" with the United States developed its own nuclear forces and (except for only a few naval and aerial tactical nuclear weapons) all of its strategic and aerial nuclear weapons were dedicated to NATO and ultimately, were commanded by its American military head.[9] Given the stakes in Korea, it is incredible that the United States would violate the principles of unified command when it comes to nuclear weapons and accept a unilateral capacity by South Korea to start a nuclear war. Indeed, in the case of the UK, NATO commanders assumed that once released from direct US control in wartime, allied forces armed with nuclear weapons would rapidly lose communication with nuclear commanders, creating a risk of loss of control that would deter Soviet aggressors.[10] This is not a precedent that the United States will want to repeat in Korea.

To the extent that both Koreas became fully armed with operational nuclear forces targeting each other across the Demilitarized Zone, independent South Korean nuclear weapons would not only make Korean situation much more volatile and conflict ridden than it already is, would also contribute to a rigid and permanent (until it fails) state of psychological warfare and nuclear threats even more ferocious than that seen over much (but not all) of the last six decades. In short, a nuclear-armed South Korea would ensure the continuing division and antagonism between the two Koreas and would undermine inter-Korean *trust politik, peace politik*, or anything other than *mutual destruction politik* for the indefinite future.

This nuclear standoff would be made even more volatile because one

---

[9] Shaun, Gregory, "The command and control of British tactical nuclear weapons," *Defense Analysis* 4:1(1988): 39-51, http://dx.doi.org/10.1080/07430178808405328

[10] Shaun Gregory, "The command and control," *op cit*, 49.

or both Koreas armed with nuclear weapons may believe that nuclear weapons provide a threshold below which covert or even overt conventional military provocations may be undertaken, because the aggressor Korea believes that the victim Korea would see the risk of escalation to nuclear war arising from retaliation as too great to run. This is the obvious lesson learned from the North's attack on the ROK warship *Cheonan* and the shelling of Yeonpyeong Island in 2010. The same lesson has been learned by India facing Pakistani-originated violence in Kashmir and Mumbai; and by Israel faced with rocket attacks from Lebanon.[11]

The ROK would face very high costs were it to move in this direction because it is deeply embedded in a network of multilateral and bilateral treaty commitments and nuclear energy supply trading networks. South Korea is a member of the Nuclear Non-Proliferation Treaty (NPT), and therefore cannot receive, manufacture or get any assistance to produce nuclear explosive devices or weapons under Article 2. It is also obliged to comply with the safeguard regulations of the International Atomic Energy Agency. It cannot emulate Israel, which has refused to sign the NPT and is believed to be one of the states with a clandestine nuclear weapons program. Seoul would have to emulate Pyongyang if it pursues nuclear weapons sovereignty. Like the DPRK in 1994, the ROK would have to leave the NPT using the pretext of emergency. But unlike North Korea which had almost no external nuclear ties or market relations to lose, South Korea is highly involved in global markets. The ROK's global reputation is exemplified by Koreans serving as UN Secretary General and World Bank president. Pulling out of the NPT and the IAEA might lead to UN action, possibly UN Security Council sanctions as were imposed on the DPRK, as well as national sanctions. It would certainly end South Korea's profitable reactor exports, never mind the loss of supply of uranium, enrichment services, and other materials and dual use technology needed for South Korea's nuclear fuel cycle from the Nuclear Supply Group such as the United

[11] Terence Roehrig, "The Case for a Nuclear-free South," *JoongAng Daily*, June 19, 2014, http://koreajoongangdaily.joins.com/news/article/article.aspx?aid=2990820

States, Australia, Russia, and France. South Korea would face an even larger energy shortfall than Japan had to deal with after shutting down all its nuclear plants in 2011.

The IAEA alarm bells will sound loudly the moment such proliferation activity commences, not least due to the Agency's experience with South Korea's enrichment research and development.[12] Consequently, South Korea would have to close down 21 of its nuclear power reactors and suspend plans to add 11 more because the supply of nuclear fuels will end refueling within a few years. The United States will cut off nuclear fuel supply and could even insist on retrieving fuel and technology already sold to South Korea under licenses. Other suppliers in the Nuclear Suppliers Group would also act. South Korea's nuclear industry, which is responsible for 40 percent of the country's electricity supply, would be paralyzed within one to two years as existing reactor cores are burned up. How would the ROK power its economy? South Korea would be lumped together with countries like North Korea and Iran, hurting its national pride and hard-earned prosperity, with potentially huge impacts on external investment, trade, and financial markets that underpin South Korea's economy. To say the least, it would undermine South Korea's claim to global middle power leadership as embodied in its hosting of such events as the 2012 Nuclear Security Summit.[13]

South Korean independent quest of nuclear weapons would not only justify North Korea's nuclear status and diminish the opposition from China and Russia to its nuclear armament, but could also trigger a nuclear domino effect in Northeast Asia. South Korea would have to take into account hostile Japan and China armed with nuclear weapons in its defense planning. It should be noted that some ultra-rightists in Japan relish the prospect that Seoul might make such move so that they can justify Japanese nuclear weapons. Generalized nuclear armament will be a nightmare

---

[12] Jungmin Kang et al., "South Korea's Nuclear Surprise," *Bulletin of the Atomic Scientists*, January-February (2005): 40-9, http://bos.sagepub.com/content/61/1.toc

[13] Terrence Roehrig, "The Case for a Nuclear-free South," *JoongAng Daily*, June 19, 2014, http://koreajoongangdaily.joins.com/news/article/article.aspx?aid=2990820

for South Korean security.

In sum, South Korea would face significant, possibly highly significant political, economic, and security costs if it were to develop and deploy its own nuclear weapons. Of course, if such a choice were made in a context in which the United States withdrew extended deterrence due to isolationism in Washington, or the North obtained substantial backing from other big powers for its provocative actions or outright military aggression against the South, or it acted outrageously (such as conducting an atmospheric nuclear test,) then some of these negative impacts might be ameliorated. The United States might be persuaded to remain in alliance, albeit with major downgrading of its stature in American eyes that it enjoys today due in large part to its restraint to date in responding to the North. Trading partners might be less damning and more willing to continue with business-as-usual. However, the probabilities are against such a positive outcome.

What About Re-Deploying US Tactical Nuclear Weapons?

Those who recognize the surreal nature of having South Korea "going it alone" with nuclear weapons in the 21st century sometimes suggest that the threat to do so is made in order to induce the United States to redeploy nuclear weapons withdrawn in late 1991 by the first President George Bush. Such redeployment is not inconceivable. After all, the United States itself asserted its prerogative to redeploy nuclear weapons to the region in a security emergency when it pulled them out in 1991. And some US officials have stated that the United States would re-deploy nuclear weapons should the South Korean government officially request that it do so.[14] Some American analysts have also suggested some interim or baby steps be taken in this direction such as integrating South Korean officials into selecting nuclear targets, etc.

[14] Myo-ja Ser, "U.S. arms control chief backs nuke redeployment,Says placing tactical atomic arms in South would be symbolic gesture," *Korea Joongang Daily*, March 1,2011, http://koreajoongangdaily.joinsmsn.com/news/article/article.aspx?aid=2932857

However, considered carefully, the idea of redeploying US tactical nuclear weapons to South Korea turns out to be as fantastic as South Korea going it alone. First, a few air-delivered nuclear weapons based in Korea would add little to deterrence and pose the same use-them-or-lose-them dilemma as would South Korean nukes. Second, since the 2009 speech in Prague articulating a vision of a 'nuclear weapons free world,' the United States has downplayed the role of nuclear weapons in every aspect of its security posture. In its 2010 Nuclear Posture Review, Washington announced plans to rely almost completely on strategic rather than tactical nuclear weapons to support nuclear extended deterrence commitments to its allies. It has slashed tactical nuclear arms, which numbered as many as 7,300 in Europe in 1971, to 200 in 2010. The remaining nuclear gravity bomb nuclear weapons in Europe serve as no more than a symbol of NATO's collective commitment.

The second practical obstacle is the lack of a US-ROK nuclear Program of Cooperation such as those struck with America's NATO allies over fifty years ago. Without a Program of Cooperation, the US military cannot share any nuclear weapons data or operations with allies.[15] The probability that the US Congress would approve such an agreement as is required under the US Atomic Energy Act is very low. Thus, redeployment of US tactical nuclear weapons would reinstate the ROK military's exclusion during the Cold War from almost all matters of nuclear war planning, communications, emergency action messages, permissive action links, and actual decisions related to deployment and use of nuclear weapons. It would be relegated to its former role in providing a security perimeter for such weapons, as occurred (likely illegally) during the Cold War. As the only tactical nuclear weapons left in storage for re-deployment to Korea are B61 gravity bombs (the rest that were deployed in South Korea for delivery via short range missiles or artillery have been dismantled,)

[15] See Peter Hayes, *Pacific Powderkeg, American Nuclear Dilemmas in Korea* (Lexington Press, 1990), 119-120 and related references therein, http://nautilus.org/wp-content/ uploads/2011/04/ PacificPowderkegbyPeterHayes.pdf

these nuclear weapons likely will be stored at Kunsan Air Base, ready to be flown out of Korea altogether at the slightest indication that a real war is imminent, likely by helicopters to an aircraft carrier, or on a long-range transport aircraft. However, even these warheads may not be available due to problems in the B61 stockpile life extension program; and the Pentagon may not certify F35 bombers to deliver them.

Thus, far from asserting South Korea's military prowess against the North Korea's nuclear weapons, these weapons would symbolize its renewed subordination to the US military and would simply confirm the North Korean (and in some quarters) Chinese view that South Korea's military follows American bidding.

Yet another practical hurdle is worth mentioning. At the height of the Cold War, the number of US tactical and theater nuclear weapons based on South Korea peaked at about 950.[16] At times, about 2,000 personnel at US Forces Korea were certified to be reliable to handle these nuclear weapons. Many more troops were assigned to defend them against seizure, thus depleting the forces needed for conventional defense. Amidst draconian fiscal austerity, it seems highly unlikely that the United States would commit personnel and dollars to re-deploying nuclear weapons to Korea, even if the number of re-deployed nuclear weapons were far smaller. From the US perspective, the nuclear extended mission is supported already by its home-based strategic nuclear forces, and there is no reason to pay twice for such an improbable mission—especially when the costs to sustain, modernize and strengthen the aging, ailing nuclear weapons organizational infrastructure run into billions of dollars already.

Finally, the counterproductive escalatory potential of such weapons is worth mentioning. Certainly, US nuclear weapons at Kunsan would be early targets for North Korean special forces and chemical attack in a war and would complicate greatly the implementation of a conventional campaign to retaliate against North Korean attack. Given their own difficulty

[16] The Brookings Institution, "50 facts about nuclear weapons today," April 28, 2014, http://www.brookings.edu/research/articles/2014/04/28-50-nuclear-facts

incredibly delivering nuclear weapons against the ROK due to unreliable warheads and delivery systems, we also surmise that the North would consider attacking instead South Korea's light water reactors and spent fuel pools with missiles and special forces. Increasing the salience of nuclear threat in the minds of the DPRK instead of focusing them on the inevitability of defeat by conventional force will induce the KPA to respond asymmetrically for no strategic gain. Far from increasing deterrence and military stability in the Korean Peninsula, the net effect would be to reduce deterrence and increase military instability, the opposite of what is needed for Korea to survive, let alone for the various parties to the Korean conflict to resume dialogue about reversing North Korea's nuclear breakout.

Political and Military Effects of Re-Deployment

Even if the United States somehow made South Korea an exception to its de-emphasis of nuclear weapons, and found a way to share nuclear weapons operations with the South Korean military, and pays to return tactical weapons to the peninsula, the new posture would not help solve the North Korean nuclear conundrum. It would only give a pretext to Pyongyang to nullify the Six-Party Talks and accelerate and deepen its weapons program. China would be highly sensitive to re-deployment of US nuclear weapons in its proximity and would move toward closer military ties with North Korea. Such a development would only aggravate the security risks for South Korea, as the US tactical nuclear weapons would provide new targets for North Korean attacks and a renewed incentive to attack these targets first in order to disable the American nuclear threat at the outset of a war.

From a strictly military perspective, US nuclear weapons based in South Korea are without merit for all conceivable missions. We will examine the disutility of nuclear weapons in each of these scenarios of possible military use.

The first mission is to deter North Korean nuclear and conventional attack on South Korea. If Kim Jong-un is a rational commander, then he knows that he faces an overwhelmingly capable South Korean, the United

States, and allied conventional military force that can crush the Korean People's Army. Moreover, the trend is towards increasing North Korean conventional inferiority. In spite of the DPRK military's forward deployment and ability to threaten northern Seoul with long range artillery and rocket fire—the essence of North Korea's deterrent force against South Korean occupation of the North—Kim Jong-un cannot hope to attack the South and achieve military victory.[17] In this sense, the Demilitarized Zone represents a set of opposed, immense military masses, both deterred from moving against the other, and therefore trapped in an inherently stable and so far, permanent standoff.

Kim Jong-un's nuclear weapons capabilities provide at best little or no marginal deterrence to that already sustained by his conventional forces against US-ROK conventional forces in this standoff. Indeed, we are skeptical that the logic of nuclear deterrence even applies with regard to North Korean military goals at this point. Our guess is that North Korea has 5 or less crude plutonium nuclear devices according to most authoritative estimates; and between zero and 10 high-enriched uranium weapons at most. Its operational capacity is limited. The North has demonstrated a 20 percent success rate of its long-range missile development over the past two decades and five launches; and a 66 percent or less success rate of nuclear device detonation (as of writing in May 2014, with a fourth test possible in the near future.) The combined probability of a North Korean missile-delivered nuclear warhead exploding over a target given all the systems that must work together—the rockets, the separating stages, the re-entry vehicle, the guidance system, the fuze, and the warhead itself—is likely less than 10 percent. You don't have to be a rocket scientist to figure out that the North would have to fire many more missiles and warheads than it could possibly have to realize it could not achieve a reasonable confidence of destroying even one target with a missile-delivered nuclear warhead. And even if it did, one asks: what then?

---

[17] Roger Cavazos, "Mind the Gap Between Rhetoric and Reality," *NAPSNet Special Reports*, June 26, 2012, http://nautilus.org/napsnet/napsnet-special-reports/mind-the-gap-between-rhetoric-and-reality/

After first-use of a nuclear weapon, whether it failed or was successful, the DPRK would then face US-ROK and allied forces that would defeat the military in detail, dismember, the regime, and kill or capture and try its leadership, both political and military, for crimes against humanity and nuclear aggression. Even before the introduction of a complete kill-chain in 2020, South Korea's missile capability has significantly improved, and its air superiority with F-16s, F-15s, and eventually F-35s would allow more effective offensive defenses. If American conventional weapons assets are added up on top of that, ROK-US combined forces are formidable. With complete control of North Korea's airspace, it would not take long to occupy key sites in the DPRK, even if infantry and unconventional warfare lingered on in mountainous areas for some months.

The second military mission is to deter to the extent possible and then defeat Kim Jong-un's forces on the assumption that he is only partly rational, or is ignorant or misinformed about military realities, conventional and nuclear, and launches an all-out attack on South Korea. Of course, deterrence as a conceptual framework presumes that the adversary is cognizant of the costs and benefits of different courses of action, and sensitive to risk, especially catastrophic risks—in the case of North Korea, this refers foremost to the removal of the current leadership. If Kim Jong-un is truly irrational, then he is immune to a rational deterrence calculus, conventional or nuclear, in which case strictly military considerations as to the uniquely nuclear weapons effects—essentially, instantaneously delivered, and massive thermal, blast and radiation damage—should drive US and ROK deliberations on the necessity of supplementing conventional forces with nuclear weapons.

Again, we are skeptical that the US tactical nuclear weapons are militarily usable for the same reasons that they were opposed from within the US army in Korea (led by General Jack Cushman) in the mid-eighties in the debates that led in part to the global withdrawal of tactical and theater nuclear weapons in 1991.[18] We will not describe in detail the devasta-

[18] John H. Cushman, *Organization and Operational Employment of Air/Land Forces*, U.S. Army War

tion that would be wrought by the use of nuclear weapons for military purposes in Korea that would involve dozens of weapons, depending on the mission. Authoritative analysis is easily available to the reader who is interested in the details.[19] Suffice it to say that B61 gravity bombs that would be used today are 0.3-340 kiloton thermonuclear weapons designed to destroy deep underground targets, or very large areas of ground forces.[20] Delivered by fighter aircraft in the numbers (low scores) likely to be available from redeployment in Korea and detonated at or close to ground level for military effect, these weapons would be too few to stop the southward advance of North Korean armored forces, but used in places likely to slow such an attack such as the narrow defiles in the invasion corridors leading towards Seoul in large enough numbers to have an effect, would result in a vast radiological plume that would lay waste large parts of Korea. That mission would be better accomplished by air-launched precision-guided munitions.

If they were used to destroy the leadership, the United States and the ROK would be responsible for killing vast numbers of innocent North Koreans. Such an attack would be held by many, especially by Koreans, to be disproportionate and reprehensible, even after North Korean nuclear first-use.[21] It is also doubtful that the United States or South Korea would have real-time knowledge of the location of North Korea's leaders or weapons of mass destruction (given the vast number of caves dug by North Korea over the decades) to use B61 bombs with precision and sufficient assur-

College, Carlisle Barracks, Pennsylvania, 1984; John H.Cushman, "Military Options in Korea's End Game," NAPSNet Policy Forum, May 23, 1994, http://nautilus.org/napsnet/napsnet-policy-forum/military-options-in-koreas-end-game/, John H. Cushman, oral history and other papers that describe his internal battles in the US Army to remove fallacious nuclear weapons strategies from his plans to fight war in Korea, http://www.west-point.org/publications/cushman/

[19] Bryan Jack et al., *The South Korean Case: A Nuclear Weapons Program Embedded in an Environment of Great Power Concerns*, volume II, *Regional Rivalries and Nuclear Responses*, Panheuristics Final Report to US Defense Nuclear Agency, DNA 001-77-C-0052, February 28, 1978, II-85~II-95, http://nautilus.org/publications/essays/napsnet/reports/Panheuristics_ROK_Regional_Rivalries

[20] Thomas B. Cochran et al., US *Nuclear Forces and Capabilities, Nuclear Weapons Databook* (Ballinger: Cambridge, 1984), 82-93.

[21] Tom Nichols, "The Case for Conventional Deterrence," *The National Interest*, April 20, 2014, http://nationalinterest.org/commentary/the-case-conventional-deterrence-9381

ance that the mission would be achieved. These factors all militate against American nuclear preemption and retaliation and render nuclear deterrence against the North an almost pointless exercise in allied reassurance.

North Korean nuclear first-use would not only forge an unstoppable US-ROK resolve to punish the North Korean leadership and utterly defeat its military; it would likely also draw China and Russia into the conflict in a united front with the United States and South Korea.[22]

In between these two missions, one aimed at deterrence and one aimed at military defeat of the DPRK, are a range of other less demanding military missions such as responding to covert military provocations from the North, or worse, managing crises with high levels of alert, or actual war due to loss-of-control of forces on either side of the DMZ. In such circumstances, the catastrophic, multi-trillion dollar potential damages from full-scale war in loss of lives, property, and production, makes the overarching imperative to use military force in ways that avoid further escalation and reinstate the *status quo ante* (or some negotiable and militarily sustainable version of it in a new Armistice.) A nuclear-armed South Korea, and the resulting pressures to escalate on both sides, makes that outcome far less likely. Indeed, the risk of escalation might constrain any response to lower-level provocations. In such fast-moving and violent circumstances, it is difficult to imagine any marginal military or political utility arising from deployment or use of tactical nuclear weapons in Korea, relative to the nuclear threat to the DPRK already posed by US-based strategic nuclear forces, that would not simply make the situation on the ground worse and complicate the negotiations needed to stop the war from escalating.

The most demanding military mission is the one in which this intermediate level of conflict escalates, in spite of the best attempts to extinguish the conflagration, and North Korea's leaders face pending certain defeat and an existential threat to their state's existence. In this situation, the

---

[22] The reader should note that this ultimate multilateral backing to defeat an irrational North Korean leadership crazed enough to use nuclear weapons would not be available to South Korea if it were to deploy nuclear weapons independently.

North might use nuclear threat to force negotiations or a stalemate, or even detonate a nuclear weapon in a way that threatens second use over a civilian or military target of value. Such a demonstration firing could indeed have a massive political and psychological impact. Some of these types of North Korean nuclear weapons use, either completely suicidal and irrational, or rational but only in a narrow range of improbable circumstances in which conventional and nuclear deterrence have already failed, cannot be avoided completely now that they have tested and deployed nuclear weapons, no matter how crude. Managing this irreducible risk is the price South Koreans are paying for the US, ROK and others' failure to stop the DPRK nuclear breakout.

Here the question is whether redeployed US tactical nuclear weapons would have a marginal impact on the probability that in extremis, North Korea would play this nuclear card. This issue is the crux of the matter of redeploying nuclear weapons. Ironically, the effectiveness of such risk-taking by the DPRK would be enhanced in the eyes of its leaders in the event of in-country deployment of US weapons. Redeployment of US tactical nuclear weapons would play into a North Korean strategy of "crazy as a fox" nuclear threats (Kim Jong-un would be taking a leaf out of Richard Nixon's nuclear playbook in the Vietnam War.) Such irrational North Korean threats would be motived by their perception that redeployment of US nuclear weapons would increase the probability of US or North Korean nuclear pre-emptive attack, and that this risk can be exploited. Redeployment might buttress the waning credibility of nuclear extended deterrence by substituting South Korean for American resolve. But by pitting nuclear armed Koreans against each other, it would make the peninsula more unstable and prone to escalation to nuclear war.

This would not be a totally ungrounded perception as this was the logic of forward-deployment for more than three decades and increased proximity to a battlefield or weapons depots under attack could reduce time and degrade decision-making in Washington as to use of weapons under threat or actual DPRK attack. To be effective, this North Korean strategy demands that it increase the risk to the United States of prosecuting the war to eliminate North Korea, not play it safe. This is not the military incentive we should be presenting to Kim Jong-un.

Put another way, redeployment of US nuclear weapons to South Korea would shift US and North Korean nuclear deterrence from an ultimate to imminent form whereas reliance on nuclear existential deterrence from strategic weapons based in the United States preserves the general deterrence posture until specific circumstances call upon forces to be displayed or deployed. This latter posture is far safer, and has been tested thoroughly for two decades without failure in Korea (the two DPRK attacks in 2010 and 2011 fell below the threshold at which nuclear weapons are salient and did not constitute a failure of nuclear extended deterrence.)

What About Credibility of US Nuclear Extended Deterrence?

The most potent argument for an independent ROK nuclear weapons capability is that whether the United States has redeployed tactical nuclear weapons in Korea or not, when the DPRK achieves a credible capacity to attack the United States itself, the credibility of its nuclear extended deterrent to the ROK will fall so much that it no longer suffices to reassure the ROK that it has a countervailing threat to neutralize the North Korean nuclear threat to the ROK. There is some truth to this argument, so it bears close consideration. Ironically, with only a few exceptions,[23] it has not

[23] All these sources are translated from Korean. One scholar who adheres to this position is Ho-yeol Yoo. "I would like to trust the US that provides extended deterrence. But if its policy cannot assure a 100 percent nuclear deterrence, we should seek to acquire more forceful instrument for survival. If we cannot have tactical nuclear weapons by ourselves, we should have capability to develop them. ... One of the surest ways to defend ourselves is to possess tactical nuclear weapons, and I believe there is room for cooperation with the US." Ho-yeol Yoo, "Is It Right Time to Propose a Dialogue with North Korea?" JTBC, April 18, 2013, http://news.jtbc.joins.com/article/article.aspx?news_id=NB10266522 and, "Redeployment of American nuclear weapons to South Korea is not the best option, but it can be the second best choice. Thus, we should raise the issue with the US, and the transfer of wartime operational control scheduled in 2015 should be re-examined." Ho-yeol Yoo, "Northeast Asia under New Leaderships: Foreign and North Korean Policy of the Park Geun-hye Government," the 72nd Monthly Discussion at Hankuk Seonjinhwa Forum, February 28, 2013, http://www.kfprogress.org/client/month/viw.asp?sidx=2682&cpage=1. Another is Choon-geun Lee: "The reason why I advocate the nuclear armament is that there is no realistic counter-measure to nuclear North Korea. The only way to counter North Korea's nuclear threat is to acquire nuclear weapons by ourselves. We cannot trust the American nuclear umbrella 100 percent. North Korea can sooner or later can strike the US mainland with nuclear wepaons. The ROK trust American goodwill. But ROK's possession of nuclear weapons can achieve a credible nuclear deterrence more than the denuclearization of North Korea which the US aims at. South Korea's nuclear weapons can be an effective tool to disarm North Korea's nuclear arsenal." And, Choon-geun Lee, ("Nuclear Armament: An Interpretation from International Political Perspective," *Bukhan* (*North Korea*) 417(2011): 22; and "The best way to assure American credibility is to redeploy its tactical nuclear weapons

figured much in the recent public debates over the ROK's need for an independent nuclear force.

This credibility problem for nuclear extended deterrence is not new.[24] It has been an integral part of US nuclear posture and policy since the early 1950s in Asia and Europe. It affects both general extended deterrence, that is, the ability of the United States to enable the ROK to ensure over time that the DPRK does not attempt to reshape the security status quo on the peninsula; and immediate extended deterrence, that is, the ability of the United States to enable the ROK to deter the DPRK from acting on an intention to attack at a specific time and place, typically, in a military confrontation or time of high tension between the two Koreas.

The credibility of nuclear deterrence threats suffers from a number of inherent flaws. For many instances of provocation and military aggression, nuclear retaliation would be implausible either because the means of annihilation would be disproportionate or even militarily counter-productive on the battlefield; or could lead to moral and political condemnation by important third parties. Such flaws are passed onto allies by the United States when it extends nuclear deterrence, and cannot be evaded whether the adversary can hit the United States itself or not.

However, once an adversary like China in the mid-sixties or the DPRK in the future can plausibly threaten to hit the United States itself, the sheer magnitude of nuclear detonations—even if they are too few to threaten the United States' national existence—could make the United States think twice about trading Guam or Los Angeles for Seoul or Tokyo. A small South Korean nuclear arsenal, goes the argument, can overcome this credibility deficit because South Korea's national existence would be at stake

---

to South Korea and to allow its use with South Korea. ... Ultimately speaking, the American nuclear umbrella is nothing but a verbal statement like 'if you trouble my friend, I will punish you.' That is not enough. We can prevent provocation from North Korea with nuclear weapons only when we show our capability and resolve that 'we can also destroy (kill) you.' That capability is nuclear weapons." (an interview with *Newsis*, April 18, 2013) "Resurgent Voices urging South Korean Nuclear Armament, Lee Choon-geun, 'American Nuclear Umbrella Cannot Guarantee South Korea's Security,'"http://news.zum.com/ articles/6326749

[24] Timothy W. Crawford, "The Endurance of Extended Deterrence, Continuity, Change, and Complexity in Theory and Policy," in *Complex Deterrence, Strategy in the Global Age*, ed.T.V. Paul, P. Morgan, and J. Wirtz. (University of Chicago Press, 2009), 277-303.

should it be attacked by a nuclear-armed state such as North Korea or China and its resolve and capacity to retaliate against nuclear aggression would be credible whereas that extended by the United States would not, or would be less so and insufficient for the ROK to rely upon.

This logic pertains whether the United States has forward-deployed nuclear weapons in Korea or not. Forward-deployment is simply a means to assert resolve. It does not itself improve credibility when the United States faces an adversary able to strike it with nuclear weapons, not just its ally. Thus, the relevant baseline is the credibility of the status quo of South Korea relying on nuclear extended deterrence based on US strategic nuclear forces based outside of Korea compared to the credibility of an independent South Korean nuclear weapons program from the viewpoint of the DPRK, and to a lesser extent, China.

It is important, therefore, to examine more closely the key elements that make nuclear threats "credible" and to compare the status quo of nuclear extended deterrence with a ROK nuclear weapons force in each of these respects. These are capacity and resolve, both of which must be sufficient for a nuclear threat to be credible to the adversary. We will first examine capacity, and then move onto resolve, before concluding with some remarks about the significance of nuclear versus conventional threat in the first place.

The first and necessary attribute of a credible nuclear threat is that the party making the threat has the capacity to deliver on the threat. There is no doubt that the United States can reduce the DPRK into a smoking, radiating ruin in a few hours if it decides to do so with only a small fraction of its missile force, either from submarines, or from land-based missiles. These missiles are well-tested, reliable and would be precision-targeted. There is no credibility gap here, whatsoever. Moreover, the credibility of such delivery was arguably improved when tactical nuclear weapons were removed from Korea in 1991. The residual nuclear weapons in Korea at that time were subject to loss-of-control and seizure and invited preemptive attack by DPRK nuclear, biological, and chemical forces that would have possibly disabled these weapons and would have complicated greatly US and ROK conventional military operations. Offshore American nuclear weapons suffer from no such disadvantage.

Even to develop a minimum deterrent that is deliverable on targets in the DPRK would take the ROK years to produce, test, and deploy. From when the ROK pulls out of the NPT and likely ruptures its alliance with the United States to make its own nuclear weapons to the time when it deploys operational nuclear weapons, it would be vulnerable to countervailing nuclear threat from the DPRK. Even when developed and deployed, compared with the ability of the United States to deliver warheads on targets in ways that could disarm the DPRK so that it could not escalate to additional nuclear attacks on the South (or Japan) or persuade the DPRK that it not strike the United States, the ROK force would be vastly inferior and less credible from a purely military viewpoint, both with respect to the DPRK, and even more so with respect to its ability to credibly threaten other regional nuclear weapons states with nuclear attack.

Additional dimensions of capacity-related credibility are fielding of redundant delivery systems to reduce the DPRK's ability to eliminate a retaliatory attack from a first strike on the United States or the ROK; the ability of a state to "ride out" an attack and survive to fight on, even under conditions of outright nuclear attack on the national leadership; and its ability to terminate a nuclear war to fight another day. In each of these dimensions, US strategic forces are far more capable than a prospective ROK nuclear force could ever hope to be. A ROK nuclear force, especially at the outset, would necessarily focus on one or two delivery platforms and would not be redundant until it developed a nuclear-armed submarine force deployed offshore. The ROK has a small, densely populated territory that is far more vulnerable to nuclear attack than the United States and consequently, far less capable of surviving a major nuclear attack. Given the proximity of Seoul to the DMZ and the concentration of almost every aspect of national life in the capital city, the ROK is also far less likely to be able to survive with a leadership intact and able to negotiate to terminate a nuclear war than the United States. In all these respects, a nuclear-armed ROK would present an inferior force and a less credible ability to project nuclear threat to the DPRK or other nuclear armed states than the United States for the foreseeable future.[25]

Moreover, the ROK armed forces have little experience compared to the US military services in the operational aspects of deploying and using nuclear weapons in a battlefield. Yes, ROK forces train alongside US forces to fight under conditions of nuclear, biological, and chemical warfare (and as a result, are likely more capable of doing so than their DPRK counterparts should they start a nuclear war.) Operating by itself, the ROK lacks the space-based and high altitude reconnaissance and other intelligence gathering systems needed for precision targeting of nuclear weapons, especially to hit mobile targets or to rapidly redial target coordinates in order to attack DPRK command-and-control systems as they present themselves.

The ROK would also find itself confronting many of the same operational dilemmas that afflicted US tactical and theater nuclear weapons when they were deployed in Korea—including the near impossibility of conducting conventional operations while simultaneously planning nuclear attacks, a tendency to use multiple warheads on single targets to achieve high kill probabilities with resultant substantial radiological, blast, and thermal collateral damage to one's own troops as well as to civilians on both sides; and the necessary security measures on nuclear command and control systems as well as on personnel, delivery systems, and warheads that are demanding and resource-intensive. In these dimensions, the ROK would be either at a disadvantage relative to reliance on US strategic weapons, or there would be no gain relative to these problems that afflict US strategic weapons used for warfighting in a renewed Korean War.

There is another set of capacity-related aspects of nuclear weapons that need to be compared to determine the relative credibility of reliance on US strategic weapons versus an independent ROK nuclear force. These are the ability to signal the salience of nuclear threat in a calibrated manner in

---

[25] All these arguments pertain to the relative vulnerability and weakness of the DPRK's nuclear threats against the ROK and the United States.

specific crises—typically done with rhetorical threats to adversaries and reassurance to allies from nuclear weapons state leaders, military commanders, and sometimes third parties, combined with various types of display. This can be done by protracted forward-basing of nuclear weapons (which presents its own set of problems inviting pre-emptive first strike by the adversary without time for national leaderships to review and make strategic decisions,) routine nuclear-capable warship or aircraft visits to allied ports or airfields; expanded exercises involving simulated nuclear strikes and operations; offshore deployment of defensive systems (such as BMD); and in near-war or very tense situations, use of silent but evident (to the DPRK or China) changes in routine deployments, communication routines, and even timing and format of transmission of Emergency Action Messages that send alerts and firing instructions to nuclear submarines over radios that can be monitored by adversaries.The United States has sixty years of such more or less subtle signaling activity and its standard operating procedures and signaling "language" is well known and likely well understood by the DPRK and China.

The ROK has no such experience, and it would take time to establish its vocabulary and develop mutual understanding with its adversaries as to its intended meaning of its nuclear threat signals in routine and crisis operations. In this regard, the ROK's ability to communicate a credible nuclear threat to the DPRK or China is much less than that of the United States. After all, the essence of credibility of threat is in the mind of the party threatened, not in the mind of the party issuing the threat.

The second and much less easily determined aspect of credibility is the resolve of the party issuing a nuclear threat to make good on it. There is no simple equation that when summed, equals the net quantity of perceived (by the adversary) resolve applicable to a given conflict, either generally in terms of shaping an adversary's perceived strategic options, or specifically, in terms of deterring the adversary's immediate intention to launch an attack, nuclear or conventional. Elements that contribute to perceived resolve include the intrinsic interest in the outcome of a conflict, reputation for making good on threats in past conflicts with adversaries, especially a repeat offender; precedent setting use; reputation for making unconditional demands for capitulation rather than negotiated solutions entailing some reciprocity; and degree to which decision-making has been delegated to local commanders or made semi-automatic ("trip wires") by forward-deployment.

With regard to precedent, the words "Hiroshima" and "Nagasaki" provide a short answer as to who is more credible in making nuclear threats from a Chinese or North Korean perspective. "Would they use nuclear weapons?" is open to doubt in relation to the relative propensity of Seoul and Washington to use nuclear weapons, and is subject to many determining variables, some of which are unknowable in advance. The answer to: "Could they use nuclear weapons?" is already known. The answer for Americans is decisively yes. The answer for South Koreans is maybe, we don't know. American nuclear threats are more credible than an ROK nuclear threat for the simple reason that Americans have already used them, South Koreans haven't. For North Koreans, this historical reality counts no matter who is in the White House and the Blue House.

Even when it comes to intrinsic interest in retaliating against nuclear attacks on South Korea, it is not evident that the balance weighs in favor of a South Korean nuclear force being more credible than relying on American nuclear forces, once North Korean forces can hit the US homeland (which starts with Guam and Alaska, a much shorter reach and easier task for DPRK nuclear forces than hitting the continental United States.) For a start, any attack by a nuclear state with such reach on an American ally is a signal that an attack on the United States may be forthcoming and requires immediate response—although that response may not be nuclear for various reasons. It follows that any threat by a state such as the DPRK to the ROK signals the possibility that an attack on the United States itself may be pending. For all intents and purposes, the two would be indistinguishable and the DPRK knows that already. Thus, words not just capacity matter, and the outrageous North Korean threat rhetoric in March-April 2013 prompted the most significant American nuclear threat response since the August 1976 crisis when US forces moved tactical nuclear weapons towards the DMZ in response to the DPRK attack at Panmunjon.

Second, the United States not only has its direct vital interests vested in South Korea, including American and allied lives and treasure spent during and since the Korean War; and its economic interests in a vital South Korean economy. What happens in the ROK affects directly its strategic relationship with China, which involves US-Chinese nuclear weapons not only in relation to the Taiwan Straits issue, but also with regard to the peninsula. A North Korean nuclear attack and nuclear threats aimed at South Korea immediately reverberates into the US-China relationship, as occurred in 2012 and 2013. This aspect of US intrinsic interest is growing over time as the ROK becomes an increasingly important trading partner and investor in the Chinese economy and increases US resolve to not allow the DPRK to threaten the ROK with nuclear weapons.

From the Chinese perspective, the DPRK threat to the ROK threatens its vital interest in South Korea's future existence; but this interest is dwarfed by the impact that threats to the ROK have on the US-China relationship, because it is linked to and thereby amplified by many other shared US and Chinese vital interests in the region. American resolve to not have its vital interests in its relationship with China trashed by the DPRK outweighs the impact that the ROK resolved to stand alone with its own nuclear weapons against the DPRK would have on China's vital interests, and thereby on the US-China relationship. Put another way, a nuclear-armed ROK would delink itself from the US-China strategic relationship, and lose some of the advantages of being important to both the great powers. In particular, an ROK with an independent nuclear force would reduce Chinese interest in influencing or coercing the DPRK in relation to its nuclear threats, and is less credible in this regard than relying on US nuclear extended deterrence which links the fate of the ROK directly to US-Chinese strategic interests.

Yet another dimension of intrinsic interest is the US versus ROK concern with the regional and global impacts of the DPRK nuclear breakout. The ROK has enormous direct interest in the local impact of the DPRK's nuclear forces on the disputed Korean Peninsula due to its vulnerability—

a condition shared with the United States when the DPRK reach extends to Alaska and Guam. The United States also has enormous direct interest in the regional and global impact of the nuclear non-proliferation regime of which it is one of the primary architects. This interest is vital and informs directly US policy toward the DPRK and reinforces the credibility of its threats towards the DPRK. The DPRK nuclear breakout directly challenges one of the pillars of US nuclear hegemony or consent-based leadership, for which there is no equivalent in the case of the ROK equipped with a stand-alone arsenal. If the ROK goes nuclear, it would further damage that global US interest, and even delink that US interest from the inter-Korean nuclear threat dynamic. Both have an existential interest in countering the DPRK nuclear threat; but the United States has a far greater interest in maintaining the global nuclear order than the ROK, and its nuclear threats are more credible to the DPRK than those of the ROK as a result.

Another subtle dimension exists in which to compare the relative credibility of reliance and US extended deterrence with an independent nuclear-armed ROK once the DPRK can hit the United States itself. That is the deterrence capacity that is derived from the United States ability to curtail any ROK impulses towards provocative or over-bearing military behavior towards the DPRK, especially in response to DPRK covert or overt low-level military provocations. The US nuclear extended deterrent encourages opportunistic DPRK attempts to exploit ROK dependence on the United States, seeing nuclear weapons as creating either a threshold below which it is safe to conduct provocations, or as a way to push the United States into political negotiations due to the risk posed by such provocations escalating into real war and even nuclear war. This is a cost to the ROK that comes with alliance with a great power. The flip side of this coin, however, is that the DPRK would perceive correctly that a stand-alone, small ROK nuclear force (like its own) begs pre-emption. Lacking US political and military oversight, the DPRK would constantly pressure the ROK to act in ways to undergird and constantly try to restore the credibility of its countervailing threats.

Put differently, credible but minimalist US nuclear threat invites low-level DPRK opportunistic non-nuclear provocations and rhetorical nuclear aggression, but do not pose a serious risk of nuclear war. They also offer the DPRK the side-benefit that the US curtailment of ROK adventurism.In contrast, an ROK stand-alone nuclear force will require constant rhetorical and operational reinforcement to project a consistent nuclear threat to the DPRK, and the DPRK will respond in kind—an inherently unstable situation. In the former case, US resolve reduces DPRK propensity to strike first and lends credibility to its threats. In the latter case, ROK will increase DPRK propensity to strike first and the credibility of its nuclear countervailing threat will be diminished constantly in the face of DPRK escalatory rhetoric and actions.

Closely related is another aspect of credibility—the negotiating style of the party issuing nuclear threats. The United States has conducted multiple negotiations with the DPRK over many decades, including crises that had potential to escalate into full-scale war. These include the seizure of the USS Pueblo in 1969, the commando attack on the Blue House in 1970, the August 1976 Panmunjon crisis, the Rangoon bombing of the ROK cabinet in 1983, and US preparations to bomb Yongbyon nuclear sites in 1994, and the dozens of negotiations between US and DPRK officials over nuclear issues since 1991 to the present day. In these negotiations, the United States exhibited a willingness to negotiate outcomes that did not require outright capitulation by the DPRK but recognized it had valid security interests at stake. This element of its reputation endows the United States with credibility in negotiations with the DPRK that the ROK cannot match. The ROK negotiating record, in contrast, is one of hot-cold, wild swings in policy towards the DPRK depending on the political proclivity of the President and the Blue House. A nuclear-armed ROK as a negotiating adversary with the DPRK may speak the same language, but does not have a consistent reputation for seeking reciprocity in outcomes that would provide greater credibility than the United States on nuclear threat and nuclear war.

Thus, in every aspect of credibility, whether capacity or resolve-related, dependence on the US for nuclear extended deterrence is more credible than an independent ROK nuclear weapons state. This conclusion should be read on context, however. In either case, the marginal contribution of nuclear weapons to deterrence, including nuclear deterrence, in the Korean Peninsula is small, and increasingly small over time, compared with the deterrence impact of conventional military forces. Indeed, many of the missions formerly only achievable by use of nuclear weapons such as attacking underground sites or assured destruction of targets by use of multiple nuclear detonations in rapid sequence are now achievable with use of precision-guided munitions. The military role of nuclear weapons in warfighting has shrunk greatly since the end of the Cold War, and the United States reserves them almost exclusively for retaliation against nuclear attack.[26] Nuclear weapons may not be used even in that instance because retaliatory use poses many real dilemmas and massive, protracted conventional retaliation may be more effective and desirable in almost every conceivable respect.

What Should South Korea Do Instead?

South Korea's best military option to respond against the DPRK's nuclear threat is to develop its conventional military forces in alliance with the United States, and in cooperative military-military relations with all states in the region. South Korea should avoid a simplistic retaliatory response to North Korean provocations, and work closely through Combined Forces Command to develop operational strategies underscoring the absolute and relative superiority of ROK-US allied forces while avoiding deployments and exercises that suggest pre-emptive attacks aimed at the leadership, or positioning of forces that imply a pending all-out attack on the DPRK (especially offshore US forces.) Specifically recommended in this regard is avoidance of CFC operations designed to degrade KPA C3I, destroy its leadership, and strike strategic forces, including nuclear weapons, that

[26] Bary Blechman and Russel Rumbaugh, "Bombs Away: The Case for Phasing Out U.S. Tactical Nukes in Europe," Foreign *Affairs* July/August (2014), http://www.foreignaffairs.com/articles/141484/barry-blechman-and-russell-rumbaugh/bombs-away

may induce nuclear strikes from the DPRK as they may believe they are in a "use or lose" situation.[27]

US and ROK military strategy should not be based on preemptively attacking North Korea's nascent nuclear force, nor on retaliating against its first-use with nuclear weapons. US nuclear attack on the DPRK is vanishingly improbable, under any but the most extreme circumstances, in which case options are available to the United States that do not require redeployment. Although it may seem counter-intuitive to many, military strategies, exercises, and capacities that are designed to attack and kill North Korea's national political-military leadership are a particularly bad idea, because they impel these leaders to reflect on the utility of early first nuclear use, and if achieved, could lead to loss-of-control of whatever nuclear weapons the DPRK has to deliver against US and ROK forces. Unless it has high confidence that DPRK deployment of nuclear weapons is not accompanied by pre-delegated use authority to nuclear units, successful decapitation could generate nuclear attack. Some strategies to attack military command posts and communications links between nuclear forces and central commanders may also risk nuclear escalation if use authority has been pre-delegated to nuclear unit and such attacks may be minimized and some avoided altogether. Such restraint may come at a cost to US-ROK conventional forces that would otherwise gain relief from the fragmentation and confusion created by such disabling retaliatory attacks against the DPRK's conventional command posts and communications (assuming these are commingled with those supporting nuclear units.) Strengthening US-ROK defenses, including counter-missile and hardening of US-ROK command posts against nuclear attack, reduce further the chance of a DPRK attempt to use nuclear weapons to decapitate the ROK and US military.[28]

---

[27] Kier A. Lieber and Daryl G. Press, *Coercive Nuclear Campaigns in the 21st Century: Understanding Adversary Incentives and Options for Nuclear Escalation*, PASCC, Naval Postgraduate School, 2013, http://www.nps.edu/Academics/Centers/CCC/Research/PASCC.html

[28] Chang Kwoun Park and Victor A. Utgoff, "On Strengthening Extended Deterrence for the ROK-US Alliance," *Joint Forces Quarterly*, 68:1(2013): 84-90, http://ndupress.ndu.edu/JFQ.aspx

Concurrently, the United States and the ROK should do everything possible to help stabilize economically the DPRK to avoid it falling into desperate straits that induce the leadership to lash out in order to unify the population. Crisis avoidance is far cheaper than crisis management, let alone war and nuclear war. South Korea's best political and psychological strategy to counter the DPRK's coercive use of nuclear threat and to reassure its own population, allies, and third parties, is to deepen and expand its non-nuclear nationalist credentials. In this regard, South Korea's use of creative and agile diplomacy that exploits its position as a medium-sized power surrounded by great powers is the best approach. South Korean leadership on nuclear security agendas, including post-Fukushima regional frameworks for emergency response to nuclear fuel cycle incidents and large-scale accidents, is a powerful symbolic strategy that devalues North Korea's crude nuclear threats as a weapon of the weak.

This non-nuclear national narrative should be extended to design and implement a regional treaty framework for comprehensive security and within that framework, lead the in-depth examination of the stabilizing and effects of a regional nuclear weapons-free zone. This strategy can be implemented in concert with China and Mongolia, and could receive the support of the United States and Russia, leaving Japan nowhere to go but to join such a zone in the future. North Korea could be invited to join and comply over time, or disarm quickly to join as a non-nuclear state in return for guarantees from the nuclear weapons states that it will neither be attacked nor threatened with attack by nuclear weapons, a non-hostility agreement, peace treaty to end the Korean War, and economic assistance to enable it to make a transition to a normal state and political economy. If North Korea balks, then eventually it will collapse into a unified Korea and become part of a regional nuclear weapons-free zone.[29]

To achieve this outcome, South Korea needs to redefine the goals of

---

[29] Binoy Kampmark, Peter Hayes and Richard Tanter, *A New Approach to Security in Northeast Asia: Breaking the Gridlock*, Summary Report, Breaking the Gridlock Workshop, October 9-10, 2012, Woodrow Wilson International Center for Scholars, Washington, D.C., http://nautilus.org/napsnet/napsnet-special-reports/gridlockworkshopsummary/

reviving the moribund the Six-Party Talks to achieve a comprehensive security settlement, not just the nuclear disarmament of North Korea. At the same time, South Korea must maintain an open door policy towards the North. The South is powerful enough today to be strategically patient with the North for as long as it takes for the North to commence a genuine reconciliation process leading to rapprochement, and eventually peaceful reunification. In this ultimate end game, nuclear weapons have no role to play.

CHAPTER 3

SURGING WAVES UNDERWATER: NUCLEAR SCENARIO IN NORTHEAST ASIA

Hua Han

Introduction

This paper provides a Chinese perspective on the underlying dynamics of nuclear weapons proliferation in Northeast Asia.It starts by examining the DPRK's efforts to develop a nuclear deterrent and the impact of this development on threat perceptions of the DPRK's neighbors in Northeast Asia. In spite of nuclear alarm bells being rung in Seoul and Tokyo, a scenario of rapid nuclear proliferation by South Korea and/or Japan is not realistic. American nuclear extended deterrence to these two allies remains strong. Moreover, strong diplomatic interventions by all parties, but especially by China, have discouraged the DPRK provocations, at least for now.

Moreover, there is no consensus in the ROK or in Japan about developing independent nuclear weapons capabilities, although both are acquiring nuclear fuel cycle and other options that provide them with extra technological capacity to proliferate quickly should they so choose. Meanwhile, US deployment of missile defenses in this region could lead to friction between Beijing and Seoul, and to emergence of security dilemmas for the US-China as well as Japan-China relations. A regional mechanism to achieve nuclear disarmament and non-proliferation is sorely needed to ensure regional stability in security affairs.

IMPACT OF THE DPRK NUCLEAR WEAPONS PROLIFERATION

North Korea's nuclear nuclearization

After three rounds of nuclear tests and several rounds of missile tests, North Korea has reached a tipping point.The DPRK's capability is on the verge of achieving an operational nuclear deterrence. Various experts have noted that the DPRK may have the capacity to miniaturize a nuclear warhead in order to place it on a missile, although it is not known if it has actually done so. Once this milestone is achieved, and once their missile and re-entry vehicle is tested successfully, the DPRK will become a nuclear armed state able to project a credible nuclear threat.

Over the years, the DPRK has made various nuclear provocations and unwanted acts with its nuclear capability. North Korean leaders have often mentioned their growing capability of nuclear weapon systems. They say that they treasure the nuclear weapon as a sword. Also, North Korea has amended its constitution by including nuclear weapons in the provisions of its constitution and legal framework. When combined with its nuclear threat rhetoric, this emerging capacity has led other countries to believe that the DPRK will never give up its nuclear weapons.

Anxiety over the DPRK Nuclear Weapon

Not surprisingly, as a result of these provocations and increasing capabilities, anxiety in this region has intensified, especially in South Korea and Japan. Although no dominos have fallen as a result of North Korean proliferation, anxiety has certainly spread widely, especially in South Korea and Japan.

Thus, ROK President Park Geun-hye has warned: "North Korea would effectively be crossing the Rubicon if they were to conduct another nuclear test" and if it were to occur, it would take, "a huge toll," on security across the Korean Peninsula. Relatedly, the chairman of South Korea's Joint Chiefs of Staff pledged to pre-emptively strike against North Korea if it showed intent to use a nuclear weapon. As a consequence, the once-fringe debate in Seoul about the ROK obtaining its own nuclear weapons has moved onto center stage in South Korean politics.

Japan too has been alarmed by North Korea's nuclear weapons. As Japan's former chief cabinet spokesman said: 'We are doing all we can to protect the safety of our nation.' More concretely, Japan's Defense Ministry deployed the Air Self-Defense Force's PAC-3s as a precaution against possible ballistic missile tests from North Korea.

Rationale behind the new anxiety

There are multiple reasons that this new anxiety has emerged in the region, especially in the ROK and Japan. First and simplest, North Korea is seen to be a real and immediate threat to the security in Seoul and Tokyo. This threat perception is reinforced by the DPRK's provocative actions. Also, the DPRK's threats to launch "pre-emptive nuclear strikes on the headquarters of the aggressors," and specific mention that Japan may be the first to be hit, as well as Seoul being identified as a potential nuclear target, have had a psychological impact in both countries.

Another reason for the evident insecurity is that the leaders of the ROK and Japan harbor real doubts about the reliability of US extended deterrence commitments. To them, the nuclear umbrella looks like it may have big holes in it. Although the United States has reaffirmed that it will defend its allies, once North Korea demonstrates that it possesses long-range missiles that can attack the United States itself, its allies may worry that the United States might capitulate in some manner to the DPRK's nuclear coercion, at the allies' expense.

Moreover, many security specialists and policymakers in the ROK and Japan, and even in the United States, complain that Beijing has taken only a "soft" approach toward the DPRK, rather than a tough stance against the DPRK's nuclear development or provocations.

A further reason for allied insecurity is lack of regional institutions for tackling nuclear proliferation and security as a whole. As we all know, the Six-Party Talks have been long stalemated and there is no institutional mechanism whereby nuclear and non-nuclear states can manage the instability created by nuclear threats or to ensure that nuclear proliferation is curbed or avoided altogether.

Also underlying the new anxiety is domestic politics. As we noted earlier, a political debate has broken out into mass media in South Korea as to whether the ROK should make its own nuclear weapons. This trend is linked to rising demands in the ROK for "nuclear sovereignty" in its negotiations with the United States over permitted activities in the realm of nuclear energy, with the corollary being gaining of weapons-related reprocessing technology and separated fissile materials on a par with Japan and the DPRK. This nuclear debate has moved into mainstream circles in South Korea led by Mong-joon Chung, a ruling party legislator. At the same time, the public opinion polls by the Asan Institute—admittedly an entity with its own political agenda—show that a majority of people favor an independent South Korean nuclear weapons capability, but only less than 30 percent are against.

Advocates of independent nuclear weapons are also gaining ground in Japan.Many of these voices want to pursue a foreign and defense policy that is strategically independent of the United States, or at least gain greater autonomy within the alliance.

Abe's political agenda

Although Japan is the only state to be victim of nuclear attack, Japan has developed a unique approach to its own nuclear weapons development. It has nurtured the national identity of a non-nuclear state but has taken care to develop enough capability to gain a *de facto* or practical "virtual" nuclear weapons status. This "technological deterrent" is based on its accumulation of excess plutonium stored in Japan and also recent reports of Japanese government internal thinking about the possibility of producing Japanese nuclear weapons. North Korea's provocations have stimulated anew this nuclear debate in Japan. Since the Fukushima disaster, Japan's ruling Liberal Democratic Party (LDP) government has pushed the restoration of Japan's plutonium strategy and to restart as many light water reactors as possible, in spite of profound domestic anti-nuclear sentiments at the popular, provincial, and even political-elite levels. Some prominent Japanese figures such as Shintaro Ishihara, former governor of Tokyo and leader of the Japan Restoration Party, have called openly for the development of nuclear weapons. Former Foreign Ministers Nakagawa and Aso have suggested "chipping away at the nuclear taboo and preparing a national agenda for a fundamental re-examination of Japan's security policy that includes consideration of the nuclear option."

Some in Japan argues that nuclear reactors are in themselves a nuclear deterrent, and when combined with Japan's long-range rocket launching capabilities, is effectively a "latent" or virtual nuclear weapons in the basement, held in reserve as insurance against future contingencies, but already in play in political and military perceptions in the region. That the government has reportedly conducted internal studies on the nuclear weapons option only increases regional concern as to Japan's ultimate nuclear weapons intentions.

From anxiety to a nuclear domino?

Thus, the impact of North Korean proliferation and the recent resurgence of nuclear weapons as a factor in relations between the great powers has not led to a short-term nuclear domino effect or proliferation chain reaction, but rather to what I will call nuclear "deregulation," that is, the necessity of now considering the "might be" medium-term scenarios that now inflects security thinking and planning throughout the region.

As adduced above, there are three reasons that no nuclear dominos have fallen to date after North Korea's nuclear breakout. These are:

a) Dependence on US extended nuclear deterrence remains the preferred option for Seoul and Tokyo;
b) North Korea's nuclear provocations have been discouraged by a variety of regional diplomatic and, at a lesser extent, technological restraints; and
c) Japan and South Korea manifest domestic dissensus on the desirability of gaining independent nuclear weapons.

US extended nuclear deterrence

To abate the anxiety wrought in the ROK and Japan by North Korea's nuclear breakout, the United States has pledged its 'unwavering commitment' to alliance with these two states, including the extension of nuclear deterrence. Thus, so long as the US-ROK and US-Japan alliances remain strong, Seoul and Tokyo are unlikely to pursue independent nuclear deterrent forces.

Some lessons from history of the dangers of allied proliferation have been observed in the case of South Korea, and these affect the current calculi of all parties in the region. As is now well documented, South Korea had secretly engaged in nuclear programs when it felt insecure after Nixon announced the Nixon Doctrine, and Carter's proposed to withdraw US forces in part from the Korean Peninsula. In addition to the earlier proliferation campaign waged by Park Chung-hee, in 2004, South Korea admitted that it had an AVLIS (Atomic Vapor Laser Isotope Separation) enrichment program from 1991 to 2000 which earned it special investigations from the IAEA.

In this regard, although US nuclear weapons are no longer forward-deployed in the region in host nations, the US military presence remains. The force levels have reduced to 28,000 personnel in South Korea, and 100,000 in the region as a whole, and there is little prospect of this falling further.Thus, there is little objective basis for allied insecurity with regard to the US intention of remaining committed and capable of leading bilateral alliances in this region.

ROK-US nuclear extended deterrent

In 2009, the ROK and the US adopted "the Joint Vision for South Korea-US Alliance" to build a comprehensive strategic alliance. The US-ROK security consultative meeting reaffirmed the robustness of the alliance and its ability to counter the deteriorating security situation on the Korean Peninsula. The allies produced "The Strategic Alliance 2015," updated "Guidelines for US-ROK Defense Cooperation," and held multiple meetings of a bilateral extended deterrence policy committee, to reaffirm US extended deterrence, including nuclear extended deterrence.From the perspective of the DPRK, this appears as a joint nuclear deterrent, not dissimilar to that operated by NATO in Europe.

US-Japan alliance

Undoubtedly Japan is the first ally among all the US allies in the Asia Pacific region. By virtue of its pacifist constitution, Japan has given up its rights to develop offensive weapons. Rather than deploy nuclear weapons as "defensive," Japan has sheltered under the US nuclear umbrella as its security guarantee since 1960. The United States prefers strongly to stick with the status quo of Japan's three non-nuclear principles whereby Japan foregoes the nuclear weapons option. However, US policy does not extend to constraining the slow growth of Japan's latent technological deterrent and it remains silent on Japan's growing reprocessing capability and accumulation of a 40 tonne of plutonium while officially dismissing the risk of possible conversion of nuclear materials and technological readiness into nuclear weapons. Yet, from a regional perspective, the Rokkasho reprocessing facility in northern Honshu can produce nine tonne of weapons-grade plutonium annually, or enough to construct up to 2,000 bombs

Diplomatic efforts to discourage the DPRK nuclear engagement

Although the Six-Party Talks have been suspended for years, the effort to curb North Koreas nuclear weapons has continued unabated. This effort has included collective measures such as sanctions and statements under the UN Security Council auspices. Under the current South Korean administration, President Park has pushed for a "trust building" process to reinstitute the multilateral dialogue, including the Six-Party Talks. China too has undertaken a new approach toward the DPRK, increasingly downgrading its bilateral alliance relationship from a special to a near-normal status. President Xi Jingping's statements and diplomatic efforts have shown a growing intolerance of the DPRK provocations, especially in the nuclear dimension. Thus, at their summit meeting in Beijing, President Park noted that: "President Xi and I agreed North Korea's denuclearization should be achieved and we are resolutely opposed to North Korea's nuclear tests." For his part, President Xi talked about "not allowing trouble-making on China's doorstep," a clear reference to Pyongyang. He also sent a senior envoy to North Korea calling for resumption of the Six-Party Talks, and exerted other pressure on the North Korean regime to agree to resumption of the talks.

Nuclear Domino Effect is Unlikely

As I noted above, in spite of nuclear weapons proliferation debates and evolving discourse in Japan and the ROK, there is no evidence that either government has any intention of going nuclear. It is completely clear that no government decision has been made to go nuclear in the ROK and Japan, even though both countries have built the scientific base for building nuclear weapons. In the ROK, there is also no prospect of bringing US tactical nuclear weapons back to the ROK's territory. In truth, the nuclear debates in both Seoul and Tokyo have been used as a way to press China to take a tougher stance on North Korea's nuclear and other provocative activities. In Japan, the populace mostly remains opposed to nuclear weapons; and many Japanese security strategists are acutely aware that "going it alone" would increase Japan's real insecurity rather than reduce it.

Regional nuclear "deregulation"

To reduce nuclear anxiety in the ROK and Japan, the United States has taken steps to assure Seoul and Tokyo in recent years and to accommodate aspects of their nascent nuclear aspirations at the same time. For example, the United States has permitted the ROK to extend the range of its ballistic missiles from 300 km to 800 km, a move to be regarded by the ROK as the means to "deter military provocation from North Korea." Moreover, the United States and the ROK have reportedly agreed that the ROK may commence reprocessing of spent nuclear fuel for research purposes and the ROK will be allowed to conduct uranium enrichment with prior US consent. At the same time, the United States is pushing hard for the ROK to install THAAD, the high altitude missile defense system, and accompanying X-band radar in South Korea.

Similarly in Japan, the United States has intensified its missile defense cooperation to deter potential nuclear attacks from North Korea. The allies have deployed an X-band radar in Aomori Prefecture and plan to deploy the second radar in Kyogamisaki submarine base in the city of Kyotango. The United States is also trying hard to triangulate the two bilateral military alliances by using missile defense system as first step to get the three countries to cooperate.

CONCLUSION

The DPRK's efforts to develop a nuclear deterrent has alarmed northeast Asian countries. It has stimulated a growing sense of insecurity and prompted nuclear alarmists to emerge as powerful voices in domestic nuclear politics of the ROK and Japan. However, it is unlikely that nuclear proliferation will result in a short-term "nuclear domino" scenario because US security commitments and nuclear umbrellas extended to the ROK and Japan remain strong. Also, intensified diplomacy has discouraged the DPRK provocations, and there is a lack of consensus in Seoul and Tokyo as to the need for an independent nuclear weapons capability.

Nonetheless, the US development and deployment of a missile defense in this region justified by the North Korean nuclear threat and other provocations could exacerbate friction between Beijing and Seoul, and lead to security dilemmas emerging between Tokyo and Beijing and between Washington and Beijing.

To solve the nuclear problems of this region and to maintain regional stability, a regional mechanism and dialogue on nuclear disarmament and nonproliferation is badly needed. Although they were flawed, the Six-Party Talks were still a useful mechanism to resolve the nuclear issues, but only on an interim basis. A regional mechanism should not only tackle non-proliferation issues. It should also address how to maintain strategic stability between nuclear weapons states and provide security to non-nuclear weapons states in the region. China should make a special effort to reach some consensus on such a mechanism to manage nuclear issues in this region.

CHAPTER 4

THE CURRENT STATE AND FORECAST OF NORTHEAST ASIA'S NUCLEAR POWER PLANTS

Won-young Yang Lee

Introduction

The myth that nuclear power is safe has been fully debunked by Japan's Fukushima power plant catastrophe and its aftermath. The damage to the reactor of Fukushima plant No. 1 was not so surprising considering that it was already long past its initial life span. But the destruction of the containment building was shocking as estimates of the probability of containment breach were as small as no more than once in a 100 million operating years. Thus, the threat of an accident at an active nuclear plant is perceived now to be real, perhaps as much or more so than from a nuclear weapon.

The Fukushima disaster is an ongoing process. The amount of radioactive gas and fluids emitted have fallen drastically but are still being dispersed into the air and sea. Recovery efforts are slow. Officials barely managed to figure out how the nuclear fuel meltdown occurred by using a remote-controlled drone. Celsium-134 stemming from Fukushima has reached Alaska and the east coast of the United States. Thyroid cases of those under 18 are also expected to increase and secondary and other collateral damage from Fukushima are expected to be incurred in the indefinite future.

While the world's reliance on atomic energy is in general falling, Northeast Asia, including Japan seems to be the center of the world's proliferation of nuclear power plants. Renewable energy growth in China, however, is much faster than that of nuclear plant adoptions. Whether China will complete its initial nuclear plant projects is also unknown, given its gas pipeline deal with Russia. Japan's state of nuclear power, which used to account for 30 percent of its electrical power, remains at zero since September 2013. Yet its energy demand and supply balance remains stable. The country not only boosted its output of thermal plants but introduced a nationwide energy efficiency policy that drastically cut electricity demand. Applications for solar energy generation have also exceeded 70,000 MW due to a fast adoption of renewable energy policies. This amounts to the output of nearly 15 1,000 megawatt-level power plants.[1] South Korea seems to move in the opposite direction. For the first time in thirty years, it has designated two new sites for nuclear plants. It also approved the activation of the Shinwolsong No. 2 reactor, bringing the number of active plants from 23 to 24. Nuclear safety regulators, despite controversy surrounding its safety, approved the extension of the Wolsong No. 1 reactor's life span. Approvals for Shingori reactors 3 and 4 are also pending.

State of Global Nuclear Power Plants and Forecast

Although nuclear power grew rapidly in the 1980s, the total number of nuclear power plants today is more or less static. Nuclear power generation is falling at a constant rate. Germany decided to shut down eight nuclear plants in light of the Fukushima disaster and also decommissioned plants that were active in the eighties.

The IAEA refers to plants that have been unused for a long time as "Long Term Shut down," or LTS, and does not count them in the tally of active nuclear plants. Among Japan's operational nuclear plants, which stood at 54 pre-Fukushima, 11 were closed down. From September of 2013 to April 2014, 43 facilities suspended operations citing inspections. (The Oi No. 2 reactor was used temporarily but the number of running

[1] Hee-gon Yu, *The Kyunghyang Shinmun*, Octorber 13, 2014, http://news.khan.co.kr/kh_news/khan_art_view.html?artid=201410122156185&code=610103

plants since September 2014 remains at zero.) The IAEA, however, counts the 43 facilities as "operational" plants, and notes the total number of up and running plants as standing at 443. But plants that have remained dormant for over a year would be better described as LTOs. Japan's nuclear energy companies have requested the resumption of 21 nuclear plants. Four received approval by regulators but remain in limbo due to the court's restraining order and consent whereabouts of local governments. The rest is still under review.

Globally, reactor construction thrived in the 1980s. But since the Three Mile Island accident in 1978, US nuclear reactor construction went into hibernation. Social tolerance and acceptance also declined after the 1986 Chernobyl incident. The sector as a whole faced stagnation in the 1990s, as profitability tumbled amid strengthening of safety requirements. Naturally the rate of nuclear electricity production fell from a high of 18 percent to 11 percent in 2013.

In contrast, the solar and wind energy sectors thrived. In fact, renewable energy today is the driving force of the energy industry. Growth of renewable energy in Europe, led by efforts in Germany, is most notable. Germany's rate of power production via renewable means exceeded 25 percent as of end of 2014. The level of nuclear electricity fell to only to 15 percent. The difference between the output of solar panels and wind energy, and nuclear power has become stark. Installations of wind power generators have soared.

In 2014, the accumulated grid-connected wind power amounts to 301 gigawatts—almost as much as the installed 332.5 GW of nuclear reactors. Wind turbines set up in China in 2013 account for some 91 GW and this figure is approximately one-third of all grid-connected wind turbines in the world. Nuclear reactors are moving in the opposite direction. The number of newly built nuclear reactors from 2000 to 2013 is actually smaller than the number of reactors that were closed.

The International Energy Agency (IEA) predicted the closing of some

200 nuclear reactors by 2040.[2] This probably stems from the fact that the number of reactors that have operated for more than 30 years stands at 162 as of May 2014. The average lifespan of the 143 reactors that closed in 2013 was 23 years.[3] The New Policies Scenario introduced by the IEA predicted a resurgence of nuclear reactors after 2020. The forecast was however smaller than that of renewables and gas generation.

The IEA predicts the closing of 150 gigawatts-worth of nuclear facilities, along with 380 gigawatts-worth of new construction in the next 25 years.

But looking back at the trend of the past twenty years, the number of new reactors is falling while the ones shutting down are on the rise. The likelihood of this trend reversing itself to yield a net increase of new reactors is slim. Past outlooks of the nuclear energy growth scenario have not been accurate and, to some degree, overestimated.

State of Northeast Asia's nuclear energy, forecast

As of March 2015, South Korea is running 23 nuclear reactors worth of 20,716 MW and is the process of constructing 5 new facilities with 6,600 MW (see Table 4-1). One of these (Shingori No. 3) is being test run under regulators' approval. Another reactor is being under review. Two retired reactors (Gori No. 1 and Wolsong No. 1) were approved to have their lifespan be extended. The Gori No. 1's 1st phase life extension ends in 2017 and its operator is currently writing up its application for a 2nd phase approval. The law stipulates that the application be filed no later than two years prior to the life span deadline. Therefore the application must be submitted no later than June 17 2015. Regulators approved Wolsong No. 1 reactor's lifespan extension in February 27 and the plant is currently under inspection to be on operation.

---

[2] "World Energy Outlook 2014," IEA, http://www.worldenergyoutlook.org/publications/weo-2014/

[3] "The Database on Nuclear Power Reactors," IAEA Power Reactor Information System (PRIS), http://www.iaea.org/PRIS/home.aspx

Table 4-1: South Korea's nuclear reactors (as of March 2015)

Reactor		Location	Type	Capacity (MWe)	Initiation of commercial use/ Construction rate
Gori	#1	Jangan, Busan	Light water reactor	587	'78. / 4.29
	#2			650	'83. / 7.25
	#3			950	'85. / 9.30
	#4			950	'86. / 4.29
Shin Gori	#1			1,000	'11. / 2.28
	#2			1,000	'12. / 7.20
	#3	Uljugunseo-saeng, Ulsan		1,400	Under Construction / 98.24%
	#4			1,400	
	#5			1,400	Planned
	#6			1,400	
	#7			1,500	
	#8			1,500	
Wolseong	#1	Yangnam, Gyeongju, North Gyeongsang Province	Heavy water reactor	679	'83. / 4.22
	#2			700	'97. / 7. 1
	#3			700	'98. / 7. 1
	#4			700	'99.10. / 1
Shin Wolseong	#1	Yangbuk, Gyeongju, North Gyeongsang Province	Light water reactor	1,000	'12. / 7.31
	#2			1,000	Under Construction / 99.71%

<table>
<tr><td rowspan="6">Hanbit</td><td>#1</td><td rowspan="6">Hongnong, Yeonggwang, South Jeolla Province</td><td rowspan="6">Light water reactor</td><td>950</td><td>'86. / 8.25</td></tr>
<tr><td>#2</td><td>950</td><td>'87. / 6.10</td></tr>
<tr><td>#3</td><td>1,000</td><td>'95. / 3.31</td></tr>
<tr><td>#4</td><td>1,000</td><td>'96. / 1. 1</td></tr>
<tr><td>#5</td><td>1,000</td><td>'02. / 5.21</td></tr>
<tr><td>#6</td><td>1,000</td><td>'02. / 12.24</td></tr>
<tr><td rowspan="6">Hanwool</td><td>#1</td><td rowspan="10">Uljin, North Gyeongsang Province</td><td rowspan="10">Light water reactor</td><td>950</td><td>'88. / 9.10</td></tr>
<tr><td>#2</td><td>950</td><td>'89. / 9.30</td></tr>
<tr><td>#3</td><td>1,000</td><td>'98. / 8.11</td></tr>
<tr><td>#4</td><td>1,000</td><td>'99. / 12.31</td></tr>
<tr><td>#5</td><td>1,000</td><td>'04. / 7.29</td></tr>
<tr><td>#6</td><td>1,000</td><td>'05. / 4.22</td></tr>
<tr><td rowspan="4">Shin Han-wool</td><td>#1</td><td>1,400</td><td rowspan="2">Under Construction / 71.81%</td></tr>
<tr><td>#2</td><td>1,400</td></tr>
<tr><td>#3</td><td>1,400</td><td rowspan="2">Planned</td></tr>
<tr><td>#4</td><td>1,400</td></tr>
<tr><td colspan="2">Total</td><td>-</td><td>-</td><td>35,916</td><td>-</td></tr>
</table>

Source: Korea Hydro and Nuclear Power (KHNP), http://khnp.co.kr/

Nuclear power generation for 2014 was at 156,406 GWh, approximately 30 percent of the year's entire power generation. In 1978, when the country first started its nuclear power generation, output stood at 2,324 GWh, or 7.4 percent of all power generation.[4] Reactors under construction as of March 2015 are the Shinweolsong No. 2, Shingori No. 3 and 4, Shinhaneul No. 1 and 2. Those under planning are Shingori No. 5-8 and

[4] Korea Hydro and Nuclear Power, http://khnp.co.kr/

Shinhaneul No. 3-4. Moreover, North Gyeongsang Province's Yeongdeok and Gangwon Province's Samcheok in 2012 were designated to house new nuclear power plants. South Korea's concentration of nuclear generation per unit area is the highest in the world and is expected to rise further. Considering the plants under construction, the country's four nuclear reactor sites all remain within the top 10 in terms of number of reactors and equipment volume per unit area. This is because additional nuclear plant constructions are continuing on the border areas of neighboring sites. The government decided to expand pre-existing sites due to difficulty of securing new sites after securing four in the 1970s. The designation of Samcheok and Yeongdeok in 2012 were the first nuclear site designations in 40 years. Such designations will become even harder in the future.

China also has hit the accelerator in terms of building new nuclear power plants. China's ever-increasing electricity demand from its economic progress and concerns over air pollution from coal thermal power are the driving causes of Beijing's nuclear expansion program. The country is operating 27 reactors (net 24,603 MW) as of April 2015 and is constructing 25 more (net 27,335 MW), making it the world's largest nuclear power nation (see Table 4-2.) The country showed restraint in seeking new plants in the wake of the 2011 Fukushima crisis but resumed its push in October 2012. 14 new plants were connected to its electric grid since the Fukushima incident.

Table 4-2: State of China's nuclear power (as of April 2015)

Name		Location	Type	Status	MW	grid connection date
CEFR		Beijing Tuoli	FBR	in operation	25	2011-07-21
CHANGJIANG	#1	Hainin Changjiang	Light water reactor CNP650	in construction	650	
	#2				650	

<table>
<tr><td rowspan="2">DAYABAY</td><td>#1</td><td rowspan="2">Guangdong SHENZHEN CITY</td><td rowspan="2">Light water reactor M310</td><td rowspan="2">in operation</td><td>984</td><td>1993-08-31</td></tr>
<tr><td>#2</td><td>984</td><td>1994-02-07</td></tr>
<tr><td rowspan="2">FANGCHENGGANG</td><td>#1</td><td rowspan="2">Guangxi Fangchenggang</td><td rowspan="2">Light water reactor CPR1000</td><td rowspan="2">in construction</td><td>1080</td><td></td></tr>
<tr><td>#2</td><td>1080</td><td></td></tr>
<tr><td rowspan="2">FANGJIASHAN</td><td>#1</td><td rowspan="2">Zhajiang Jiaxing</td><td rowspan="2">Light water reactor CPR1000</td><td rowspan="2">in operation</td><td>1080</td><td>2014-11-04</td></tr>
<tr><td>#2</td><td>1080</td><td>2015-01-12</td></tr>
<tr><td rowspan="5">FUQING</td><td>#1</td><td rowspan="5">Fuqing</td><td rowspan="4">Light water reactor CPR1000</td><td>in operation</td><td>1080</td><td>2014-08-20</td></tr>
<tr><td>#2</td><td rowspan="4">in construction</td><td>1080</td><td></td></tr>
<tr><td>#3</td><td>1080</td><td></td></tr>
<tr><td>#4</td><td>1080</td><td></td></tr>
<tr><td>#5</td><td>Light water reactor Hualong 1</td><td>1150</td><td></td></tr>
<tr><td rowspan="2">HAIYANG</td><td>#1</td><td rowspan="2">Haiyang</td><td rowspan="2">Light water reactor AP1000</td><td rowspan="2">in construction</td><td>1250</td><td></td></tr>
<tr><td>#2</td><td>1250</td><td></td></tr>
<tr><td rowspan="6">HONGYANHE</td><td>#1</td><td rowspan="6">DALIAN</td><td rowspan="4">Light water reactor CPR1000</td><td rowspan="3">in operation</td><td>1119</td><td>2013-02-17</td></tr>
<tr><td>#2</td><td>1119</td><td>2013-11-23</td></tr>
<tr><td>#3</td><td>1080</td><td>2015-03-23</td></tr>
<tr><td>#4</td><td rowspan="3">in construction</td><td>1080</td><td></td></tr>
<tr><td>#5</td><td rowspan="2">Light water reactor ACPR1000</td><td>1080</td><td></td></tr>
<tr><td>#6</td><td>1080</td><td></td></tr>
</table>

LINGAO	#1	Guangdong SHENZEN	Light water reactor CPR1000	in operation	990	2002-02-26
	#2				990	2002-09-14
	#3				1080	2010-07-15
	#4				1080	2011-05-03
NINGDE	#1	Fujian Ningde	Light water reactor CPR1000	in operation	1080	2012-12-28
	#2				1080	2014-01-04
	#3				1080	2015-03-21
	#4			in construction	1080	
QINSHAN-1		Jiaxing	Light water reactor CNP300	in operation	310	1991-12-15
QINSHAN2	#1		Light water reactor CNP650	in operation	650	2002-02-06
	#2				650	2004-03-11
	#3				660	2010-08-01
	#4				660	2011-11-25
QINSHAN3	#1		Heavy water reactor CANDU6	in operation	728	2002-11-19
	#2				728	2003-06-12
SANMEN	#1	Taizhou	Light water reactor AP1000	in construction	1250	
	#2				1250	
SHIDAO BAY-1		Weihai	High temperature gas-coaled reactor HTGR	in construction	211	

TAISHAN	#1	Taishan	Light water reactor EPR	in con-struction	1750	
	#2				1750	
TIANWAN	#1	Lianyungang	Light water reactor WER1000	in opera-tion	1060	2006-05-12
	#2				1060	2007-05-14
	#3			in con-struction	1060	
	#4				1060	
YANGJIANG	#1	Guangzhou Yangjiang	Light water reactor CPR1000	in opera-tion	1086	2013-12-31
	#2				1080	2015-03-10
	#3			in con-struction	1080	
	#4				1080	
	#5				1087	
	#6				1087	
Total		-	-		51,938	-

Source:"China, People's Republic of," IAEA PRIS,http://www.iaea.org/PRIS/CountryStatistics/CountryDetails.aspx?current=CN, http://www.heneng.net.cn/index.php?mod=npp, Korea Institute for International Economic Policy's Beijing bureau briefing (December 10, 2010.) The inaugural KHNP-CNNP Nuclear safety conference (March, 2015.) Ministry of Foreign Affairs, http://www.mofa.go.kr

* Notes for Table 4-2: M310 of France's Areva, AP1000 of US Westinghouse, WER1000 of Russia's pressurized light water reactor, CANDU6 of Canadian pressurized heavy water reactor, CNP300/CNP650 of CNNC, CPR1000 of third-generation Chinese pressurized light water reactor (modeled after Areva technology), ACPR1000 of upgraded model of CPR1000, HUALONG, pressurized light water reactor developed for export. Co-developed by CNNC and CGN

China is producing its plants with home-grown technology, having adopted most of the world's leading reactor models with source technologies. The country, besides its light and heavy-water reactors, has either built or is in the process of building its own fast breeder reactor and high-temperature gas-coaled reactor. The breeder reactor remains dormant after running 26 hours when first activated in 2011. China, in December 2012 began construction of its high-temperature gas-coaled reactor but the expected completion date remains uncertain. China, along with the United States, Russia, France, and Korea, is among the top five nuclear energy nations. But its rate of nuclear generation stands at a mere 2.4 percent. The United States currently runs 99 reactors with a generation rate of 19.5 percent. Rate of nuclear generation Russia, with 34 reactors, stands at 18.57 percent.[5] According to China's long-term nuclear power supply plan, the country aims to reach a power capacity of 40,000 MW by the end of 2015. It also expects to reach an output capacity of 5.8 MW and secure an additional 30,000 MW of ongoing or new plant constructions.[6] China suspended construction of reactors in the immediate aftermath of the Fukushima nuclear disaster but resumed in October 2012 and on March 10 approved the construction of Hongyanhe No. 5 and 6 after a 4-year review period, marking the first nuclear plant approval after the Fukushima incident.[7] Hongyanhe reactors 1-3 are currently in operation, with No. 4 set for completion soon. The Hongyanhe No. 4 is a pressurized water reactor plant made with homegrown technology based on France's Areva. Hongyanhe 5 and 6 are reportedly models upgraded from No. 4. When resuming its push for nuclear power, China, along with long-term nuclear energy development plan, also announced its nuclear safety plan. Pre-Fukushima, Beijing had established a wide-scale nuclear energy development initiative with a planned installed capacity of 40,000 MW by 2007. The figure was later boosted to 70,000 MW by 2009. But since Fukushima, the government puts first priority on realizing a high-efficiency management policy, showing a more conservative stance in approving constructions of new

---

[5] "The Database On Nuclear Power Reactors," IAEA PRIS, http://www.iaea.org/pris/

[6] "The bright and dark side of China Nuclear Power Plant," Keun-young Yu, January 29, 2015, http://www.globalwindow.org/gw/overmarket/GWOMAL020M.html?BBS_ID=10&MENU_CD=M10103&UPPER_MENU_CD=M10102&MENU_STEP=3&ARTICLE_ID=5025662&ARTICLE_SE=20302

[7] "Approval on new project of building Nuclear Power Plan of Chna," Ministry of Foreign Affairs, http://www.mofa.go.kr/webmodule/htsboard/template/read/korboardread.jsp?typeID=24&boardid=11661&seqno=10411&c=&t=&pagenum=1&tableName=TYPE_KORBOARD&pc=&dc=&wc=&lu=&vu=&iu=&du=

plants.[8]

On March 16, 2011, Prime Minister Wen Jiabao convened a cabinet meeting to assess and analyze the Fukushima disaster and announced four major emergency measures regarding nuclear energy development: 1) conduct immediate inspections of all on-going nuclear plant constructions; 2) strengthen safety management of nuclear energy development through cooperation between operator and safety watchdog; 3) assess safety of reactors under construction by applying the strictest standards and halt insufficient ones; and, 4) hasten the preparation of the nuclear development safety plan. Meanwhile, China suspended all new projects, including those in preparation, until the plan was reviewed and approved. The Chinese government also began reviewing adoption of alternative power sources and an increase in reduction of energy use.[9] China recently resumed approval of a new plant, the first in four years, but submissions for building new reactors in the inland were all on hold as of late 2014.[10]

According to the World Nuclear Agency, newly planned reactors in China amount to 45 as of April 2015 (42 when excluding ones that have begun construction.) The number of newly proposed reactors is estimated at 142 (see Table 4-3.) Many among those planned are located in the inland area. Upon completion of all planned nuclear reactors, China is poised to outpace the United States (99 reactors, 98,639 MW) and become the world's largest possessor of nuclear equipment in terms of volume (94 reactors, 100,769 MW.)

Table 4- 3: Number/equipment volume of planned, proposed Chinese reactors

Planned reactors	Proposed reactors

[8] Jong-seon Kim, "China's nuclear safety policy and implication," (in Korean), *STEPI Insight* 96 (2012), http://www.stepi.re.kr/module/publishDownFile.jsp?categCd=A0501&ntNo=96&r=

[9] Zhidong Li, "China's nuclear development condition and policy trends," June 2011

[10] Zhu Yue, "China's nuclear expansion threatened by public mease, "*China Dialogue*, September 23, 2014, at; http:// www.chinadialogue.net/article/show/single/en/336-china-s-nuclear-expansion-threatened-by-public-mease.

Number	MWe	Number	MWe
42	48,569	142	152,000

*Source: IAEA, WNA[11], KOTRA, Ministry of Foreign Affairs

Similar to Korea, China's nuclear energy development projects are run by the government (see Table 4-4.) In Korea, the Korea Hydro & Nuclear power, 100 percent owned by the Korea Electric Power Corporation under the Ministry of Trade, Industry and Energy runs all construction and management of nuclear reactors. In China, the country's three largest nuclear operators, under state supervision, are in charge of all nuclear energy development. Korea's nuclear reactor construction projects are decided under the biennial electric power demand/supply plan within the country's basic energy plan devised every five years. China's nuclear generator plans are devised by the National Development and Reform Commission and the National Energy Bureau proposing the country's new energy industry development plan (2011-2020), the 12th 5-year energy development plan (2011-2016) and the mid-long term nuclear energy development plan (2011-2020). China's nuclear safety is overseen by the Ministry of Environmental Protection. This is similar to Japan's nuclear regulatory committee being housed under the ministry of environment. Before Fukushima, the Ministry of Economy, Trade and Industry oversaw regulation of nuclear energy policy. This arrangement was also similar in South Korea. But the IAEA over several occasions advised the two countries to ensure their respective nuclear regulators have independent authority from the government. Since the Fukushima disaster, Japan and South Korea both formed their own nuclear regulatory committees and nuclear safety committees and placed them under the Ministry of Environment and the presidential office, respectively. Korea's nuclear safety committee was moved a notch down to a prime ministerial-level body. The prime minister

[11] "World Nuclear Power Reactors & Uranium Requirements," World Nuclear Association, http://www.world-nuclear.org/info/Facts-and-Figures/World-Nuclear-Power-Reactors-and-Uranium-Requirements/

doubles as chairman of the Atomic Energy Promotion Committee, raising questions regarding the body's regulatory independence.

Table 4-4: Breakdown of China's nuclear energy business

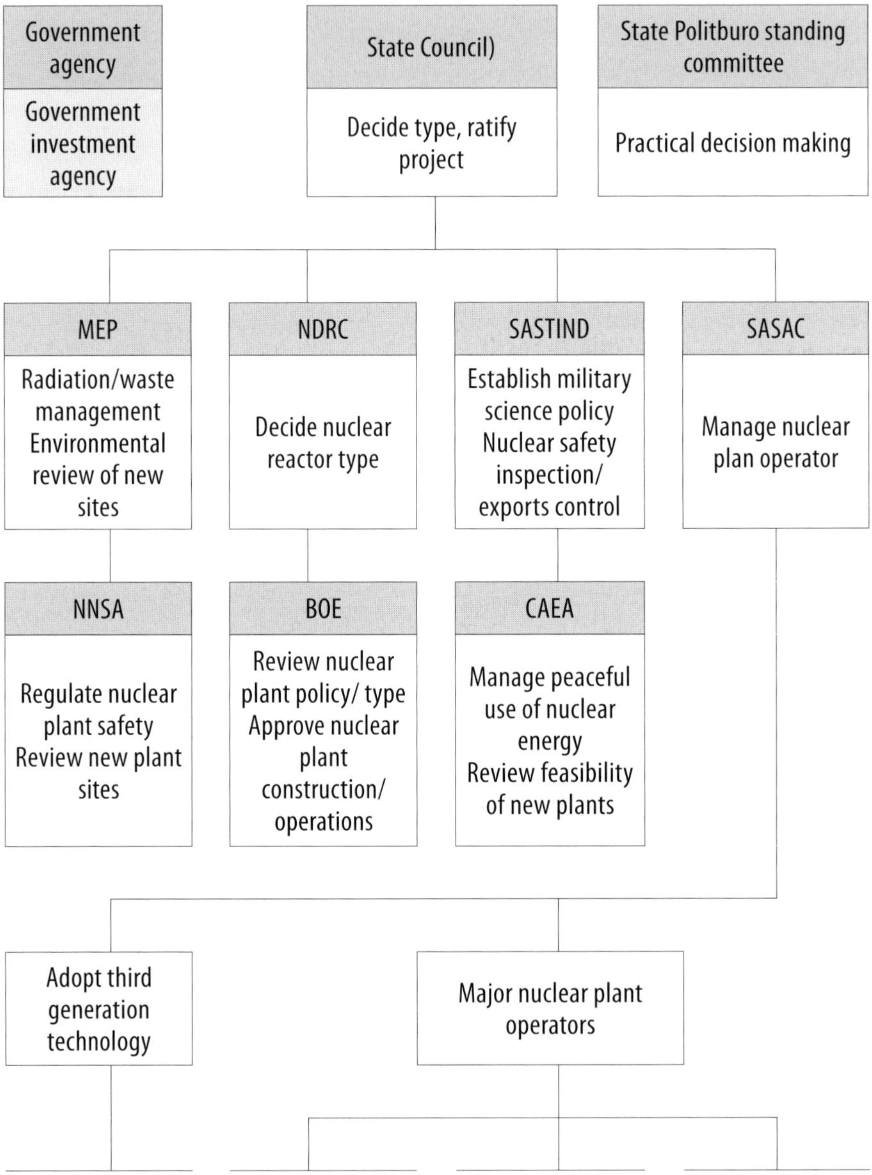

SNPTC	CNNC	CGN	CPI
SNERDI	CNNP	CNPDC	CPEC
SDEPCI	CNNO	CTEC	CPCEC
SNPEMC	CNNO	CNPEC	LHNP
SNBEIC	JNPC	LANPC	SNDPC
SNAISEC	SNPC	LDNPC	CNPC
SNPEC	FQNP	TSNPC	
SNPPOSTC	HNPC	DNMC	※ CPI, SNPTC in merger process as of March 2015
	LNPC	YGNPC	
	CNUC	NDNPC	

*Source: The 1st KHNP-CNNP nuclear safety enhancement conference Reference, March, 2015, KHNP

Historically Japan's nuclear history can be treated as pre- and post-Fukushima. Pre-Fukushima, Japan (excluding the practically defunct Monju fast breeder reactor) was running 54 nuclear reactors (48,960 MW)[12] and constructing two reactors (2,756 MW.) See Table 4-5.

[12] Monju in 1994 underwent nuclear fission but was suspended for over 15 years after a liquid sodium leak accident in December 1995. It was resumed on May 2010 but was suspended in just three months over malfunction. Regulators on May 15, 2013 ordered a complete suspension of all activities involving resumption preparation. This was effectively an order to shut down the plant for good. The Abe administration on February 5, 2014 reversed this order in its new energy basic plan.

Table 4-5: Japan's nuclear power plants (as of April 2015)

Power plant		Location	Type	Status	MW	Grid connection date	Long-term inspection	Post-Fukushima shutdown status	Pre-Fukushima shutdown status	Application for resumption	In construction
FUGENATR		TSURUGA	HWLWR	Closed	165	1978-07-29			1		
FUKUSHIMA-DAIICHI	#1	OHKUMAMACHI	BWR	Closed	460	1970-11-17					
	#2				784	1973-12-24					
	#3				784	1974-10-26					
	#4				784	1978-02-24					
	#5				784	1977-09-22					
	#6				1100	1979-05-04		6			
FUKUSHIMA-DAINI	#1	NARAHAMACHI	BWR	Long-term inspection	1100	1981-07-31					
	#2				1100	1983-06-23					
	#3				1100	1984-12-14					

	#4				1100	1986-12-17	4				
GENKAI	#1	GENKAI-CHO	PWR	To be closed after long-term inspection	559	1975-02-14		1			
	#2			Long-term inspection	559	1980-06-03					
	#3			Long-term inspection (Applied for re-sumption)	1180	1993-06-15					
	#4				1180	1996-11-12	3			2	
HAMAOKA	#1	OMA-EZAKI-SHI	BWR	Closed	540	1974-08-13					
	#2				840	1978-05-04			2		
	#3			Long-term inspection	1100	1987-01-20					

	#4			Long-term inspection (Applied for re-sumption)	1137	1993-01-27				1	
	#5			Long-term inspection	1380	2004-04-30	3				
HIGASHIDORI-1(TOHOKU)		Higashi-dori-mura	BWR	Long-term inspection (Applied for re-sumption)	1100	2005-03-09	1			1	
IKATA	#1	IKATA-CHO	PWR	Long-term inspection	566	1977-02-17					
	#2				566	1981-08-19					
	#3			Long-term inspection (Applied for re-sumption)	890	1994-03-29	3			1	
JPDR		TOKAI-MURA	BWR	Closed	13	1963-10-26			1		

KASHIWA-ZAKIKARI-WA	#1	KASHI-WAZAKI-SHI	BWR	Long-term inspection	1100	1985-02-13					
	#2				1100	1990-02-08					
	#3				1100	1992-12-08					
	#4				1100	1993-12-21					
	#5				1100	1989-09-12					
	#6			Long-term inspection (Applied for re-sumption)	1356	1996-01-29					
	#7				1356	1996-12-17	7			2	
MIHAMA	#1	MIHAMA	PWR	To be closed after long-term inspection	340	1970-08-08					
	#2				500	1972-04-21		2			
	#3			Long-term inspection	826	1976-02-19	1				

MONJU		TSU-RUGA	FBR	Decision to close down reversed	280	1995-08-29			1		
OHI	#1	OHI	PWR	Long-term inspection	1175	1977-12-23					
	#2				1175	1978-10-11					
	#3			Court rules for operational halt (1st trial) (Applied for resumption)	1180	1991-06-07					
	#4				1180	1992-06-19	4			2	
OHMA		OHMA	BWR	In construction (Applied for safety review)	1383					1	1

ONAGAWA	#1	ONA-GAWA, ISHINO-MAKI	BWR	Long-term inspection	524	1983-11-18					
	#2			Long-term inspection (Applied for re-sumption)	825	1994-12-23				1	
	#3			Long-term inspection	825	2001-05-30	3				
SENDAI	#1	SATSU-MASE NDAI	PWR	Long-term inspection (Applied for re-sumption/ approved)	890	1983-09-16					
	#2				890	1985-04-05	2			2	
SHIKA	#1	SHIKA-MACHI	BWR	Long-term inspection	540	1993-01-12					
	#2			Long-term inspection (Applied for re-sumption)	1206	2005-07-04	2			1	

SHIMANE	#1	MATSUE	BWR	To be closed after long-term inspection	460	1973-12-02		1			
	#2			Long-term inspection (Applied for re-sumption)	820	1988-07-11	1			1	
	#3			In con-struction	1373						1
TAKAHAMA	#1	TAKA-HAMA	PWR	Long-term inspection	826	1974-03-27					
	#2				826	1975-01-17					
	#3			Long-term inspection (Applied for re-sumption/ approved) Court rules injunction	870	1984-05-09					
	#4				870	1984-11-01	4			2	

TOKAI	#1	TOKA IMURA	GCR	Closed	166	1965-11-10			1		
	#2		BWR	Long-term inspection (Applied for re-sumption)	1100	1978-03-13	1			1	
TOMARI	#1	TOMA-RIMURA	PWR	Long-term inspection (Applied for re-sumption)	579	1988-12-06					
	#2				579	1990-08-27					
	#3				912	2009-03-20	3			3	
TSURUGA	#1	TSURU-GACITY	BWR	To be closed after long-term inspection	357	1969-11-16		1			
	#2		PWR	Long-term inspection	1160	1986-06-19	1				
Total (number)					62		43	11	6	21	2

Total (installed capacity)				53,720		42,048	6,912	2,004	21,483	2,756

Source: "Japan," IAEA PRIS, http://www.iaea.org/PRIS/CountryStatistics/CountryDetails.aspx?current=JP, "Fugen,"Atomic Knowledge Information Portal (AKIP), https://www.atomic.or.kr/atomica/word_read.html?idx=1695, "Dissolution of JPDR," AKIP, https://www.atomic.or.kr/atomica/read.html?chapter=5-2-4-10, KHNP Official Blog, March 4, 2014, http://blog.khnp.co.kr/blog/archives/5166, SBS, September 16, 2013, http://news.sbs.co.kr/news/endPage.do?news_id=N1001983887, *Newsis*, September 3, 2013, http://www.newsis.com/ar_detail/view.html?ar_id=NISX20130903_0012328608&cID=10102&pID=10100, JTBC, March 17, 2015,http://news.jtbc.joins.com/article/article.aspx?news_id=NB10810080, Institute of Nuclear Material Management-Korea Chapter, May 23, 2014,http://www.inmm-kc.or.kr/bbs/board.php?bo_table=m52&wr_id=205&page=10, Map of Nuclear Related Facilities (in Japanese), http://genpatumap.seesaa.net/article/367792940.html

*Notes:Heavy Water Light Water Reactor (HWLWR), Japan Power Demonstration Reactor (JPDR)

On March 2011, after the shutdown of four reactors at the Fukushima Daichi plant, reactor No. 6 (4,696 MW) was shut down. On March 17, the government also decided to close down the worn out No. 5 (2,216 MW) which was over 40 years old. No. 21 (21,483 MW) has filed to resume operations after a prolonged inspection process in line with the new safety regulation standards.[13] Also included was the Oma reactor that was being built in Shimokita, Aomori. It marked the resumption of ongoing construction projects in the post-Fukushima era. Nuclear plant operator J Power filed for a safety review of the Oma plant. It was the first ever safety filing of an uncompleted plant since the launch of the atomic regulation committee.[14] Among the 21 plants that have requested for approval for resumption, Sendai No. 1, 2 and Takahama 3, 4 were the ones that were inspected by regulators and ultimately approved resumption. Sendai No. 1 and 2 were okayed by the local government but the resumption date was postponed as regulators noted that safety measure planning was insufficient for the post-resumption period. Takahama No. 3 and 4 failed to receive support from local governments, while handed injunctions by the court. The Oi reactor No. 3 and 4 on May 2014 were handed injunctions by the Fukui local court and Takahama No. 3 and 4 on April 2015 were handed similar court decisions.

The number of nuclear reactors before the Fukushima incident, which stood at 54 (48,960 MW) has fallen to 43 (42,048 MW) as of April 2015. Since the Fukushima disaster, besides Oi reactors 3 and 4 having had operated for about a year,[15] all nuclear plants in Japan have entered a phase of long-term safety inspection. With not a single nuclear reactor in operation, this 'zero reactor' phase has continued for about a year and a half since September 2014 and as of September 2015, only one is now back in operation (at Sendai.)

---

[13] Map of Nucler Related Facilities (in Japanese), http://genpatumap.seesaa.net/article/367792940.html

[14] Yonhap News Agency, December 18, 2014, http://www.yonhapnews.co.kr/bulletin/2014/12/18/0200000000AKR20141218090900073.HTML

[15] SBS, September 16, 2013, http://news.sbs.co.kr/news/endPage.do?news_id=N1001983887

On May 21, 2014, the Fukui local court ruled it cannot recognize the resumption of Oi reactors 3 and 4 under regular inspections. Then-Prime minister Noda Yoshikiho, in consideration of the nation's power shortage, decided to resume operating the Oi 3 and 4. But the residents of Fukui and Fukushima prefectures filed a lawsuit against Kansai Electric Power restarting the plants, arguing that safety was not assured. Residents stated the arguments: 1) cooling of the reactor was impossible in the case of losing external power supply, 2) damage of used fuel tanks could lead to radiation leaks; and, 3) the possibility of ground split, as the Oi reactors were located on active faults. Kansai refuted these arguments, claiming that safety measures were strengthened since Fukushima but the court nevertheless ordered a suspension.[16]

In order to reopen a reactor, operators must prove that the facility was up to par with strengthened standards, and also have approval from local governments within a 30-kilometer radius. This 30-kilometer radius region is designated as a special defense zone in contingencies. Requiring consent from local governments is not stipulated by law, but since the Fukushima disaster, the central government abides by this process in resuming nuclear plant operations.

Kyushu Electric Power's Sendai reactors No. 1 and 2 on October 28, 2014, received approval by the city council of Satsumasendai. It was also okayed by the Kagoshima prefecture. Japan's atomic regulatory committee on July 2014 decided on activating Sendai reactor No. 1 and 2, stating that safety measures were sufficient. The Sendai prefecture council on November 7 voted on whether to allow resumption and ultimately approved the reactors with support from the ruling Liberal Democratic party and the Clean Government Party.[17]

But the nuclear regulatory committee pointed out insufficiencies in

[16] *The Hankook-ilbo*, May 22, 2014, http://www.hankookilbo.com/v/c1dba53b78534b0c8b9f50b8f046594e

[17] Consulate General of the ROK in Fukuoka, October 29, 2014, http://jpn-fukuoka.mofa.go.kr/webmodule/htsboard/template/read/korboardread.jsp?typeID=15&boardid=3796&seqno=1106332&c=&t=&pagenum=1&tableName=TYPE_LEGATION&pc=&dc=&wc=&lu=&vu=&iu=&du=, Newsis, November 7, 2014, http://www.newsis.com/ar_detail/view.html?ar_id=NISX20141107_0013282166&cID=10102&pID=10100

Kyushu's safety measures, thus delaying resumptions of Sendai reactors No. 1 and 2. Kyushu Electric Power plans to review these items and later resubmit resumption filings for No. 1. But even after the paperwork was complete, approval awaits the committee's on-site inspection. The actual date of resumption can take more than several months. Kansai's Takahama reactors No. 3 and 4 also received preliminary approval for resumption on December 22 and were ultimately okayed by the nuclear regulatory committee on February 12. The nearby local governments of the Sendai plants are Satsumasendai city and Kagoshima Prefecture but the Takahama plants need approval not just from the Fukui prefecture but also the city of Kyoto and Saga prefecture. Receiving consent from these local governments is not expected to come easily.[18] Not only that but the local court on April 14 accepted the request from residents of Fukui Prefecture, ordering injunctions on the Takaham reactors No. 3 and 4.[19] The court effectively reversed the atomic regulators' decision that the sites were safe. Oi reactors No. 3 and 4 were also ordered against restarting and this was too ruled by the Fukui local court. Kansai Electric Power was facing an uphill court battle ahead of winning consent from local governments.

Japan implements its energy policy based on the basic energy plan established every three years. The country's basic energy plan, first established in 2003, was revised in 2007 and 2010. In the second revision in 2010, the government, by 2030, aimed to increase its energy independency rate from 38 percent to 70 percent, reduce carbon dioxide emission to zero and boost the rate of nuclear and renewable energy from 34 percent up to 70 percent. To this end, it planned to build new nuclear power plants and propel the rate of atomic energy to 50 percent. But in light of the Fukushima disaster, Prime Minister Kan Naoto on May 10, 2010, announced

[18] "Global Brief," Korea Institute of Science and Technology Information (KISTI), December 12, 2014, http://mirian.kisti.re.kr/futuremonitor/view.jsp?record_no=254051&cont_cd=GT, Korea Energy Economic Insitutue, *World Energy Market Insight* 15(7), February 2015, http://www.keei.re.kr/keei/download/WEMI1507.pdf, Yonhap News Agency, February 10, 2015, http://www.yonhapnews.co.kr/bulletin/2015/02/10/0200000000AKR20150210099400073.HTML

[19] Yonhap News Agency, April 14, 2015, http://www.yonhapnews.co.kr/bulletin/2015/04/14/0200000000AKR20150414124300073.HTML

that his government would review its nuclear plant expansion plan from square one.[20]

In September 2012, the Japanese government announced a new energy and environment plan with the goal of moving away from nuclear energy and reducing dependence from fossil fuel. The plan, announced after going through a total of 33 meetings and discussions by Agency for Natural Resources and Energy, was sent back to the drawing board in 2013 following the change of government. A new blueprint was announced on December 13 after 10 additional deliberations. In the blueprint, the 'zero-nuclear energy' policy was replaced by a 'nuclear resumption' policy. The plan however failed to reach a Cabinet review.[21]

The fourth basic energy revision was approved by the Cabinet on April 11, 2014 under the Abe administration. It drastically revised the plan written by the Democratic Party and made official the government's nuclear energy resumption policy. It vowed to increase adoption of renewables to reduce atomic energy dependency but has effectively discarded the 'zero-nuclear' position. It reiterated the 'base-load' role of atomic energy and suggested on placing priority on deciding on achieving a stable energy supply. For plants deemed safe by atomic regulators, the government vowed support for swift resumption and to win consent by local governments. Regarding the nearly-closed Monju fast-breeder reactor, the government announced that the plant won't be shut down but will be used as a research facility. Whether it will remain operational was left unclear. The Monju facility, however, remains virtually unusable as technical failures remain unresolved.

The atomic energy industry as a whole expressed frustration over the fourth revision, pointing to the lack of concrete figures regarding plant operations. Public opinion regarding the Abe government's fourth revision of

---

[20] Media Today, May 11, 2011, http://www.mediatoday.co.kr/news/articleView.html?idxno=95316

[21] Seung-eun Choi, "Gist of Japan's basic energy plan revision (draft),"*World Energy Market Insight* 13-45, December 13, 2014, http://www.keei.re.kr/keei/download/WEMI1345.pdf, Seung-eun Choi, "Basic content of Japan's basic energy plan (full text)," *World Energy Issue Insight* 13-4, December 2013, http://www.keei.re.kr/keei/download/WEIS1304.pdf, "Japan's basic energy plan [abstract]," Korea-Japan Foun- dation's Japan Economic Research Institute, 2014

the basic energy plan remains unfavorable. Prior to the Fukushima disaster, the Japanese public in general was relatively favorable towards atomic energy. According to a 2009 poll, 60 percent responded that the country had to increase the rate of its nuclear energy. Only 16 percent answered the opposite.[22] But in most surveys held after Fukushima, more than half of respondents were against restarting atomic reactors. NHK surveyed 2,459 persons over the age of 16 for a year from November 2013. 46 percent called for a reduction of nuclear reactors while 30 percent wanted a full closing of all nuclear plants in the country. Nearly 80 percent of the public held a negative view on nuclear energy.[23] This sentiment, however, is not reflected directly in the country's nuclear energy policy as the Liberal Democratic Party, which pushes for resumption of nuclear plants, usually overwhelms the opposition party in elections.

State of nuclear industry in South Korea, China and Japan and its significance

Korea currently runs 23 reactors (20,716 MW) and China 27 reactors (24,603 MW). Pre-Fukushima, Japan was running a total of 54 reactors. Since the disaster, Japan shut down 11 and has temporarily suspended 43 others. Twenty one plants have filed for resuming operation but face obstacles in the process. South Korea is currently building five new reactors, China and Japan 25 and 2, respectively. But in terms of land areas and amount of electricity use, South Korea has the highest concentration of nuclear reactors among the three. Its rate of nuclear generation in comparison to total power supply, 30 percent, also towers above that of China and Japan, with 2 percent and 0 percent respectively. Japan's pre-Fukushima figures stood at 30 percent but were reduced to 0 percent. Reduction of electricity use and thermal power has filled the void since.

According to the International Energy Agency (IEA), 54 percent of all new nuclear reactor under construction are concentrated in South Korea, China and Japan. Despite the shock from the Fukushima disaster, Japan

---

[22] Atom Story (run by Korea Nuclear Energy Agency), March 13, 2015, http://atomstory.or.kr/p/47763/

[23] Environment TV News, March 10, 2014, http://www.greenpostkorea.co.kr/news/article.html?no=36364

announced its policy to resume nuclear power generation and China also resumed approvals of new plants. The IEA predicts that by 2040 the three country's installed nuclear reactor capacity will account for 37 percent (231 GW/624 GW) global total. This prediction likely took into consideration the recent spikes in electricity consumption, with South Korea and China showing explosive growth of per capita use. South Korea has shown an even steeper hike than that of China.

Japan, when compared with China and Korea, has shown a net decrease in electricity consumption after the Fukushima incident. Japan is the only nation that has actually recorded a drop in population. But the overall downfall in power consumption likely stems from the shutdown of nuclear reactors, which accounts for 30 percent of the country's power generation in the wake of the Fukushima disaster. South Korea (see Table 4-6) has a very high rate of electricity consumption per capita, just below that of the United States (12,947 kWh per capita, 2012.)

Table 4-6: Electricity consumption comparison between Korea, China and Japan (2011~2012)

Country	Year	Population (million)	GDP (billion 2005USD)	GDP per capita (2005USD/capita)	Electricity consumption (TWh)	Electricity consumption per capita (kWh/capita)
Korea	2011	49.78	1,056.12	21,215.75	505.86	10,162.00
	2012	50.00	1,078.21	21,564.20	517.33	10,346.00
China	2011	1,344.13	4,194.94	3,120.93	4,432.90	3,298.00
	2012	1,350.70	4,522.14	3,348.00	4,693.68	3,475.00
Japan	2011	127.83	4,621.97	36,157.16	1,003.09	7,847.00
	2012	127.55	4,694.39	36,804.31	988.92	7,753.00

*Source: Key World Energy Statistics 2013, 2014, IEA

Electricity use leads the overall energy consumption. Comparing energy use against economic development can be used as a reference to evaluate the country's energy efficiency. Economic progress normally leads to advancement in technology. In a growing economy with rising energy consumption, the amount of energy required to produce a dollar worth of power decreases. This means that the production output value increases with the same amount of input. But among South Korea, China and Japan, only South Korea has a downward trend in GDP energy intensity. This trend can also be seen Greece, Iceland and other nations in economic downturns. This trend first appeared during the Lee Myung-bak administration. The amount of value produced from the same amount of energy consumption is falling despite economic and technological progress. Korea's GDP is growing but its energy consumption is also increasing. In terms of energy consumption, the country is moving towards becoming structurally more inefficient and unproductive. China's energy and electricity use has surged but it is moving in line with its GDP growth. China's energy use per GDP is in an upward trajectory. Japan has shown a general decrease in energy use from shutting down its nuclear reactors. But its GDP growth has been consistent and is seen as maintaining a highly-efficient and highly value-added economy.

Japan, like Germany and other nations with successful renewable initiatives, adopted a feed-in tariff system. The government received some 70 GW of solar panel project applications in two years. This amounts to 70 and 15 nuclear plants in terms of installed capacity and quantity, respectively.[24] Concurrently, efficiency in electricity consumption has risen; thus the per capita electric. China, together with the United States, the world's largest emitter of greenhouse gas, announced its greenhouse gas reduction goal last year. It aims to begin a net reduction of greenhouse gas emission starting in 2030 and boost zero-carbon energy sources by 20 percent.[25]

The fifth IPCC assessment report and analyses by climate scientists

[24] Pressian, March 19, 2015, http://www.pressian.com/news/article.html?no=124835

[25] Yonhap News Agency, November 12, 2014, http://www.yonhapnews.co.kr/international/2014/11/12/0603000000AKR20141112093151083.HTML

recommend that a drastic reduction of China's greenhouse gas emission. Beijing has recently started a cap-and-trade system and began regulating total emission of coal consumption. And with a spike in renewable energy use, China has significantly raised its energy consumption efficiency and may be able to increase further its greenhouse-gas reduction. Along with improving its energy consumption efficiency, the rate of renewables in energy consumption has long surpassed that of nuclear energy. Decisions on new reactor construction plants in the inland are being put off. Constructions are also taking much longer than before. For the APR1000, 18-30 months, EPR, 13-15 months are being delayed. Wind and solar facilities, on the other hand, are being built at a rapid pace (see Table 4-7.)[26]

Table 4-7: Approved volume of China's wind power construction

Year	Approval volume (MW)
2011	26,830
2012	25,280
2013	27,970
2014	27,600
Total	107,680

*Source: Ministry of Foreign Affairs.[27]

China's National Energy Administration (NEA) on February 13, 2014, announced its fourth approval plan for new wind energy initiatives. In 2011, the NEA launched the approval initiative for wind generation construction projects. Accumulated approval has surpassed 100,000 MW during four years. The IEA also forecasts that investments in renewables will

[26] Mycle Schneider et al., "The World Nuclear Industry Status Report 2014," http://www.worldnuclearreport.org/IMG/pdf/201408msc-worldnuclearreport2014-lr-v4.pdf

[27] Ministry of Foreign Affairs, March 17, 2014, http://www.mofa.go.kr/webmodule/htsboard/template/read/korboardread.jsp?typeID=6&boardid=181&seqno=349678&c=&t=&pagenum=1&tableName=TYPE_DATABOARD&pc=&dc=&wc=&lu=&vu=&iu=&du=

greatly exceed that of nuclear energy. Japan and China's investment in renewable energy from 2014 to 2025 is projected at US$ 196 billion USD and US$ 700 billion USD, respectively. The figures are much higher than that of their nuclear energy development, standing at US$ 14 billion and US$ 193 billion USD, respectively. South Korea, according to Bloomberg in 2012, has one of the lowest investment in renewables among the G20 countries. South Korea has much potential in the renewable energy sector. According to the 2014 government white paper on the country's state of renewables, technological potential in renewables amounts to 1.37 billion tons (toe.) Technical potential in solar ray and solar heating energy along amounts to 1.16 billion tons. This is some five times more than the 254,410 tons of projected energy consumption for 2035.

Although South Korea has high potential renewable energy supply, due to the 2012 abolition by government of the act to compensate for cost difference and a consequent lack of investment, the rate of renewables in energy generation remains lower than 1 percent. China has the highest rate of renewables against the country's primary energy. But Japan is showing fast growth of renewables as well. China in the past had a higher rate of renewable energy dependence but the rate dropped due to the country's fast industrialization. The absolute portion of renewables for China has, in fact, risen.

South Korea, China and Japan remain the global hotspot for nuclear energy development. Despite shutting down all of its reactors since Fukushima, Japan persists on resuming operation. China and South Korea remain on their courses of nuclear energy expansion. However, South Korea is the only country in which the rate of energy of energy dependency from nuclear power is on the rise. China in the past had a higher rate of renewable energy dependence and is adopting renewables much faster than its announced rate of increase of nuclear power which remains implausible.

PART II

SEEKING SOLUTIONS

CHAPTER 5

A PROPOSAL FOR A NORTHEAST ASIA NUCLEAR-WEAPON-FREE ZONE

Hiromichi Umebayashi

Introduction

2015 is the 70th anniversary of the Hiroshima and Nagasaki bombings. It is timely to put the Northeast Asian nuclear disarmament issue in the global context. Unfortunately, we have only a very dim glimpse of a world free of nuclear weapons. The Nagasaki Peace Declaration of August 9, 2014 expressed concerns about the growing gap between nuclear weapon states plus states under their nuclear umbrella and genuine non-nuclear weapon states.

Regional nuclear crisis is a core part of the global nuclear stalemate. The current situation of DPRK's continuing nuclear program and ROK and Japan's increased reliance on US extended nuclear deterrence are mirror reflections of the global reality, where nuclear weapon states envision indefinite possession of their nuclear arsenals and compete among themselves to seek balance and stability through their modernization under the old-fashioned nuclear deterrence theory. In this respect, attempts to establish a nuclear-free Northeast Asia have important implications for the global effort to realize a world without nuclear weapons. Thus, the discussion of possible Northeast Asia nuclear weapon free zone (NEA-NWFZ) will be a subject of global interest.

Scheme Proposals

When the Cold War ended, the concept of a NEA-NWFZ became more than a political slogan and several concrete proposals with different arrangements were proposed. A chronology of such proposals is appended at the end of this paper.

The first was made by a research group led by John Endicott in 1995 after three years research cooperation.[1] One typical scheme was based on a circular zone with a 2,000 km radius centered on Panmunjom, which encircles the whole land area of the Republic of Korea (ROK), the Democratic People's Republic of Korea (DPRK), Japan and Taiwan, and part of China, Russia and Mongolia. The United States is also included in the treaty arrangement because it has military bases in the ROK and Japan. The Track II study of such a circular scheme, together with a later elliptical modification, led to a proposal of a limited NWFZ in which only non-strategic nuclear weapons are prohibited on the territory of nuclear weapons states covered by the zone (all nuclear weapons would have been banned from the territory of the non-nuclear weapons states in the zone.)

Chronology of Proposals on a Northeast Asia Nuclear-Weapon-Free Zone

March 1995	John Endicott, et al.[2]	Limited Nuclear Weapon-Free Zone (LNWFZ), involving only non-strategic weapons. A Circular Zone with 2000 km radius centered on Panmunjom or an elliptical zone.
1995	Andrew Mack[3]	NWFZ involving the ROK, DPRK, Japan and Taiwan
March 1996	Kumao Kaneko[4]	A Circular Zone with 2000 km radius centered on Panmunjom. Different obligations posed on nuclear weapons state and non-nuclear weapons states.

[1] John E. Endicott and Alan G. Gorowitz, "Track II Cooperative Regional Security Efforts: Lessons from the Limited Nuclear-Weapon-Free-Zone for Northeast Asia," *Pacific Review* 11:3(1999).

[2] See note 1.

[3] Andrew Mack, "A Northeast Asia Nuclear-Free Zone: Problems and Prospects,"in *Nuclear Policies in Northeast Asia*, UMDIRI95I16, United Nations (1995).

[4] Kumao Kaneko, "Japan Needs No Umbrella," *Bulletin of Atomic Scientists,* March/April (1996).

May 1996	Hiromichi Umebayashi[5]	Three plus Three nations arrangement involving ROK, DPRK and Japan as non-nuclear weapons states and China, Russia and United States as nuclear weapons states.
October 1997	John Endicott, et al.[6]	NEA League of Non-Nuclear States, involving the ROK, Japan and Mongolia (and DPRK if possible) as a phase I formation of the LNWFZ.
June 2000	Seongwhun Cheon & Tatsu-jiro Suzuki[7]	A NWFZ supported by a tri-party treaty among ROK, DPRK and Japan.
April 2004	Hiromichi Umebayashi, et al.[8]	A model NWFZ treaty drafted based upon a Three plus Three nations arrangement.
Spring 2007	J. Enkhsaikhan[9]	An approach to form a zone through relevant non-nuclear constituent states' attaining single state NWF status.
August 2008	DPJ Disarma-ment Group[10]	A draft treaty proposal based upon a Three plus Three arrangement
Nov. 2008	Jaejung Suh[11]	Multilateralization of 1992 Joint Declaration for Denuclearization of the Korean Peninsula by making protocols to it.

[5] See note 2.

[6] John E. Endicott, "The Moscow Memorandum," Moscow, Russia, October 11, 1997. The text in its entirety can be found in the document cited in note 1.

[7] Seongwhun Cheon and Tatsujiro Suzuki, "The Tripartite Nuclear-Weapon-Free Zone in Northeast Asia: A Long-term Objective of the Six-Party Talks," *International Journal of Korean Unification Studies*, 12:2(2003): 41-68.

[8] See note 15.

[9] J. Enkhsaikhan, "Mongolia's non-nuclear status – en important element of Northeast Asia security," *Single State NWFZ: progress and prospects* (Blue Banner, Ulaanbaatar, 2007).

[10] http://www.peacedepot.org/theme/net/DPJ_NEANWFZ_EN.pdf.

[11] Jaejung Suh, "Wither the Korean Peninsula? – The U.S., Korea and Northeast Asia at a Critical Juncture," (paper presented at The Fourth Busan International Symposium, November 20, 2008).

May 2010	Nautilus Institute[12]	An approach to form a zone by establishing first a NWFZ composed of Japan and ROK (with additions).
Nov. 2011	Morton H. Halperin[13]	An approach to conclude a comprehensive agreement among member states of the Six-Party Talks and others on key elements including the establishment of a NEA-NWFZ.

This author proposed another scenario in 1966 called the "three plus three,"[14] which envisioned a trilateral NEA-NWFZ treaty between Japan, the ROK and the DPRK. It included a special protocol with provisions including negative security assurances by the three neighboring nuclear weapon states (NWS) - China, Russia and the United States of America. Later, in 2004, a model treaty was developed by the same author in co-operation with non-governmental partners in Japan and the ROK.[15] In that model treaty, while continuing to be based upon the three plus three scenario, a six-party treaty, rather than a three-party treaty, was proposed. The parties to the treaty would be divided into two categories: "Intra-zonal states" (Japan, ROK and DPRK) and "neighboring NWS" (China, Russia and the United States.) Geographically, the NEA-NWFZ is composed of the territory of the intra-zonal states. Provisions stipulating obligations of neighboring NWS, including security assurances, were incorporated into the main text of the treaty, rather than provided in a protocol because they

[12] "Korea-Japan Nuclear Weapon Free Zone (KJNWFZ) Concept Paper," Nautilus Institute, May 6, 2010. More advanced discussions appear in a later article by Peter Hayes, Richard Tanter and Joan Diamond, "General Assessment of the DPRK Nuclear Situation," December 7, 2012, http://www.recna.nagasaki-u.ac.jp/bd/files/Peter-Hayes1.pdf.

[13] See notes 32 and 33.

[14] Hiromichi Umebayashi, "A Northeast Asia NWFZ: A Realistic and Attainable Goal," (paper presented at the INESAP Conference, Gothenburg, Sweden, May 30-June 2, 1996), "A Northeast Asia NWFZ: A Realistic and Attainable Goal An Asia-Pacific Approach to the Nuclear Weapon Free Word," *INESAP Bulletin* 10 (1996), http://www.inesap.org/sites/default/files/inesap_old/bulletin10/bul10art03.htm.

[15] The model treaty has been revised several times. Draft 4 is available in the *Peace Depot Working Paper* No.1 E, "A Model Treaty on the Northeast Asia Nuclear-Weapon-Free Zone," November 2005, http://www.peacedepot.org/e-news/nwfz/workingpaper1.pdf. The most recent version, draft 7, is available in the appendix of the book in Japanese. Hiromichi Umebayashi, *Nuclear Weapon Free Zone – A Pathway to the World Without Nuclear Weapons (Hi-kakuheikichitai – KakunakiSekaienoMichisuji)* (Iwanami-Shoten, 2011).

are deemed essential to the treaty negotiation process from its outset.

The three plus three arrangement is considered to be the most realistic and fundamental arrangement for a NEA-NWFZ because it involves key three countries of the region, namely the ROK, the DPRK and Japan, as the central players and three neighboring nuclear weapon states under the NPT, namely the United States, China, and Russia, as supportive players of the arrangement. It is not a coincidence that these six nations later became the member countries in the Six-Party Talks on the nuclear issues of Korean Peninsula in August 2003. Although the ROK and Japan are non-nuclear states under the NPT, the DPRK's non-nuclear position assumed in this arrangement is against its current policy. However, the international community continues to urge "the DPRK to fulfil the commitments under the Six-Party Talks, including the complete and verifable abandonment of all nuclear weapons and existing nuclear programmes ... and to return, at an early date, to the Treaty and to its adherence with its IAEA safeguards agreement."[16] More on this subject will be discussed later in the paper.

This three plus three approach could be pursued by taking advantage of the policies once adopted in the past or currently adhered to by the intra-zonal states. Specifically, the ROK and the DPRK effectuated in 1992 the "Joint Declaration on the Denuclearization of the Korean Peninsula," in which they agreed that they "shall refrain from the testing, manufacture, production, acceptance, possession, stockpiling, deployment and use of nuclear weapons," and that they "shall use nuclear energy only for peaceful purposes." Also, Japan adheres to its "three non-nuclear principles," which state that Japan will not manufacture, possess, nor allow the bringing-in of nuclear weapons. Also, the 1995 Atomic Energy Basic Law of Japan prohibits the use of nuclear energy for military purposes.

Another merit of the scheme is that in this arrangement one can construct a security system where three "intra-zonal states," rather than out-

[16] "2010 Review Conference of the Parties to the Treaty on the Non-Proliferation of Nuclear Weapons Final Document Volume I Part 1, NPT/CONF.2010/50 (Vol. I)," http://www.un.org/ga/search/view_doc.asp?symbol=NPT/CONF.2010/50%20(VOL.I)

side powers such as the United States and Russia, could play the central role in the management of the Zone. Any NWFZ treaty will establish a commission to ensure the implementation of the provisions set forth in the treaty, as well as the executive committee, a subsidiary organ of the commission to serve the functions mandated by the treaty. The representative from one of the "intra-zonal states," rather than neighboring nuclear weapon states, is naturally deemed to take chairpersonship of such commission or committee on the rotational basis because those three states assume most fundamental obligations under the treaty to remain non-nuclear weapon states. This will help develop the autonomy of the three regional countries relative to the outside powers and ensure the durability of the NEA-NWFZ as an interim step in the long march to nuclear weapons abolition by all states.

Regional Context and Deadlock of the Six-Party Talks

The design sketched above of a NEA-NWFZ has been undertaken with mid- or long-term goals of the region in mind. These are:

a) To reverse the on-going attempt by the DPRK to acquire and strengthen its nuclear deterrent, as well as the counter military actions by Japan and the ROK by means of the strengthened US extended deterrence including nuclear components;
b) To prevent an entirely predictable competitive escalation of virtual nuclear threat and even arms racing among Japan, the ROK and the DPRK, or between Japan and a reunified Korea; and
c) To establish mechanisms to implement the provisions of a NEA-NWFZ treaty, including verification and possibly energy cooperation, as the first step toward further confidence building and broader cooperative security mechanisms in the region.

These objectives continue to be relevant today. The primary international forum to pursue them has been the Six-Party Talks involving all the six countries in the three plus three scheme. At the time of the introduction of this scheme in 1996, there were no Six-Party Talks, which started in

2003. After two years consultation, the six parties to the talks issued the September 19 Joint Statement in 2005, the fundamental agreement among the six parties that was referred to at the 2010 NPT Review Conference.[17] The Joint Statement acknowledges the relevance of security cooperation in Northeast Asia to "the verifiable denuclearization of the Korean Peninsula," by saying: "The Six Parties agreed to explore ways and means for promoting security cooperation in Northeast Asia." A NEA-NWFZ typifies such ways and means for security cooperation. Moreover, the agreement of February 2007 on "Initial Actions for the Implementation of the Joint Statement" established five working groups including one devoted to a "Northeast Asia Peace and Security Mechanism." A NEA-NWFZ is an excellent and well-established institutional form for a peace and security mechanism in this region.

Another innovative element is found in the 2005 Joint Statement. In addition to the DPRK's commitment to "abandoning all nuclear weapons and existing nuclear programs," the United States affirmed that it has "no intention to attack or invade the DPRK with nuclear or conventional weapons." This means that future security assurances by nuclear weapon states could be extended to include assurances against conventional weapons and that a new dimension of the regional security cooperation mechanism could possibly be envisioned in this regard. The importance of this statement centers on its implication on a permanent peace arrangement that would supplant the 1953 Armistice.

In spite of these achievements, the Six-Party Talks has been deadlocked since December 2008, when the parties failed to agree on any verification process at a meeting of the heads of delegation during the sixth session of the talks. The DPRK conducted three underground nuclear tests in 2006, 2009 and 2013. Although the weaponization of the DPRK's nuclear explosive devices has not yet been proven, it will not be surprising if this is demonstrated in the near future. Also, the DPRK demonstrated its ongoing indigenous plan to implement its "Juche-based nuclear power

---

[17] *Ibid.*

industry,"[18] involving the construction of a prototype small light water reactor (LWR) and a modern centrifuge uranium enrichment facility, as was observed by a team of US experts who visited Pyongyang in November 2010[19] and its expansion has been observed by satellite image analyses.[20]

The latter development relative to the LWR is considered to be more or less consistent with arguments maintained by the DPRK both before and after the start of the Six-Party Talks and could be used as a renewed path for the international community to engage the DPRK with multi-faceted deliberations.[21] Regarding the development of escalated nuclear deterrence threats by the United States and the ROK on the one side, and the DPRK on the other, it is important to note that the DPRK has never hinted that it would possess a nuclear deterrent for the purpose of parity, but it continues to assert that nuclear deterrence is needed to assure national security and regime preservation. Following intervening events, such as the regime succession by Kim Jong-un, the United States and the DPRK resumption of bilateral talks in late 2011, the failed "leap day agreement" in 2012, the DPRK's rejection of the UN Security Council sanction resolution 2094 (2013), and the execution of North Korea's senior official Sung-taek Jang in December 2013, the DPRK has returned to a less confrontational posture and sought to recommence talks. Kil-yon Pak, Vice Minister of Foreign Affairs of the DPRK, stated at the UN General Assembly High-level Meeting on nuclear disarmament on September 26, 2013;"The denuclearization of the Korean Peninsula is the consistent policy of our government. The ultimate goal of denuclearization of the Korean Peninsula is to completely remove the US nuclear threats against our country and to return the entire Korean Peninsula, including South Korea into the zone free from

---

[18] Foreign Ministry Statement of the DPRK, "DPRK Foreign Ministry Vehemently Refutes UNSC's Presidential Statement," *Korea Central News Agency*, April 14, 2009.

[19] Siegfried S. Hecker, "Redefining denuclearization in North Korea," *Bulletin of the Atomic Scientists*, December 20, 2010.

[20] David Albright and Serena Kelleher-Vergantini, "Yongbyon: Centrifuge Enrichment Plant Expands while 5 MWe Reactor is Possibly Shut Down," *ISIS Imagery Brief*, October 3, 2014.

[21] David von Hippel and Peter Hayes, "Engaging the DPRK Enrichment and Small LWR Program," *Nautilus Institute Special Report*, December 23, 2010.

nuclear weapons."[22] In principle, the statement is consistent with the September 19 joint statement. Recently, Se Pyong So, DPRK's ambassador to the UN in Geneva is reported to say "For the six-party talks we are ready, and as far as I think, China and Russia are ready."[23]

Global Context and Obligation of Japan and ROK under NPT

The establishment of a NEA-NWFZ is increasingly important in the global context, because on the one hand it will contribute to contemporary global nuclear disarmament efforts at the time when very little tangible progress has been seen in this field, and on the other, non-nuclear weapon states under the NPT reliant upon nuclear extended deterrence experience international pressure to play more role in reducing the role of nuclear weapons in their security policies.

The moves to eliminate all nuclear weapons have been manifested in numerous declarations and statements in recent years. For example, the final document of the 2010 NPT Review Conference, adopted by consensus and thus politically binding for all the state parties to the NPT, reads: "All state parties commit to pursue policies that are fully compatible with the Treaty and the objective of achieving a world without nuclear weapons,"[24] and "all States need to make special efforts to establish the necessary framework to achieve and maintain a world without nuclear weapons. The conference notes the five-point proposal for nuclear disarmament of the Secretary-General of the United Nations, which proposes, *inter alia*, consideration of negotiations on a nuclear weapons convention or agreement on a framework of separate mutually reinforcing instruments, backed by a strong system of verification."[25] These two statements are applicable to all

[22] Statement by Kil-Yon Pak at the high level meeting on nuclear disarmament of the 68th UN General Assembly, New York, September 26, 2013.

[23] Stephanie Nebehay, "Exclusive: North Korea envoy says door is open on nuclear issues, rights, abductees," Reuters, October 2, 2014.

[24] Action 1 of Conclusions and Recommendations for Follow-on Actions, 2010 Review Conference of the Parties to the Treaty on the Non-Proliferation of Nuclear Weapons Final Document, Volume I Part 1, NPT/CONF.2010/50 (Vol. I).

[25] Conclusions and Recommendations for Follow-on Actions, 2010 Review Conference of the Parties to the

NPT member states including non-nuclear states such as ROK and Japan and politically oblige them to make their own efforts to pursue nuclear weapon free world with an enduring legal framework. In addition, nuclear weapon states are called upon "to further diminish the role and significance of nuclear weapons in all military and security concepts, doctrines and policies."[26] This request is mostly directed at nuclear weapon states, but also may be interpreted in combination with the obligation posed upon non-nuclear states mentioned above. That is, those non-nuclear weapon states whose security policy relies upon extended nuclear deterrence of the nuclear weapon states are equally called upon to "diminish the role and significance of nuclear weapons in all military and security concepts, doctrines and policies."

Based upon such globally shared political commitments, countries and people are urged to demonstrate efforts to reduce the role of nuclear weapons in their security policies and to pursue the possibility of regional peace and security without reliance on nuclear weapons, especially in Northeast Asia where nuclear weapons have been playing significant roles.

In fact, recent international consultation emphasizes explicitly the roles played by non-nuclear countries that rely upon extended nuclear deterrence. In 2013, the UN Open-ended Working Group on Nuclear Disarmament discussed "the role of non-nuclear-weapons States under extended nuclear deterrence guarantees in reducing the salience of nuclear weapons in security doctrines."[27] In the same context, they also discussed "the role of nuclear-weapon-free zones in challenging the value and legitimacy of nuclear weapons."[28]

Treaty on the Non-Proliferation of Nuclear Weapons Final Document, Volume I Part 1, NPT/CONF.2010/50 (Vol. I).

[26] Action 5 of Conclusions and Recommendations for Follow-on Actions, 2010 Review Conference of the Parties to the Treaty on the Non-Proliferation of Nuclear Weapons Final Document, Volume I Part 1, NPT/CONF.2010/50 (Vol. I).

[27] "Report of the Open-ended Working Group to develop proposals to take forward multilateral nuclear disarmament negotiations for the achievement and maintenance of a world without nuclear weapons(A/68/514)," United Nations General Assembly, October 9.pdf

[28] *Ibid.*

As an effort to implement the agreed action plan for nuclear disarmament at the 2010 NPT Review Conference, a ten-nation group initiated by Japan and Australia, called the NPDI (Non-proliferation and Disarmament Initiative,)[29] presented a working paper entitled, "Transparency of Nuclear Weapons"[30] at the 2012 Preparatory Committee (PrepCom) for the 2015 NPT Review Conference. In this working paper, they proposed a standard report form to be used by the nuclear weapon states (NWS) in order to secure progressive nuclear disarmament in a transparent manner. In that standard form, one of the items to be included is "the measures taken to diminish the role and significance of nuclear weapons in military and security concepts, doctrines and policies." Moreover, the NPDI requests the rapid implementation of the report by encouraging NWS to start it at every PrepCom, namely beginning the next year. As is obvious from the discussion above, this request should be directed not only to NWS, but also to non-nuclear states under extended nuclear deterrence, including some NPDI members themselves such as Japan and NATO countries. In fact, this point was addressed by a South African delegate at the same PrepCom, who said, "those states that are part of military alliances which includes NWS, should report, as a significant transparency and confidence-building measure, on steps taken or future steps planned to reduce and eliminate the role of nuclear weapons in collective security doctrines."[31] Again, the establishment of a nuclear-weapon-free-zone is a typical way toward a security arrangement to eliminate the role of nuclear weapons regionally.

Halperin's Proposal on a Comprehensive Agreement

In late 2011 a new initiative appeared regarding efforts to establish a Northeast Asia nuclear-weapon-free zone (NEA-NWFZ). Since then,

---

[29] Later, NPDI became 12 nations group in September 2013.

[30] "Transparency of nuclear weapons: the Non-Proliferation and Disarmament Initiative (NPT/CONF.2015/PC.I/WP.12)," UN NPT PrepCom, April 20, 2012.

[31] Statement by Ambassador Xolisa Mabhongo, on behalf of the New Agenda Coalition, at the First PrepCom for the 2015 Review Conference of NPT, 3 May 2012.

the framework of the discussion has generally shifted from the question of whether such a zone might even be possible and, if so, what kind of scheme it would be, to what kind of approach might to be taken to actually realize it. This shift has been brought about by a proposal made by Morton H. Halperin, a well-known US foreign policy expert, at a workshop on East Asia security that was organized by Nautilus Institute in Tokyo in November 2011.[32] His contribution was soon published in an article entitled "A Proposal for a Nuclear Weapons-Free Zone in Northeast Asia."[33] Since then, discussions of this proposal took place at various workshops held in Washington D.C.[34], Nagasaki, Seoul, Tokyo[35] and Beijing.[36]

It was in the context of how to overcome the deadlock and to realize the denuclearization of the Korean Peninsula that Morton H. Halperin proposed a comprehensive agreement including the establishment of a NEA-NWFZ. There are two major underlying insights that motivated his proposition. The first is that nuclear proliferation in this region will have devastating consequences, both regionally and globally, and will follow if the DPRK is permitted to emerge as a *de facto* permanent nuclear power. Thus, he argues, "Until and unless it is absolutely clear that reversing North Korea's nuclear program is not possible, Western security policy in

---

[32] Morton H. Halperin, "The Role of A NE Asia NWFZ In Eliminating Nuclear Weapons From The Korean Peninsular" (paper presented at the East Asia Nuclear Security Workshop, cosponsored by Nautilus Institute, Mansfield Foundation, and Asia-Pacific Leadership Network for Nuclear Non-proliferation and Disarmament, Tokyo, Japan, November 11, 2011), http://nautilus.org/projects/by-name/korea-japan-nwfz/workshops/east-asia-nuclear-security-workshop/.

[33] Morton H. Halperin, "A Proposal for a Nuclear Weapons-Free Zone in Northeast Asia," Global Asia 6:4(2011). Also there is a revised paper "A New Approach to Security in Northeast Asia: Breaking the Gridlock," *The Asia Pacific Journal* 10:34(2012).

34 The workshop "A New Approach to Security in Northeast Asia: Breaking the Gridlock," Washington D.C. October 9-10, 2012, cosponsored by Nautilus Institute and Woodrow Wilson Center.

[35] A series of workshops were organized by RECNA in cooperation with other institutions including Nautilus Institute. "Developing a Comprehensive Approach to a Northeast Asia Nuclear Weapons Free Zone-Workshop I," Nagasaki, December 7-8, 2012; "Envisioning Northeast Asia Peace and Security System: Developing a Comprehensive Approach to a NEA-NWFZ – Workshop II," Seoul, June 20, 2013; "Denuclearization of Northeast Asia and of the World: Developing a Comprehensive Approach to a NEA-NWFZ – Workshop III," Tokyo, September 14-16, 2014.

[36] Morton H. Halperin, "A comprehensive agreement for security in Northeast Asia," *NAPSNet Policy Forum*, March 16, 2015 (paper presented originally at Nautilus-China Institute of International Studies Workshop on Comprehensive Security Settlement and DPRK Nuclear Issue, Beijing, January 23, 2014,) http://nautilus.org/napsnet/napsnet-policy-forum/a-comprehensive-agreement-for-security-in-northeast-asia/.

the region must be directed at persuading the North to give up its nuclear weapons."[37] As was cited above, a recent speech by the DPRK ViceForeign Minister at the UN General Assembly, affirms the possibility of non-nuclear DPRK still remains.

His second premise is that negotiation is possible, as evidenced by the near success achieved in the relationship between the United States and the DPRK in 2000, after comprehensive negotiations. At that time, the US–DPRK Joint Communiqué followed by the visit to Pyongyang by Madeleine Albright, then US Secretary of State, came close to resolving the DPRK nuclear issue. Halperin served as Director of the Policy Planning at the US Department of State at that time. The Joint Communiqué reads, "As the first important step both sides declared that any of the two governments entertains no hostile intention toward the other and affirmed the commitment to make all efforts to establish new relations free from past antagonism in the future."[38]

Halperin argues that as the United States (and its allies) and DPRK cannot agree why the past the Six-Party Talks failed to lead to effective implementation of commitments undertaken by the parties to those agreements, it follows that "an effort must be made to bypass this dispute." To this end, he suggests pursuing a 'Comprehensive Agreement (or Treaty) on Peace and Security in Northeast Asia' covering all outstanding issues affecting relations with North Korea." In a sense, this approach appears similar to the 1994 US-DPRK 'Agreed Framework,' which created KEDO (Korean Peninsula Energy Development Organization) that eventually failed. However, the proposed new Comprehensive Agreement is designed to meet today's circumstances in its comprehensiveness and multilateralism. It would create a permanent organization to implement and enforce the comprehensive agreement unlike KEDO that was meant to deal with the energy issue only.

[37] Morton H. Halperin, "A Proposal for a Nuclear Weapons-Free Zone in Northeast Asia," *Global Asia* 6:4(2011).

[38] "Joint communique between DPRK and USA," KCNA, October 12, 2000.

Halperin argued that there are six necessary elements in the proposed comprehensive agreement. These are:

1. Termination of the state of war.
2. Creating a permanent council on security.
3. Mutual declaration of no hostile intent.
4. Provisions of assistances for nuclear and other energy.
5. Termination of sanctions/response to violations of the treaty.
6. A nuclear-weapons-free zone

While the original papers should be consulted for the detailed accounts of these elements, it is useful to note some features of the proposed NEA-NWFZ. The fundamental structure of the zone is the same as that of a three plus three arrangement. Namely, the geographical zone consists of the territorial areas of Japan, the ROK and the DPRK, and all the five nuclear weapon states, instead of three, are obligated not to store nuclear weapons in the zone as well as not to use or threaten to use such weapons against the countries within the zone. As is the case in other preceding discussions, it is open to modification, such as expansion to include Mongolia and Canada into the zone.[39] It includes a provision concerning the destruction of existing stockpiles as in the case of Pelindaba Treaty which involves South Africa, a past nuclear weapons holder. One of the new challenges that Halperin's NWFZ proposal might address is to restrict reprocessing by non-nuclear weapon states by some means. The inspection provisions to verify compliance with the treaty would be applied equally to countries within the zone and conducted by an organization controlled by the permanent council on security created by the Agreement (or Treaty.)

Also it is important to note that the term "Comprehensive Agreement" in Halperin's concept is used in a limited context so that it can be strictly relevant to solving the current stalemate in relation to nuclear issues and not in a general context for broader regional security. This avoids the situ-

[39] For example, see note 15.

ation where a concept of comprehensiveness is unnecessarily broadened and goes beyond the original intent of the agreement. Of course, it doesn't preclude it becoming a forum to deal with broader security issues in the future if appropriate.

Further Subjects for Deliberation

Naturally there are, and will be, discussions pros and cons regarding the concept proposed by Halperin. In fact, one can observe a variety of views that appeared in the workshop held in Washington D.C. in October 2012.[40] However, there is no doubt that we need a new approach to solve the current stalemate regarding nuclear problems in Northeast Asia and that Halperin's proposal provides a reasonable starting point to move in the right direction. In the course of recent discussions, there have been raised some areas that will be worthy of further deliberation. Some of them are the following.

Freedom of Space Exploration

Although the comprehensive agreement should be as simple as possible, it may be appropriate to think about possible elements to be added, or to be subordinated, to the six elements proposed by Halperin. For example, since UN sanctions against the DPRK enforced by the UN Security Council Resolution are related not only to nuclear programs, but also to ballistic missile programs, the means by which to address the missile or space rocket issue in the agreement would need to be considered. Even if the nuclear weapons issue is resolved and thus, the missile issue might not be rendered less serious, the ultimate solution to this problem needs to be clear from the outset. As is properly stated in the recent UNSC resolution,[41] every country has the equal freedom to explore and use outer space in accordance with international law. In this respect, transparency

[40] Peter Hayes, "A Breakthrough Six-Party Summit in 2013? Why Not?," *Global Asia*, 7:4(2012). Papers presented at the workshop can be seen at http://nautilus.org/projects/by-name/korea-japan-nwfz/workshops/gridlock/.

[41] UN Security Council Resolution 2087 (2013), S/RES/2087(2013)

and confidence building measures for space exploration which are applied equally to the state parties to the comprehensive agreement will have to be developed in the region.

Modalities of the General Comprehensive Agreement

One of the characteristics of Halperin's approach is that a legally binding treaty with general agreement on a package of six elements should come first, before any negotiations start on steps to be taken to achieve them. In many cases, a binding treaty of this kind will have to be approved by the national parliament of each of the states party to the treaty. If the leaders in each state are in an authoritative position with regard to legislative processes, then simply signing and ratifying a treaty first may be feasible. However, it may be more efficacious if a summit of heads of states was to convene and issue a declaration of collective intention to bring about such a treaty and its constituent elements, to create broad public support and international consensus that in turn will make the process of domestic legislation for an international treaty to be easier over time. It will be worthwhile to further study the modalities of the general agreement, which will serve as the firm and sound basis for future negotiations on the specific elements.

Ideas on Treaty Provisions of a NEA-NWFZ

The negotiation histories of the existing NWFZs provide us with rich lessons, including a fundamental understanding that each NWFZ devises provisions unique to its own region, reflecting its regional histories and geopolitics. There have already been such unique ideas proposed for Northeast Asia in Halperin's paper as well as in others,[42] for example, regarding entry-into-force provisions and regional verification mechanisms.

[42] See for example; Peter Hayes and Richard Tanter, "Key Elements of Northeast Asia Nuclear-Weapons Free Zone (NEA-NWFZ)," September 26, 2012, http://nautilus.wpengine.netdna-cdn.com/wp-content/uploads/2012/10/Hayes-Tanter-NWFZ-2-pager-Oct1-2012.pdf ;Hiromichi Umebayashi, "A Northeast Asia Nuclear Weapon Free Zone with a three-plus- three Arrangement," March 13, 2012, http://nautilus.org/napsnet/napsnet-special-reports/a-northeast-asia-nuclear-weapon-free-zone-with-a-three-plus-three-arrangement/#ii-report-by-hiromichi., Also see note 15 and note 42.

Nautilus Institute's proposal of the DPRK's phased compliance with a NWFZ and a calibrated security assurances by nuclear weapon states during the intermediate phases[43] (drawing in turn on the process and precedent whereby Brazil and Argentina came into compliance with the Latin American NWFZ) are especially worth studying. The systematic review and revision of such ideas will be necessary.

Steps for Preparatory Diplomatic Work

Although prior close consultations should take place among and between the United States and its allies, as pointed out by Halperin, the dialogue between the United States and China at an early stage is mandatory as well, considering their recent delicate relationship over the security of East Asia, including that of the South China Sea. In order to pursue such dialogues in parallel, we will need a draft text of the Comprehensive Agreement as a shared reference point to ensure mutual trust. The possibility of a drafting party, including from interstate organizations and non-governmental organizations, coming forth in the role of broker or catalyzing agent, deserves serious consideration.

Way Forward

In this context, incremental progress has already taken place in instigating the UN to play a more active role in bringing about a NEA-NWFZ. The UN Advisory Board of Disarmament Affairs discussed on a NEA-NWFZ by including it as one of the topics of their 2013 agenda, "the relations between nuclear-weapon-free zones in advancing regional and global security." It issued a recommendation to the Secretary General[44] in July 2013 that: "The Secretary General should also consider appropriate action for the establishment of a nuclear-weapon-free zone in North-East Asia. In particular, the Secretary-General could promote a more active role for

[43] Peter Hayes, Richard Tanter, and Joan Diamond, "General Assessment of the DPRK Nuclear Situation," December 7, 2012, http://www.recna.nagasaki-u.ac.jp/bd/files/Peter-Hayes1.pdf.

[44] "Work of the Advisory Board on Disarmament Matters – Report of the Secretary General," A/68/206, July 26, 2013.

the regional forums in encouraging transparency and confidence-building among the countries of the region." This is the first time that a NEA-NW-FZ became a UN documented agenda.

This positive development was soon echoed by Mr. Elbegdorj, President of Mongolia, at the UN High Level Meeting on nuclear disarmament in September 2013. He said, "Mongolia is prepared, on an informal basis, to work with the countries of Northeast Asia to see if and how a nuclear-weapon-free zone could be established in the region. Though we know well that that would not be easy and would require courage, political will and perseverance, it is doable, if not right away."[45] In fact, Mongolia's willingness to play roles for the denuclearization of Northeast Asia was also expressed one year earlier. In 2012, Mongolia marked the twentieth anniversary of its declaration of its unique single-state nuclear weapon free status. Its remarkable diplomatic endeavors drew a five plus one parallel declaration on September 17, 2012 to obtain P5's reaffirmation of their respect of Mongolia's status, including negative security assurances. On that occasion, Ambassador Enkhsaikhan, Mongolia's focal point and the coordinator of the country's nuclear-weapon-free status, expressed Mongolia's commitment to the nuclear weapon free Northeast Asia as follows[46]: "Mongolia is a part of the Northeast Asian region and believes that an open, unbiased and comprehensive approach is needed to addressing the region's pressing issues, especially ridding the region of nuclear weapons. In this respect it is prepared to participate in the joint search for mutually beneficial arrangements and solutions." Considering the fact that Mongolia is a neighbor to the six parties of the three plus three arrangement, in fact making it a four plus three arrangement, that it maintains

[45] H.E. ElbegdorjTsakhia, Statement at the High-level Meeting of The United Nations General Assembly on Nuclear Disarmament, September 26, 2013, http://www.reachingcriticalwill.org/images/documents/Disarmament-fora/HLM/26Sep_Mongolia.pdf.

[46] Ambassador J. Enkhsaikhan at the ceremony of signing of the P5 and Mongolian declarations regarding the latter's nuclear-weapon-free status, September 17, 2012, http://www.mfat.gov.mn/index.php?option=com_content&view=article&id=1878%3Astatement-of-amb-jenkhsaikhan-mongolias-coordinator-of-its-nwfs-at-the-ceremony-of-signing-of-the-p5-and-mongolian-declarations-regarding-the-latters-nuclear-weapon-free-status&catid=42%3A2009-12-20-21-54-33&Itemid=95&lang=en.

good relationship with the DPRK, and that it will acquire legally binding negative security assurances in a NEA-NWFZ unlike the non-binding P5 declaration above, Mongolia could play a critical role in initiating the comprehensive agreement process in NEA.

As is described in the Report of UN Disarmament Commission in 1999, a proposal of a NWFZ has to be initiated by any of the countries of the region concerned.[47] In this regards, that Japan and/or the ROK (or even the DPRK) take the initiative is crucial in Northeast Asia.

[47] UN Disarmament Commission, "Establishment of nuclear-weapon-free zones on the basis of arrangements freely arrived at among the States of the region concerned," Report of the Disarmament Commission, Annex I, General Assembly Official Records, Fifty-fourth session Supplement No.42 (A/54/42), 1999

CHAPTER 6

Ending Nuclear Threat via a Northeast Asia Nuclear Weapons-Free Zone[1]

Peter Hayes

SUMMARY

This background paper sketches how nuclear threat is woven into inter-state relations in the Northeast Asian region, and the case for reducing and ending such threats against non-nuclear weapons states (hereafter NNWSs.) It then outlines how a regional nuclear weapons-free zone could bring about an end to such nuclear threats, and describes how the DPRK's active participation might be an integral part of such a zone from the outset. The paper also addresses the central issue of nuclear extended deterrence in the region, and suggests that it is possible to square the circle—that is, to end nuclear threats by nuclear weapons states (hereafter NWSs) in the region against NNWSs by creating a NWFZ—but maintaining strategic deterrence between the NWS should one of them threaten to use or attack a NNWS party to the zone, or should a NNWS party to the treaty break out and proliferate nuclear weapons. Finally, the paper argues that it is the interests of all states in the region to create a NWFZ because all of them are subject to nuclear threat today; and, it is the only way whereby they can create a stabilizing framework

[1] The author thanks Richard Tanter and Michael Hamel-Green for trenchant comments.The author alone remains responsible for its contents. He may be contacted at phayes@nautilus.org.

within which to manage, reduce, and eventually abolish nuclear threat in Northeast Asia, including those aimed at and coming from the DPRK.

NUCLEAR THREATS

Nuclear weapons enable states to project threats, the scale and type of effects of which are qualitatively and quantitatively greater than other weapons, by orders of magnitude. Some qualitative aspects—their speed of delivery, their ability to instantly annihilate whole cities, their radiological effects, etc., are unique to nuclear weapons. It is primarily the scale and speed of nuclear weapons that ensures that states recognize the risks run if nuclear weapons are involved in a conflict—although the interpretation of the nature of this involvement may differ greatly in a specific case. In short, nuclear weapons command decision-makers' attention; and give them pause when the risk of nuclear war is present in a conflict elationship. Nuclear threat is one of the most extreme forms of hostility present in the region. A non-hostility agreement that is not accompanied by measures to reduce nuclear threat would lack credibility.[2]

Impact of Nuclear Threats

States use nuclear weapons to project threats to affect the calculations of adversaries, third parties, and allies. They use nuclear threat for "deterrence" (a statement or action designed to force someone to change their intended action); for compellence (a statement or action designed to force someone to change what they are doing already); and for reassurance (a statement or action designed to persuade someone to accept

[2] A good primer on nuclear weapons and nuclear threats in international affairs is found in "Chapter 4. Doctrines and Strategies Concerning Nuclear Weapons," in (*Nuclear Weapons: A Comprehensive Study*,) UN Secretary General Department for Disarmament Affairs. (New York: United Nations, 1991), 41-56, http://www.un.org/disarmament/HomePage/ODAPublications/DisarmamentStudySeries/PDF/SS-21. pdf which updates earlier UN expert studies on nuclear weapons dating back to the original study, *Report of the Secretary-General, Effects of the Possible Use of Nuclear Weapons and the Security and Economic Implications For States of the Acquisition and Further Development of These Weapons,* Sales No. E.68.IX (New York:United Nations, 1968).

a circumstance is positive or acceptable, and aimed at a neutral party, an ally, or an adversary of a state; and is the basis of what is called "nuclear arms control" in the West.) Deterrence, compellence, and reassurance are credible depending on the resolve and capability of the state projecting nuclear threat, and the ability of the threatened state to respond in kind or a-symmetrically, to offset these threats. All three types of effects are almost always present in a nuclear threat made by one party to another; sometimes all three effects may be in play at the same time, either in the intention of the state projecting nuclear threat, or in the perception of the state that is the target of the threat, or in the perceptions of third parties. It is rare, probably impossible, for the intentions and perceptions of these two or more affected states to be the same. Therein lies much of the risk of misperception, misunderstanding, and inadvertent escalation to nuclear war. This risk arising from miscalculation is compounded by the accidental risks of nuclear war due to technical or computer malfunctions, misinterpreted signals of an impending attack, problems in communication systems, problems in fail-safe and control systems, and cybernetic organizational feedbacks that could lead to loss-of-control of nuclear forces?[3]

Nuclear Threat in Northeast Asia

All states in the Northeast Asia region fall under the shadow of the threat of nuclear war. Sometimes, this threat is intended, manipulated, and calibrated, by a variety of signals—nuclear testing, delivery system testing, visible transiting deployments, forward deployment in host countries, declaratory doctrines, operational doctrines, political statements, propaganda statements, sharing via deliberate open line communications, or even what is not done or said at a particularly tense moment. Nuclear threat is one of the bases of interstate relations between the long-standing NWSs

[3] Paul Bracken, *The Command and Control of Nuclear Forces* (New Haven:Yale University Press, 1983); Peter Lewis et al., "Chatham House Report: Too Close for Comfort: Cases of Near Nuclear Use and Options for Policy," *The Royal Institute of International Affairs*, April 28, 2014, http://www.chathamhouse.org/sites/files/chathamhouse/home/chatham/public_html/sites/default/files/20140428TooCloseforComfortNuclearUseLewisWilliamsPelopidasAghlani.pdf/.

in this region, the United States, China, and Russia, forming a triangle of strategic nuclear deterrence, compellence, and reassurance that operates continuously and generally; and sometimes becomes part of an immediate confrontation. Accordingly, these types of threat are termed general and immediate in western literature.[4] Thus, general and strategic nuclear deterrence may be said to operate to ensure that NWSs avoid actions that might suggest that they could involve nuclear weapons and intentions to use them—thereby creating a cautionary behavior that operates all the time.

Immediate Nuclear Deterrence

Conversely, immediate nuclear deterrence only arises in specific crisis, when intentions are perceived to be in play. Historical examples include the 1958 Quemoy-Matsu crisis and the August 1976 crisis in Korea. Of course, if there is no intention in the targeted party, there can be no deterrence achieved by a nuclear threat (or if there is no existing action, there can be no compellence of that party, no matter what the threatening party thinks.) But because perceptions matter so much in this world of imagined nuclear war, often intentions are attributed to be present all the time in the shorthand conversations that occur about nuclear threat. This habit leads to stereotyping and mistaken interpretations by policy advisors, and even disastrous decisions by leaders that risk starting an actual nuclear war in action-reaction arms racing.

Us Nuclear Threats To The DPRK

The DPRK has been the target of general and immediate nuclear threats since the Korean War. Some of these US nuclear threats were aimed at Russia or China as part of the bilateral, and then trilateral strategic nuclear triangle. Some were aimed more directly at Pyongyang, as in the August 1976 crisis during Operation "Paul Bunyan." For most of this early period, however, American nuclear threats were not specific to the DPRK, but in-

---

[4] The distinction between immediate and general nuclear deterrence was made by Patrick Morgan, *Deterrence: a conceptual analysis* (Sage Publications, 1977).

cluded it as part of planning and preparing for an all-out war between the United States and China and/or Russia (depending on the period.) US nuclear threat became specific to the DPRK only in the 1970s, at which time the United States and its allies, especially the ROK, feared that the DPRK might launch a conventional attack that could only be deterred by the threat of nuclear war, or stopped by use of nuclear weapons if deterrence failed. From 1975 onwards through the early 1990s, US nuclear threats were aimed at the DPRK specifically for deterrence and compellence purposes, both immediate and general at various times. Over the same period, US nuclear threats aimed at the DPRK were also intended to reassure US allies that Soviet, Chinese nuclear attacks or North Korean conventional attack would face possible US nuclear retaliation; and to compel (in the case of the ROK) and to deter (the modern term is dissuade) Japan from not proliferating their own nuclear weapons. This was particularly important in the case of the ROK that observed the DPRK starting to acquire a nuclear fuel cycle that was suitable for production of plutonium and implicitly threatened future DPRK nuclear armament (as of 1986, when the Yongbyon reactor was observed to be under construction.)

WITHDRAWAL OF US TACTICAL AND THEATER NUCLEAR WEAPONS

In the early 1990s, the circumstances shifted dramatically due to the collapse of the former Soviet Union. The United States unilaterally withdrew all forward-deployed non-strategic nuclear weapons from the ROK (about 200, mostly gravity bombs, all of which were removed by February 1992,) as well as declaring that no tactical or theater nuclear weapons were deployed on US surface warships.[5] In this move, announced on September 28, 1991, President George Bush transformed the strategic landscape

[5] US Pacific Command, *Command History, 1991*, Office of the Historian, volume 1, 90, released under US FOIA to Nautilus institute, *et passim*, http://nautilus.org/wp-content/uploads/2011/12/koreawithdrawal.pdf/.

overnight.[6]

Reduced Reliance On Nuclear Threat in Korea

This change transformed American nuclear deterrence in Korea from immediate (due to proximity of weapons to battleground) to general in nature; and made the notion of nuclear extended deterrence far less salient to US extended deterrence. Henceforth, American war-plans and deployments in Korea relied almost exclusively on conventional forces, not nuclear weapons which were effectively recessed (whereas in Europe, tactical nuclear weapons remain forward-deployed and NATO has never stopped relying upon them in relation to Russian conventional forces.)[7] The United States reserved the right to redeploy nuclear weapons in a contingency,[8] but thereafter, nuclear targeting, war-planning, and delivery of nuclear weapons was conducted from the United States, not from Korea. Given the increase in the lethality and precision of conventional weapons in the nineteen nineties and 21st century, the notion of fighting wars with crude nuclear weapons was viewed by the US military as well as its political leadership as improbable, likely disproportionate, and increasingly surreal. Indeed, delivery of nuclear weapons against North Korea would be slow via long range bombers as it would be difficult for many reasons to use long range sea or land based missiles to attack the DPRK.

In many respects, American nuclear weapons were now reserved for

[6] Susan Koch, *The Presidential Nuclear Initiatives of 1991-1992*, WMD Case Study 5, Center for the Study of Weapons of Mass Destruction, National Defense University, Washington, D.C., October 1, 2012, http://wmdcenter.dodlive.mil/files/2012/10/CSWMD-Case-Study-5-for-web.pdf/.

[7] Here, recession means progress along the following spectrum of reduction of reliance on nuclear weapons: slow but continuous minimization of various elements of nuclear extended deterrence including maintaining studious silence on public on the topic, substitution of conventional for nuclear forces in allied doctrine and postures, development of regional security institutions, resolution of major security dilemmas between states, and the lessening of residual salience of nuclear weapons over time to the point where they fade away. See Patrick Morgan, "Considerations Bearing on a Possible Retraction of The American Nuclear Umbrella Over the ROK," prepared for Nautilus Institute, June 21, 2009 and published by National Committee on North Korea, Washington D.C., in October 2009, http://goo.gl/PW9gcg

[8] Eric Schmitt, "Bush's Arm Plan; Cheney Orders Bombers Off Alert, Starting Sharp Nuclear Pullback," New *York Times*, September 29, 1991, http://goo.gl/rIRxaN

countering only existential threats, that is, when the United States or its ally faced a threat to its national existence, in particular, due to a nuclear attack. Many American experts believe that it is likely that even that contingency would be responded to with a countervailing conventional campaign.[9] However, after the 1991 withdrawal, the United States and its allies deliberately left ambiguous how they would respond to nuclear aggression and attempted to extract marginal deterrence and compellence from nuclear threats from home-based nuclear weapons above that already obtained from advanced conventional forces. Thus, the "nuclear umbrella" was maintained in principle, but in reality, began to wear very thin in the nineteen nineties.

US-DPRK NUCLEAR COMPELLENCE

Both the United States and the DPRK used actual or implicit nuclear threat throughout the nineties to attempt to compel the other to change its policies and actions in specific ways.[10] Not surprisingly, this mutual threat exchange was not conductive to engagement and cooperation, and helped to poison the well of building a new US-DPRK relationship. Both parties failed to realize their objectives with respect to each other.

DPRK Nuclear Armament

Since 2000, hostility has dominated the US-DPRK relationship, and the increasing acrimony has seen increased reliance on nuclear threat by all

[9] Tom Nichols, "The Case for Conventional Deterrence," *The National Interest*, April 20, 2014, http://nationalinterest.org/commentary/the-case-conventional-deterrence-9381/.

[10] Patrick Morgan notes that US and the DPRK used nuclear threat primarily for compellence in the 1991-2002 time frame in "Deterrence and System Management: The Case of North Korea," *Conflict Management and Peace Science* 23:2 (2006): 121-138. The DPRK's nuclear threats from 2008 onwards have been primarily compellent in nature, not deterrent, as documented in the following studies: Peter Hayes and Scott Bruce, "North Korean Nuclear Nationalism and the Threat of Nuclear War in Korea," *Pacific Focus* 26:1 (2011): 65–89, doi: 10.1111/j.1976-5118.2011.01056.x.; Peter Hayes and RogerCavazos, "North Korean and US Nuclear Threats:Discerning Signals from Noise," *The Asia-Pacific Journal* 11:14:2, April 8, 2013, http://japanfocus.org/-Roger-Cavazos/3924#/.

parties to the Korean conflict, albeit in different ways. For its part, the DPRK shifted its phrasing and increasingly referred directly to nuclear weapons as against more ambiguous terms such as "massive deterrent." Then, it tested nuclear weapons in 2006, 2009, and 2013. It also tested long range space launch rockets that have dual use technological application to long range nuclear warhead delivery missiles, succeeding finally in putting a small satellite into circumpolar orbit in 2012. In 2012, the DPRK articulated its own nuclear doctrine, stating it did not care if it was viewed as a "nuclear weapons state" as recognized under the Nuclear Non Proliferation Treaty, from which it had departed, only that it had nuclear weapons for its own purposes. In 2013, the DPRK threatened to use nuclear weapons to attack cities in the ROK and the United States, and suggested that it might do so pre-emptively.

American Recalibration of Nuclear Threat

For its part, the United States adjusted its declaratory posture as stated in the *Nuclear Posture Review* (2010). In this text, nuclear weapons are reserved for deterring only nuclear attack on the United States or its allies. Specifically to accommodate the DPRK, the 2010 Review also changed the long standing US policy that states that the United States will not attack a NNWS in good standing with its NPT and IAEA safeguards obligations unless it was in an alliance relationship with a NWS and engaged in aggression. This latter phrase previously had rendered moot US negative security assurances to the DPRK given that it was in an alliance relationship with China. By the time this change was made, the DPRK had committed unambiguously to nuclear armament.[11]

In 2010, after the clashes between DPRK and ROK military forces, the United States increased its symbolic commitment to using nuclear threat to deter the DPRK, forming an Extended Deterrence Committee with the

[11] Peter Hayes and Jeffrey Lewis, "The DPRK and the Warsaw Clause: An Unnoticed Change in US Nuclear Policy," *NAPSNet Policy Forum*, July 28, 2011, http://nautilus.org/napsnet/napsnet-policy-forum/the-dprk-and-the-warsaw-clause-an-unnoticed-change-in-us-nuclear-policy/.

ROK. In 2013, it also deployed nuclear-capable bombers to the ROK to reinforce this commitment, presumably with an intention of "tailoring" its threats to what the United States perceived to be a stream of nuclear threats issued from the DPRK. Much of of US Forces Korea effort on the Extended Deterrence Committee was devoted to ensuring that ROK revision of its rules of engagement did not lead to rapid escalation, and to increasing South Korean understanding that the US was not planning to fight a war in Korea with nuclear weapons. However, these US and US-ROK nuclear threat statements interrupted the gradual trend towards eventual nuclear recession begun by the United States in 1991.

This state of mutual nuclear threat subsided by April 2013, but rhetorical reference is made constantly to nuclear war and nuclear attack by DPRK agencies. For its part, the United States continues to conduct exercises with nuclear elements, either tabletop, or involving real nuclear delivery systems (not nuclear weapons, these remain rear-deployed except for mid-Pacific deployed ballistic missile submarines that run silent, deep, and are not used actively as part of the signaling for nuclear threat against the DPRK or to reassure the ROK.)

TRIANGULAR STRATEGIC NUCLEAR DETERRENCE

The nuclear threat relationship between the United States and the DPRK exists in a wider context of triangular strategic nuclear deterrence between Russia, China, and the United States. Russia has increased its reliance on nuclear threat since the end of the Cold War, in part to substitute it for its ailing conventional forces. China is modernizing its nuclear forces, making them mobile and subterranean, and making them harder to target and to distinguish from land-based intermediate range but conventional missiles, thereby complicating possible escalation decisions by the United States. This may be intended to reduce the propensity of the United States to use conventional force in the Taiwan Straits by increasing the risk of nuclear use by both parties. There appear to be no other immediate conflicts in which US and Russian nuclear weapons are in play in the region today. From an American perspective, all other conflicts are more than adequately covered by US and allied conventional forces. Thus, apart from the DPRK, US nuclear extended deterrence to the ROK, Japan, and Taiwan is only in play to counter potential Chinese first or retaliatory use of American nuclear weapons, in the context of a larger US-China standoff or war. As the prospect of such a war is real, so nuclear extended deterrence is real…but equally, because the probability of such a war is remote, so the salience of nuclear extended deterrence to the countering of Chinese nuclear targeting of the ROK, Japan and Taiwan is also very low.

US-DPRK NUCLEAR THREAT IS MOST DANGEROUS IN THE REGION

The most urgent and dangerous nuclear threat relationship is between the United States and the DPRK. Due to the state of war, the immense military standoff and proximity of conventional forces at the Demilitarized Zone, and the lack of any common concepts or shared understandings related to nuclear weapons, it is easiest to envision the next-use of nuclear weapons in the Korean Peninsula. The nuclear weapons of the United States, China, Russia, and the DPRK are all involved in this regional threat system.

Ending US-DPRK Nuclear Threat Requires Mulutilateral Framework

Because the US-DPRK mutual nuclear threat relationship involves all states in the region, including the NNWSs the ROK and Japan, ending nuclear threat is beyond the power of the United States and the DPRK acting alone or even bilaterally. Instead, what is needed is a robust adaptive strategy that reshapes the role of nuclear weapons in the range of possible multipolar, bipolar, and unipolar future regional orders. Rather than shaping behaviors incrementally, as was tried and failed at the Six-Party Talks, future negotiations need to focus on creating a new "comprehensive" security settlement in a treaty format that meets the needs of all states in the region to reduce reliance on nuclear threat, and wherever possible, to end it. By reshape, we mean that a comprehensive security settlement should create a new regional framework that

a) Recognizes that all parties wish to eliminate nuclear weapons as a basis of their security relationships;
b) Reflects the reality that nuclear weapons are of decreasing political and military value; and
c) Facilitates reduction of the role of nuclear weapons in their respective political and military policies and postures.

Nuclear Weapons-Free Zone

The long-standing and well-tested framework for such a commitment is a legally binding nuclear weapons-free zone, for which there are many precedents around the world spanning for decades.[12] It is therefore timely to discuss the negotiated, multilateral, and legally binding end to nuclear threats by NWSs to NNWSs in the context of a comprehensive security settlement in Northeast Asia. Such a settlement requires a regional treaty framework, not just a political agreement, if it is to be meaningful to all

---

[12] KerstinVignard et al., *Disarmament Forum* 2: *Nuclear Weapons Free Zones* (Geneva: UNIDIR, 2011), http://www.unidir.org/files/publications/pdfs/nuclear-weapon-free-zones-en-314.pdf/. "As of late 2011, 138 out of 193 UN member states have entered into, and ratified, legally binding treaties to reduce or constrain nuclear weapon proliferation, development and basing in their own regions (or other regions over which they have territorial claims.) These include the 1959 Antarctic Treaty (47 states with interests in Antarctica,) the 1967 Tlatelolco Treaty (33 Latin American states,) the 1985 Rarotonga Treaty (13 South Pacific States,) the 1995 Bangkok Treaty (10 Southeast Asian states,) the 1996 Pelindaba Treaty (30 African states, with a further 21 signed but not yet ratified,) and the 2006 Semipalatinsk Treaty (5 Central Asian States.) NWFZs now cover almost the entire Southern Hemisphere, and wide swathes of the Northern Hemisphere, including the most recent Central Asian zone, which is entirely in the Northern Hemisphere." Michael Hamel-Green, "Regions That Say No: Precedents and Precursors for Denuclearizing Northeast Asia"(paper presented at the East Asia Nuclear Security Workshop, Tokyo, Japan, November 11, 2011), http://goo.gl/zmvuj4/.

Other treaties also denuclearize geographic areas, viz: the Outer Space Treaty, the Moon Agreement, and the Seabed Treaty.Mongolia's 1992 self-declared nuclear-weapon-free status has been recognized internationally through the adoption by consensus of UN General Assembly Resolution 53/77D in December 1998 on "Mongolia's international security and nuclear weapon free status."

Arguably, *the Korean Joint Denuclearization Declaration* (1992) also established a limited NWFZ in Korea, now moribund.

Thousands of cities and provinces have established local NWFZs, and some states (New Zealand) have written their non-nuclear status into their legal system or (The Philippines) into their constitution. However,these are not treaty-based zones nor recognized by the UN under international treaty law. The Comprehensive Test Ban Treaty, not yet in force, will ban nuclear explosions, and prohibit and prevent any such nuclear explosion at any place under a state party's jurisdiction or control.

the parties including the DPRK.[13] Anything less likely will fail and leave the states in the region to ride the roller coaster of confrontation and stand-off, of semi-permanent crisis.

Only A NWFZ Legally Terminates Nuclear Threat

The DPRK insists that US nuclear threat towards it must cease before it will revert to non-nuclear weapons status; and that this guarantee must be legally binding. The only framework in which this combination is possible is a NWFZ. Last July, the UN Secretary General urged states in the region to consider appropriate action to establish a nuclear-weapon-free zone in North-East Asia, "including by promoting a more active role for the regional forums in encouraging transparency and confidence-building among the countries of the region."[14] On October 21, 2014, the DPRK announced via KCNA that it proposed "building a nuclear-free zone through peaceful dialogue and negotiations…combined with the method of removing the US nuclear threat by relying on international law."[15]

Comprehensive Security Settlement Treaty

This treaty, which might be titled A Northeast Asia Treaty of Amity and Cooperation, would have six key elements, all of which are necessary.

1. Termination of state of war
2. Creation of a permanent security council on security to monitor and verify compliance and deciding on violations
3. A mutual declaration of no hostile intent
4. Provisions of assistance for nuclear and other energy
5. Termination of sanctions

[13] Binoy Kampmark et al., "Summary Report: A New Approach to Security in Northeast Asia: Breaking the Gridlock"(paper presented at the Breaking the Gridlock Workshop, Woodrow Wilson International Center for Scholars, Washington, D.C., October 9-10, 2012), http://goo.gl/YrX6Ko/.

[14] United Nations Genenral Assembly, "Work of the Advisory Board on Disarmament Matters, Report of the Secretary-General to UN General Assembly (A/68/206)," July 26, 2013, https://goo.gl/EM7qA6/.

[15] KCNA, "U.S. Can Never Evade Blame for Blocking Solution to Nuclear Issue: Rodong Sinmun," October 21, 2014, http://www.kcna.co.jp/item/2014/201410/news21/20141021-11ee.html/.

6. A nuclear weapons free zone.

Within this comprehensive framework, a Northeast Asian nuclear weapons-free zone (NWFZ) would be created to manage three of the hardest security issues facing the region, viz, nuclear threats by the NWSs to NNWSs in Northeast Asia, the provision of US nuclear extended deterrence to its allies in the region, and the DPRK's nuclear armament.

Purposes of a NEA-NWFZ Treaty

As we noted above, a nuclear weapons-free zone (NWFZ) is a treaty, affirmed in the Nuclear Non Proliferation Treaty, whereby states freely negotiate regional prohibitions on nuclear weapons.[16] Its main purposes are to strengthen peace and security, reinforce the nuclear non-proliferation regime, and contribute to nuclear disarmament. A NEA-NWFZ would provide a stabilizing framework in which to manage and reduce the threat of nuclear war, eliminate nuclear threats to NNWSs which are in compliance with their NPT-IAEA obligations, and facilitate abolition of nuclear weapons. (It would apply to nuclear weapons only, not to other "WMD".) It would also enable the DPRK to freeze expansion, start to reverse, and ultimately dismantle its nuclear arms; build confidence that no party in the region will use nuclear weapons for political coercion or to fight wars; and reassure NNWSs that they are secure, thereby deepening commitment to non-nuclear weapons-status.

Differential Obligations

In a NEA-NWFZ, states would undertake differential obligations.[17] Non-nuclear weapons states (that is, NPT NNWSs) undertake to not research, develop, test, possess, or deploy nuclear weapons, and to not allow nuclear

---

[16] United Nations, "Annex 1. Establishment of nuclear-weapon-free zones on the basis of arrangements freely arrived at among the States of the region concerned," in Report of the Disarmament Commission, General Assembly, 54th session, Supplement No. 42 (A/54/42) (New York, United Nations, 1999), 7, https://goo.gl/MmCDj0/.

[17] This section draws on Peter Hayes and Richard Tanter, "Key Elements of Northeast Asia Nuclear-Weapons Free Zone (NEA-NWFZ)," *NAPSNet Policy Forum*, November 13, 2012, http://nautilus.org/napsnet/napsnet-policy-forum/key-elements-of-northeast-asia-nuclear-weapons-free-zone-nea-nwfz.

weapons to be stationed on their territory.[18] Nuclear-Weapons States (that is, NPT NWSs) give negative security assurancesto not use or threaten to use nuclear weapons against the NNWSs party to and in compliance with the NWFZ treaty.[19]

NEA-NWFZ Membership

In early "3+3"proposals,[20] 3 NWS (US, China, FSU then Russia) + 3

---

[18] The exact mix of these prohibitions varies across zones. Recent zones prohibit more activities. Two issues are important in the NEA context. The first is *stationing* of nuclear weapons. Secret US-Japan agreements provided for US storage and/or re-introduction of nuclear weapons. President George Bush's 1991 statement that "under normal circumstances, our ships will not carry tactical nuclear weapons," and that land and sea-based warheads not withdrawn, dismantled and destroyed "will be secured in central areas where they would be available if necessary in a future crisis" also left open the possibility that the US might, presumably subject to consultation with allies, redeploy such weapons into Japan and the ROK. At the time, then Chairman of the Joint Chiefs Colin Powell said that only 24 hours would be needed to reverse the order. Notes since 1991, many of the tactical and theater nuclear weapons in the US arsenal no longer exist. The only salient non-strategic weapon today is the now old B-61 thermonuclear warhead that is stored in the US and forward-deployed in some NATO countries. Practically speaking, re-deployment and forward stationing of nuclear weapons would be very difficult to achieve.Home-porting strategic nuclear submarines in allied ports is physically possible, but politically difficult, and would affect greatly a US second strike capability by increasing the vulnerability of these submarines to first strike.
The second important issue is transit. To avoid conflict between Japan's domestic non-nuclear principles and transit of its narrow straits leading from the Sea of Japan/East Sea of Korea to the Pacific Ocean by US and then-Soviet warships, Japan limited its coastal jurisdiction in these straits to three nautical miles, allowing free international passage through a narrow strip of international waters. Leaving aside apparently commonplace past transit of US nuclear weapons transit via airfields and ports, not just innocent passage in the territorial waters of Japan, the adoption of a zone-wide 12 mile nautical limit for a NEA-NWFZ would change current Japanese legal treatment of the straits and the related legal regime under which transit could occur. President Bush's statement is "BUSH'S ARMS PLAN; Remarks by President Bush on Reducing U.S. and Soviet Nuclear Weapons," *New York Times*, September 28, 1991, http://goo.gl/PB5a82. Powell is cited in Eric Schmitt, "Bush's Arm Plan; Cheney Orders Bombers Off Alert, Starting Sharp Nuclear Pullback," *New York Times*, September 29, 1991, http://goo.gl/05kuzy/.
On Japan's transit policy and territorial waters, seeChi-Young Pak, *The Korean Straits* (Martinis Nijhoff, 1988): 79-81; on recent Chinese naval surface and submarine transit of the straits and Japanese response, *see* Peter Dutton, *Scouting, Signaling, and Gatekeeping, Chinese Naval Operations in Japanese Waters and the International Law Implications*, China Maritime Studies Institute (Rhode Island, U.S. Naval War College), https://www.usnwc.edu/Research---Gaming/China-Maritime-Studies-Institute/Publications/documents/CMS2_Dutton.aspx.

[19] Article 2 of the Protocol of the Southeast NWFZ specifies that: "Each State Party undertakes not to use or threaten to use nuclear weapons against any State Party to the Treaty. It further undertakes not to use or threaten to use nuclear weapons within the Southeast Asian Nuclear-Weapon-Free Zone." To date, the NWSs have resisted this provision, partly because the SEA-NWFZ covers the Exclusive Economic Zone, but also because it implies restrictions on the use of nuclear weapons from within the zone against adjacent zones. Eventually, the mosaic of such stringent zones could reinforce each other to prohibit all threat and all use of nuclear weapons, as envisioned by Seongwhun Cheon as a "Pan-Pacific nuclear weapon free zone (PPNWFZ), encompassing East Asia, South Pacific and Latin America." in Seongwhun Cheon, "The Limited Nuclear Weapon Free Zone in Northeast Asia: Is It Feasible?" *The Mongolian Journal of International Affairs* 14 (2007): 115, http://www.mongoliajol.info/index.php/MJIA/article/viewFile/31/31/.

[20] Endicott's 15 year series of workshops first proposed a 1,000 km range from the Korean DMZ that covered parts of Alaska, China, Mongolia, and Russia as well as Korea and Japan; and later, an ellipse that covered NE China, Mongolia, the Russian Far East, part of Alaska, the two Koreas, Japan, and Taiwan at the southern end. See John Endicott, "Limited nuclear-weapon-free zones: the time has come," *Korean Journal of Defense*

NNWS (2 Koreas, Japan) were proposed as parties. In 2010, Nautilus Institute proposed a 3+2 version (starting with ROK and Japan only, leaving an open door for the DPRK to join later or, should the two Koreas reunify peacefully and the DPRK eliminate its nuclear forces, be integrated into the zone.) Today, it seems sensible (and consistent with other NWFZs) for all five NPT-NWSs to join, and at least 4 NPT-NNWSs join at the outset (Japan, ROK, Canada, Mongolia); and possibly DPRK in a contingent status (explained below.) This "5+4.5," later "5+5" (ignoring Taiwan, see below) model of a NEA-NWFZ takes time (but not without limit) to integrate fully the DPRK.

Monitoring and Verification

A NEA-NWFZ would require a stringent monitoring and verification regime satisfactory to all parties. At minimum, all NNWS in a NEA-NWFZ should accept the IAEA Additional Protocol. Specific monitoring and verification provisions would be needed during and after dismantlement in the DPRK.[21] The DPRK would also need to meet the requirements of the IAEA to restore "confidence" in its nuclear weapons intentions, as has South Africa since it dismantled its nuclear weapons. Conversely, the

---

Analysis 20:1(2008): 17, doi: 10.1080/10163270802006305/. Endicott's concept was reviewed critically by Seongwhun Cheon, op cit, 106-115.

The 3+3 concept is advanced by Hiromichi Umebayashi, "A Northeast Asia Nuclear-Weapon-Free Zone with a Three Plus Three Arrangement," (paper presented at the East Asia Nuclear Security Workshop, Tokyo, Japan, November 11, 2011), http://goo.gl/XOVkMF; and similarly, Kumao Kaneko, "Japan needs no umbrella," *Bulletin of the Atomic Scientists*, March/April (1996): 46-51, http://www.thebulletin.org/.

The first proposal phased implementation of a 3+3 conceptis found in Seongwhun Cheon and Tatsujiro Suzuki, "The Tripartite Nuclear-Weapon-Free Zone in Northeast Asia: a Long-Term Objective of the Six Party Talks," *International Journal of Korean Studies* 12:2 (2003): 41-68, http://www.kinu.or.kr/eng/pub/pub_03_01.jsp?page=2&num=42&mode=view&field=&text=&order=&dir=&bid=DATA03&ses=&category=11/.

Nautilus' 3+2 concept was advanced in *Korea-Japan Nuclear Weapon Free Zone (KJNWFZ) Briefing Paper*, May 6, 2010, in English, Korean, and Japanese, http://nautilus.org/projects/by-name/korea-japan-nwfz/.

[21] There is extensive precedent in the case of South Africa, Iraq, and Libya for documenting such dismantlement.See David Albright and Corey Hinderstein, "Cooperative Verified Dismantlement of Nuclear Programs: An Eye Toward North Korea," (paper presented at the Institute for Nuclear Materials Management Annual Conference, June 1, 2003), http://isis-online.org/conferences/detail/cooperative-verified-dismantlement-of-nuclear-programs-an-eye-toward-north-/10, and Andre Buys, "Proliferation Risk Assessment of Former Nuclear Explosives/Weapons Program Personnel: South African Case Study," *NASPNet Special Report*, July 14, 2011, http://www.nautilus.org/publications/essays/napsnet/reports/Buys-research-report-final.pdf and Andre Buys, "Tracking nuclear capable individuals," *NAPSNet Special Report*, Nautilus Institute, April 19, 2011, http://nautilus.wpengine.netdna-cdn.com/wp-content/uploads/2011/12/Tracking_Nuclear_Individuals_Buys.pdf

DPRK (and other parties) could demand inspection of US facilities in the ROK and Japan. Specific arrangements will be needed to control the DPRK's nuclear weapons-capable personnel. Challenge inspections might be built into the NWFZ treaty itself. Non-intrusive inspections of transiting ships and aircraft might use state-of-the-art anti-terrorist monitoring techniques at airfields and in ports but not in innocent oceanic or aerial transit. The treaty may want to invite parties to adopt more stringent inspection arrangements as technology evolves. For example, parties to a NWFZ could create a regional nuclear forensics network and database to control non-state actor nuclear proliferation. Also, plutonium-based fuel cycles as in Japan and under discussion in the ROK may require more stringent transparency in real-time than current safeguards systems allow to preserve a meaningful diversion-detection to response-time ratio. The parties would need to create a regional inspectorate, as has occurred in the Latin American NWFZ, or determine that non-compliance would be determined by the council governing a regional treaty of amity and cooperation; or refer non-compliance to the UN Security Council.

Enforcement by States Parties

The existing toolkit of sanctions, interdiction, and coercive diplomacy combined with engagement may not be sufficient to maintain compliance with a NEA-NWFZ. Nuclear threats against non-NNWSs by nuclear armed states or by NPT-NWSs should be met in accordance with the 1994 UNSC resolution whereby the NWSs undertook to respond to "nuclear aggression" against NNWSs. A NWFZ places the legal onus on all NWSs party to the NWFZ to respond, not merely those in bilateral alliances (US-ROK, US-Japan, PRC-DPRK.) Thus, it provides NNWSs with a *multilateral, legally-binding* guarantee that they make invoke if they are subjected to nuclear threat or attack. States generally are loath to break treaties, and a treaty-based commitment is more likely to be observed than one based on unilateral or executive branch declaratory policies which may vary between administrations and even abandoned overnight.

As was noted above, if the conference of parties is unable to resolve a dispute, then a NWFZ treaty must specify how non-compliance should be dealt with. The options would be to refer non-compliance to a superordinate regional council if such is created concurrently as part of a regional treaty of amity and cooperation; or to the IAEA (if the matter relates to a nuclear fuel cycle activity); or direct to the UNSC if it relates directly to nuclear weapons acquisition, deployment, or threats by NNWSs or aimed at these states.

No monitoring and verification system will provide absolute confidence; and no means of guaranteed enforcement of a NWFZ treaty is possible. What is important is whether sufficient confidence can be achieved that monitoring and verification systems will work and that enforcement is credible. This confidence should be compared with the security outcomes and confidence associated with these outcomes of not controlling nuclear threat and nuclear weapons via a NEA-NWFZ, not with an abstract ideal world in which nuclear weapons simply do not exist.

CONTINUATION AND TRANSFORMATION OF NUCLEAR EXTENDED DETERRENCE IN A NEA-NWFZ

It is worth emphasizing that such a NWFZ would not end completely US nuclear extended deterrence. It would continue to operate for the ROK and Japan to counter the general nuclear threat arising from China and Russia's nuclear forces, assuming that the DPRK were to disarm and revert to full NPT NNWS status. In effect, this arrangement requires the ROK and Japan to recast their perceptions of what constitutes nuclear extended deterrence from a Cold War concept based on forward-deployed weapons and instant nuclear retaliation to a post-Cold War concept that we termed above as "nuclear existential deterrence"; and for the ROK, Japan and the DPRK to accept that such existential deterrence exists, no matter what a NWS says or does, so long as strategic nuclear weapons exist.

Separate to the general operation of nuclear deterrence between the

United States, China, and Russia, and to the continuing existence of nuclear existential deterrence that arises from the former with regard to the NNWSs in a NEA-NWFZ, the question arises of whether nuclear extended deterrence would exist should a NEA-NWFZ be violated, either by nuclear threats from a NWS against a NNWS party to the treaty, or by a NNWS breaking out of its non-nuclear weapons status.

Should a NNWS renege on its commitments under a NEA-NWFZ treaty, then all the NWSs party to that treaty are committed to countering this breakout. Should the DPRK either halt its denuclearization to comply with a NWFZ or commence a new breakout having re-established its non-nuclear status, then US guarantees (and likely those of the other NWSs) to not use nuclear threat or attack would rendered moot.[22] If China or Russia threaten to use nuclear weapons against the DPRK, the ROK or Japan, then the United States and other NWSs would be free to extend nuclear deterrence to these non-nuclear parties. The same logic would apply in reverse if the United States threatened to use nuclear weapons against a non-nuclear armed DPRK in compliance with its NPT and IAEA obligations. Alternately, if the ROK or Japan made their own nuclear weapons, then China and Russia (and the United States and any other NWS party to the treaty) would be bound to come to the DPRK's assistance, or would be bound no longer by the NWFZ treaty to not use nuclear weapons against the non-nuclear parties.

Due to the significance of this issue for the ROK and Japan, further reassurance for all parties could be addressed by including a clause in the negative security protocols of a NWFZ treaty stating that in the event of a verified breach of the obligations, the five guarantor NWS recognised under the NPT would be free to re-establish previous extended deterrence

---

[22] Actual arrangements between NWSs and NNWSs vary from zone to zone. Dhanapala argues that they cannot do so in Jayantha Dhanapala, "NWFZS and Extended Nuclear Deterrence: Squaring the Circle?" NAPSNet Special Report, May 1, 2012, http://nautilus.org/napsnet/napsnet-special-reports/nwfzs-and-extended-nuclear-deterrence-squaring-the-circle/. The experts cited in the 1975 UN study of NWFZs split on whether nuclear deterrence could be extended to NNWSs party to a NWFZ. See United Nations General Assembly, "Comprehensive Study Of The Question Of Nuclear-Weapon-Free Zones In All Its Aspects, Special report of the Conference of the Committee on Diarment (A/100027/Add.1)." October 8, 1975, http://www.un.org/disarmament/HomePage/ODAPublications/DisarmamentStudySeries/PDF/A-10027-Add1.pdf/.

guarantees—as indeed is already explicit in number of reservations NWS have already made to other NWFZs.

One risk that should be addressed in dialogue concerning a prospective NEA-NWFZ is how serious transgression of such a zone by a NWS or a NNWS could induce some NNWSs to develop their own nuclear forces rather than reverting to the *status quo ante* of dependence on US nuclear extended deterrence, even in a stronger form that exists today. There may be creative ways to ameliorate this risk which have not been considered before because the security circumstances of preceding NWFZs did not have to address such issues in a stark manner as is the case in Northeast Asia.

THE DPRK'S NUCLEAR WEAPONS AND A NEA-NWFZ

As a self-declared nuclear-armed state, the DPRK's nuclear weapons and delivery systems are the most obvious major obstacle to realization of a NEA-NWFZ, although they are not the only one. However, the main reason to establish a NEA-NWFZ is not just to respond to the DPRK, but also to address the proliferation potential of Japan, the ROK, and Taiwan, and to create a stabilizing framework in which to manage strategic deterrence between the NWSs. The DPRK is only one state that affects the strategic environment, including its nuclear dimension, in Northeast Asia, and a relatively small one at that, including with respect to nuclear weapons. A sound strategic environment should be created that shapes the DPRK's choices in constructive ways, but it must also serve the interests of all states in the region, many of which may be affected more by considerations pertaining to each other than by those related to the DPRK, irrespective of the DPRK's nuclear capacities.

How Would the DPRK Join a Nea-Nwfz?

In a legal sense, there are two ways to deal with the DPRK and its nuclear weapons in a NEA-NWFZ treaty. The first is to simply leave the door open for NNWSs to join the treaty. Thus, if only Japan, the ROK, and possibly Mongolia were to sign at the outset, the DPRK could later join after denuclearization or integration into a non-nuclear, peacefully re-unified Korea. More desirably, the DPRK could join the NEA-NWFZ treaty at the outset, but not waive the provision that the treaty only come into force when all parties have ratified it, while the other parties would waive this provision.[23] The DPRK thereby would reaffirm its commitment to become a NNWS in compliance with its NPT-IAEA obligations, but would take time to comply fully.

The other NNWSs could set a time limit for the DPRK to come into compliance (and specify milestones.) The entry into force provision could allow them to reserve the right to abandon the treaty if the DPRK has not denuclearized sufficiently by that time. Concurrently, the NWSs (hopefully all of them, not just the United states) would qualify their guarantees to not use nuclear weapons to attack the NNWSs party to the treaty so as to specifically exclude the DPRK from the guarantee, or would calibrate their guarantee to the extent that it has come into full compliance.

[23] This approach is transposed from the Tlatelolco Treaty which established an ingenious and innovative legal mechanism by which reluctant states could be encouraged to join the zone at a later date. It consists of a provision in Article 28 (3) that allows a signatory state to "waive, wholly or in part" the requirements that have the effect of bringing the treaty into force for that state at a particular time. As Mexican diplomat Alfonso Garcia Robles noted in his commentary on Article 28: "An eclectic system was adopted, which, while respecting the viewpoints of all signatory States, prevented nonetheless any particular State from precluding the enactment of the treaty for those which would voluntarily wish to accept the statute of military denuclearization defined therein. The Treaty of Tlatelolco has thus contributed effectively to dispel the myth that for the establishment of a nuclear-weapon-free-zone it would be an essential requirement that all States of the region concerned should become, from the very outset, parties to the treaty establishing the zone. In this way, the normative framework for a non-nuclear region can be established before all states are ready to actually implement the framework." Michael Hamel-Green, "Implementing a Korea-Japan Nuclear-Weapon-Free Zone: Precedents, Legal Forms, Governance, Scope, Domain, Verification, Compliance and Regional Benefits," *Pacific Focus* 26:1 (2011): 97-8, doi:10.1111/j.1976-5118.2011.01057.x

EQUAL TREATMENT FOR ALL NON-NUCLEAR PARTIES

In a NEA-NWFZ, the DPRK's nuclear armament, such as it is, would not be recognized as legitimate in any manner under the Nuclear Non Proliferation Treaty (which it disavows in any case.)[24] The standards that it must meet when denuclearized would equal or exceed those for all non-NNWSs in the NWFZ, including monitoring and verification requirements. Most important, the DPRK would be offered a legally binding, multilateral guarantee by all the NWSs that it will not face nuclear threat or the use of nuclear weapons against it, but would have to earn this guarantee by actually coming into full compliance within the specified time. These considerations would be important to the political process that would be required to implement a NEA-NWFZ.

THE TAIWAN PROBLEM

Designing, negotiating and implementing a NEA-NWFZ would not be easy. Indeed, there are many difficult issues that would require a NWFZ to be tailored to the region's specific circumstances. Taiwan for example, presents a special problem for a NWFZ. However, Taiwan could solve this problem by declaring that it will fulfill the NNWSs' obligations in NEA NWFZ treaty. China can declare that its commitment covers Taiwan as part of China (NWSs have made such declarations in other NWFZs with regard to trust territories.)

[24] KCNA, "FM Spokesman on Right to Bolster Nuclear Deterrent," May 26, 2010, http://www.kcna.co.jp/item/2010/201005/news24/20100524-15ee.html

KEY QUESTIONS FOR A NEA-NWFZ

A regional NWFZ should be tailored to the specific needs and circumstances of the region to be covered. Thus, past NWFZs offer precedents and lessons-learned, but do not constrain Northeast Asian states from introducing innovations or specific approaches to achieve the basic goals of a NWFZ in their region—the avoidance of nuclear war, the reversal of nuclear proliferation, and the eventual elimination of all nuclear weapons. Following are some key questions that states would need to resolve before negotiating and implementing a NWFZ. An Eminent Persons Group might be a good vehicle by which to obtain preliminary answers before states commence official dialogue.

a) Whatare the risks of potential accidental or miscalculated use of nuclear weapons in the region, and how may such risks be reduced or eliminated through the processes and phases of establishing a NWFZ

b) Should nuclear fuel cycle cooperation be included as part of the NWFZ treaty or as a separate set of parallel side agreements (some regional in scope, some likely DPRK-specific)?

c) Would a NWFZ need to head off rocket programs that prefigure long-range missile development in NNWSs in NEA; if so would a parallel agreement on regional space launch cooperation program or consortium under the regional comprehensive security settlement treaty facilitate Japanese, ROK and DPRK commitment to a NEA-NWFZ?

d) Are side agreements needed to restrain arms racing with offensive conventional weapons that undermine strategic stability and even restore the threat of mass destruction, only this time, by non-nuclear weapons?

e) Would a NEA-NWFZ commit NWSs to not fire nuclear weapons out of a zone, not just to not station them in the Zone or to transit them through via innocent passage?

f) Should NWSs impose on their own territory a geographic restriction on deployment of nuclear-armed ground-launched ballistic and cruise missiles in a verifiable zone as part of the NWFZ—in effect, the price charged by the United states and Russia to China for delivering Japan, the ROK, and *de facto*, Taiwan, into a NWFZ?

g) What provisions for emergency re-deployment, as apparently exist in the case of Japan and were implied in the 1991 withdrawal, would be allowed? (Otherwise, wittingly or unwittingly, a NNWS can become party to nuclear threat or nuclear use, transgressing its non-nuclear status in the treaty and opening the way for others to accuse it of non-compliance and to cite it as a basis for their own non-compliance or even withdrawal?)

h) What are the geographical boundaries of a NEA-NWFZ? (At first glance, it would appear to cover only the national territories of the NNWSs party to the treaty, including only maritime areas encompassed by their respective territorial seas extending 12 nautical miles offshore.)

i) How would a NEA-NWFZ complement adjacent NWFZs, and how would it facilitate a Middle East-NWFZ (and vice versa)?

CHAPTER 7

Securing Nuclear Safety in Northeast Asia -ROK Proposal on Northeast Asia Nuclear Safety Mechanism[1]

Yoon-won Park

Background

The Fukushima nuclear disaster in Japan on March 11, 2011 produced much skepticism on the global community's nuclear power safety capacity as well as much distrust towards nuclear power in general from the people of respective nations. The Republic of Korea (hereafter Korea) and China raised the most amount of concern back then, given their close vicinity with Japan. I hesitate to call it a saving grace, but most of the radioactive material was channeled to the Pacific due to westward winds, bringing down the radioactive damage in the Korean peninsula and China down to virtually zero. Nonetheless, there is growing concern and a common understanding within Northeast Asia (NEA) on the need for a more progressive cooperation agreement on nuclear safety.

From an energy-demand standpoint, NEA (Korea, China and Japan) has many reasons to increase its use of nuclear power, despite the temporary reduction since the Fukushima crisis. Korea and Japan's overseas energy reliance stand at 97 percent and 84 percent, respectively. China's rate is lower than that of Korean and Japan but its heavy reliance on coal is

[1] A version of this essay in English containing images is found at: Yoon-won Park, "Securing Nuclear Safety in Northeast Asia: ROK Proposal on Northeast Asia Nuclear Safety Mechanism," NAPSNet Special Reports, May 04, 2015, http://nautilus.org/napsnet/napsnet-special-reports/securing-nuclear-safety-in-northeast-asia-rok-proposal-on-northeast-asia-nuclear-safety-mechanism/

blamed for its extreme air pollution. Therefore, China cannot but increase its use of pollutant-free energy sources.

The state of trilateral nuclear safety cooperation remains at a rudimentary level. The countries' Top Regulators' Meeting, or the TRM, launched in 2008 is held annually, but had remained mostly ceremonial and protocol-centric before the Fukushima disaster. Since then, it has touched upon the topic of information sharing in times of crises but has not yet produced a common outcome.

While the three countries share much in common culturally and historically, when it comes to nuclear safety, the nations have either resorted to self reliance or cooperation with the IAEA and other international agencies, or far more distant nations such as the United States or France, instead of consulting with regional neighbors. President Park Geun-hye in her August 15, 2013 Independence Day speech proposed forming a NEA nuclear safety consulting body. This proposal will become the foundation for the region's nuclear safety consultive body and ultimately contribute to securing regional nuclear safety.

State of regional nuclear development and outlook

As of 2014, Korea, China and Japan currently operate 24, 21 and 48 (halted) nuclear power plants, respectively. By 2050, the total is expected to increase to about 300, thus concentrating approximately 40 percent of the world's nuclear power facilities in Northeast Asia. According to the Berkeley Energy and Resources Collaborative, if China pushes on with its current nuclear power plant constructions, then by 2035, nuclear power of China and OECD Asia (Korea, Japan, etc.) will surpass that of the United States and Europe (see Table 7-1).

Table 7-1: Nuclear Power Plants in Northeast Asia, 2014

	China	Korea	Japan
Operational	13	21	54

Under Construction	27	7	3
Planned	188	4	12

Northeast Asia's nuclear safety policy and safety related issues

By looking at Korea's energy resource make-up, we can observe Korea's energy import dependncy. Of the country's $519.6 billion imports in 2012, 36 percent, or $184.8 billion was spent on merely energy imports. Among these $5.4 billion worth of oil was reprocessed for exports, but still, a whopping $130 billion of energy imports reveal Korea's dire energy situation. Korea, Japan and China's imports of the three major fossil fuels - coal, oil and natural gas- all rank in the top 5 list of import nations. NEA's level of dependence on fossil fuel and how much it spends on energy imports is clearly profound.

Korea's nuclear safety legal system (see Table 7-2) is formed largely by the nuclear safety law, the presidential enforcement ordinance, enforcement regulation and the notification from the nuclear safety committee. Underneath are the technical regulatory standards, guidelines and the industry standards that govern machineries, production, installation and maintenance.

Table 7-2: Korea's nuclear safety legal system

Nuclear Safety Act	To provide for matters concerning safety management in the research, development, production and use of nuclear energy
Enforcement of Decree of the Nuclear Safety Act	To provide for matters delegated by the Nuclear Safety Act and matters necessary for the enforcement thereof
Enforcement Rule of the Nuclear Safety Act	To provide for matters delegated by the Nuclear Safety Act and Enforcement of Decree of the Nuclear Safety Act and matters necessary for the rule thereof.
NSSC Notification	To prescribe for matters of the engineering standards and the administrative procedures in detail

Regulatory standards / Regulatory guidelines	Regulatory standards, Regulatory guidelines, KEPIC, ASME etc.

Nations around the world have concentrated their efforts in improving nuclear safety since the Fukushima nuclear disaster. In the past, construction of a plant had been focused mostly around 'design-basis accidents.' In the post-Fukushima era, safety of nuclear facilities have been drastically improved, with natural disasters and possible after-effects and other factors being taken into much more consideration. In Korea, operational plants were thoroughly examined for any possible signs of a similar crisis-level disaster such as the Fukushima disaster, with regulators and experts producing step-by-step contingency plans as seen in Table 7-3.

Table 7-3: Safety Measures of Korean plants after the Fukushima Debacle

Goal	Measure
Acquire means of emergency safety shut-down even in extreme natural disasters	Installing of earthquake-related automatic suspension equipment, waterproof doors and sea walls

↓ When in failure

Prevent progression towards severe accident in any given situation	Acquire mobile generator and storage battery, external channel to inject cooling water, strengthen cooling capacity of spent fuel pool

↓ When in failure

Suppress massive leaking of radioactive material in case of severe accident	Passive hydrogen removal system, installation of exhaust in housing facility, reinforcing of emergency procedures

↓ When in failure

Reinforce measures under crisis scenario
-Acquire additional protective gear -Bolster emergency crisis countermeasures

As seen in Table 7-3, reinforcement of safety standstill mechanism of reactors in times of extreme environmental hazards and also in case of its failure, emergency power delivery and cooling mechanisms to prevent the core's meltdown were drastically improved. Assuming that these measures failed and the disaster further escalate, hydrogen explosion prevention, structural reinforcement of the primary reactor containment and supplementary crisis scenario manuals and directives have been put in place as well.

In case the measures fail and radioactive materials become loose, further emergency planning and contingency measures have been put in place. Despite such proactive measures, establishment of the country's nuclear safety apparatus and policy still has a long way to go. This is especially due to the down trodden public trust amid revelations of use of parts with fabricated safety documentations.

China's energy source make up for electricity production is 70-80 percent thermal power, 10-20 percent hydro power. A mere 1.3 percent comes from nuclear power. In contrast to China, the United States, which in terms of electricity production nearly equals that of China, produces 20 percent of its electricity via nuclear power. Household, commercial and industrial consumptions are spread across fairly equally, 35 percent, 35 percent, 25 percent respectively. China, on the other hand, channels 75 percent of its power to industrial use, 12.5 percent towards household consumption and 10 percent towards commercial use. The imbalance in power spending underlines the need for China to prop up its investment in power production facilities. China, in the future, plans to produce 10 percent of its electric power via nuclear means. Chinese leadership's strong will towards this is evident as seen in Table 7-4.

Table 7-4: Chinese leadership's apparent intent in developing nuclear power

On Friday, China's President Xi Jinping told a government meeting that development of nuclear energy should be accelerated. "By adopting top international standards and ensuring safety, China should lose no time in constructing nuclear power projects in eastern coastal regions," Xi said, as state-run Xinhua newswire reported. At the end of 2013, China's 17 operational nuclear power plants were generating about 2 percent of the country's total energy, according to Xinhua. But Ye Qizhen, an expert in nuclear energy at the Chinese Academy of Engineering, told the newswire that China should aim to get 10 percent of total energy from nuclear power.

*Source: Bloomberg Businessweek, June 17, 2014

China's legal system governing nuclear safety, however, remains relatively feeble amid the country's grand nuclear energy vision. China in 1984 first came up with a draft for its nuclear law but failed to ratify it due to conflict of ideas and interest within the government. Such problems still persist, hence a basic nuclear law governing production, use, and safety management yet remains to be seen. The current law is formed merely of the radiation pollution prevention act legislated in 2003 along with 8 administrative regulation, 27 partial provisions, and 6 local regulations.

China's nuclear plant development programs similar to that of Korea's. The country is developing its very-own CAP-1000 model by benchmarking the Westing House AP1000 from the United States and plans to bolster its capacity to create an upgraded CAP-1400 model. This is similar to the Korean model based on CE technology, completing development of ORP-1000 and further expanding it to APR-1400.

In the end, Korea, China, and Japan all have its nuclear technology based on that of America. They later boosted their in-house development to improve upon the technologies and similarly produced nuclear products for exports. In this respect, the three countries are in unique positions of competition while at the same time in the need for close consultations.

84 percent of Japan's energy is reliant on overseas imports. In terms of electricity, the country's 54 reactors produce approximately 30 percent of its power, but this has all been replaced by fossil fuel since the Fukushima crisis. As of now, safety revisions of 48 reactors are being conducted, as Fukushima 1's four reactors and 5 and 6 reactors from Fukushima 2 were shut down. Japan, since the end of World War II has persisted in its nuclear endeavors and have acquired high levels of enrichment and reprocessing technology. Public objection towards nuclear power remains high but the country is not in a situation to simply give up its nuclear program.

Since the Fukushima crisis, Japan has significantly changed its nuclear safety regulation agency and required each nuclear plants to drastically improve upon safety measures. For example, it required plants to raise the level of breakwater walls to cope with severe natural disasters, while also ensuring the safe supply of emergency power and cooling capabilities towards the core. As the Fukushima crisis was further escalated due to a common cause failure from the massive tsunami, regulators improved upon various options in order to avoid common cause failures in the future. While safety evaluation in the past was conducted strictly through deterministic means, post-Fukushima evaluation have taken into consideration a higher level of performance-based requirements. It also modified the basic requisites of nuclear safety regulations so that individual nuclear operators can set their own performance goals and meet their respective safety requirements.

Pre-Fukushima, there have been a string of criticism towards Japan's nuclear safety governance, such as lack of consistency, a convoluted command/control structure, lack of regulatory independence and confounding business and regulations. Japan ignored much of these. As its nuclear safety regulators failed to fulfill its contingency missions, the country came to drastically repair its regulatory system as pointed out by the IAEA and other international agencies. Regulatory functions were dispersed among different agencies before. They are now consolidated under the NRA.

Progress in the direction of forming NEA nuclear safety consultive body

In order to build a NEA nuclear safety consultative body, one must first observe and seek if there are other similar groups in other regions. Europe in 1999 launched and is operating WENRA (Association of Regulators of Western Europe). WENRA for the past 10 years set the common standard for nuclear development within Europe. It has received high accolades from respective European countries for having achieved much public approval in terms of nuclear safety. Within 10 days following the Fukushima disaster, WENRA ordered all nuclear plants within its jurisdiction to conduct stress tests and prove their safety. It has played a critical role in ensuring nuclear safety and alleviating Europe's anxieties towards nuclear plants.

NEA since 2008 operates TRM as regulators' consultative group, but is merely a perfunctory apparatus. The three NEA nations have become keenly aware of the need for mutual cooperation in nuclear safety, thus raising the qualitative talks and operations within TRM, but still remains shy of the high level of safety standards incorporations and requirements of the parties' compliance.

As mentioned before, the three NEA nations collectively face the inevitability of expansion of nuclear energy use, and winning public approval regarding nuclear safety remain the utmost priority in raising regional partnership and cooperation. Korea and Japan faces an uphill public battle concerning nuclear expansion and China, while the public anger remains dormant due to its political system, is also sure to face similar obstacles in terms of establishing its nuclear policy. The countries ultimately share a common fate in terms of nuclear power, which is why the need for cooperation remains large. But talks on a consultative body surpassing the TRM among the three countries still remains to be seen.

Why Do We Need a NEA Consultative Body?

President Park Geun-hye first underscored the need for and proposed on the formation of a NEA nuclear safety consultative body. But China and Japan have not shown favorable reaction. Thus, analyses of why China and Japan, despite the apparent need for close consultations, remain lukewarm are necessary. Unlike Korea, the proposer, China and Japan lacks the common understanding on why there must be a nuclear safety consultative body. The most pressing matter is drawing out, from the two countries, the common understanding on the practical goals that such body can deliver.

NEA will soon be the most concentrated area in the world in terms of nuclear facilities. Therefore, it is required to build up and maintain world's most leading nuclear safety measures. The United States, which accounts for a quarter of the world's 400 active nuclear plants, at the moment leads in global nuclear safety initiatives. But if China comes in possession of over 200 nuclear plants, it will naturally take on the leading role in nuclear safety. This serves as a good reason for China to step forward in forming a NEA nuclear consultative body. Japan has already received much flak for the Fukushima disaster. Tokyo has put a great deal of effort into overcoming such hurdle, despite relatively negative public opinion. But this is no longer Japan's own problem; Japan must not only build upon its own nuclear safety measures but also help China to vastly improve nuclear safety to a highly reliable level. The fact that plants within the three NEA countries are relatively younger than that of the United States or Europe, and also that plants under construction are all of third-generation-and higher and with drastically improved safety, allows a higher level of safety endurance than that of European counterparts.

Since the Fukushima crisis, nearly all in the nuclear industry has come to agree that winning the public's trust relating to nuclear safety is the most important factor in sustaining the industry as a whole. To this end, upping the game in terms of nuclear safety is important. But also as important is allowing the people better access towards nuclear safety information and raising the level of its transparency. While China is soon to become the world's largest possessor of nuclear plants, it is also one of IAEA members that does not disclose its IAEA nuclear safety agreement report. Therefore, it is imperative that China raises its transparency regarding nuclear safety. On August 25, 2011, Wikileaks revealed documents revealing China's opaque nuclear bidding procedure and the government's excessive influence. As state policy, China is aggressively pursuing the development of nuclear plants. But its speed of nuclear expansion is accelerating to the point where the country is unable to build upon its experiences and ultimately raising the possibility of future disasters to an alarming level. In the end, China's nuclear expansion policy could become a safety liability for Korea and Japan, hence demanding contingency plans to mitigate such concerns.

Nuclear plant developments are again gaining ground, as well as parts replacement for active plants. But no single country in the world has the capacity to self-produce all parts that go into their nuclear power plants. All parts are made and traded within the global market, hence signifying the need for increased efforts in transnational cooperation in tackling fake parts and documentation. For example, in Korea, a consumer plate holder product sold in e-mart contained abnormal levels of radiation. The product was checked and was later discovered that it was made of China-made stainless steel. China of course did not purposely export such a product. Nonetheless, the incident was a cautionary tale on the need to improve cooperation in terms of customs, tracking and overall measure in dealing with nuclear-related issues. In the case of a large number of imported parts, it is virtually impossible for the importing nation to inspect every single vendor. This calls for a system to utilize and inspection results from the export nation. The US Nuclear Regulatory Commission has issued a report (SECY-11-0154) after having discovered several cases of fraudulent Chinese parts used in American nuclear plants. This is a case signaling the importance of trilateral cooperation of NEA nations relating to nuclear safety.

What should be done?

The following three plans may be proposed with a view to forming a trilateral NEA nuclear safety consultative body.

Proposal 1: Upgrading the current TRM into a WENRA-level body (centered around Korea, China and Japan)

Proposal 2: A two-track approach centered around the three countries' regulators and trade groups (centered around Korea, China and Japan)

Proposal 3: An expanded trilateral body with the willing participation of other Asian members as observing states (variation on the TRM+ model)

To this end, nuclear safety regulators must bolster three-way ties in order to overcome and outpace the TRM Work Frame-model and establish a consultative body with more binding decision power similar to that of WENRA:

a) Setting common safety goals: Developing common safety standards, harmonization process
b) Drawing up and action plan, working group formation
c) Enacting of a common nuclear safety decree

Also, unlike its European counterparts, the three NEA nations, besides Korea, do not appear to agree strongly on the need for a nuclear safety consultative body. The South Korean Foreign Ministry should focus on forming a common understanding on such need with Beijing and Tokyo with regard to:

a) The need in reaching a common understanding of the "why" element
b) Inducing the establishment of diverse consultative groups not just among regulators but within the industry and academia
c) Announcing a trilateral joint statement relating to nuclear safety.

CHAPTER 8

HOW CAN WE SOLVE THE NORTH KOREAN NUCLEAR ISSUE?

Wooksik Cheong

Introduction

Nuclear weapons might be viewed as similar to the One Ring in the movie "The Lord of the Rings." The ring gives its owner deadly power to dominate the world, but unless this power is relinquished, the inevitable outcome is death for all living things. The ring evokes both attraction and fear at the same time for all who know of its existence. This concept is best represented by the split personality of the character Gollum, also known as Smeagol. When he appears as Gollum, he is enslaved and overwhelmed by his desire to possess this powerful ring, but when under the identity of Smeagol, he is tormented by these same obsessions.

Clear parallels may be drawn between this story and nuclear weapons. The weapons are perceived in a variety of ways, but these perceptions can vary even within a single person's mind. The history of the United States proves this. Although the famous scientist Albert Einstein once sent US President Franklin Roosevelt a letter to urge the American government to start its nuclear weapons program as soon as possible, specifically before Nazi Germany, the physicist later changed his mind and defined himself as an 'anti-nuclear fighter' after witnessing the atomic bombings in Hiroshima and Nagasaki. Similarly, J. Robert Oppenheimer, the 'American Prometheus,' led the Manhattan Project and presented the United States with 'God's fire.' As the US government developed a hydrogen bomb, which should have never been pursued, the 'father of the atomic bomb' opposed its creation and desired to become the 'father of nuclear disarmament.'

This duality is also found among former presidents of the United States, a nuclear-armed nation. John F. Kennedy sparked debates over the 'missile gap' between the United States and the Soviet Union during the 1960 presidential election, resulting in a significant increase in the US nuclear weapons stockpile. The very next year, however, during a speech at the UN General Assembly he announced that, "[t]he weapons of war must be abolished before they abolish us." Likewise, the Reagan administration first proposed the so-called "Star Wars" to prepare for a winnable nuclear war against the Soviet Union, but in the latter part of his tenure the president left the door wide open for the prospect of nuclear disarmament. Of course the opposite exists as well. Barack Obama won the Nobel peace prize for promising a "world without nuclear weapons" before taking any actual steps. He is now trying to modernize the US nuclear arsenal on a huge scale.

It seems from these examples that thoughts on nuclear weapons can shift even in the mind of a single individual. Is Kim Jong-un an exception? Is it true, as many argue, that Kim will never abandon his desire for nuclear capabilities? Probably, even Kim himself doesn't know know the answers to these questions. This chemistry, produced through a combination of human cognition and the fruit of nuclear physics, is unknowable and therefore, unpredictable.

Needless to say, the primary reason for the North Korea's obsession with nuclear weapons is that it believes it has more to gain than to lose. This means that if the contrary becomes true, if the benefit of giving up these weapons greatly outweighs the cost of possessing them, there is a distinct possibility that Pyongyang might change its strategic calculus. Hence the importance in inducing Kim Jong-un to make such a change through a type of 'chemical reaction' in his conceptual state.

Some say that North Korea would not relinquish its nuclear weapons program in order to ensure its own survival. This thinking is utterly absurd. The logic is that the North could not survive without nuclear weapons, which leads to the conclusion that it should not give them up. The critical matter in this case is to create the conditions and an environment in which North Korea can survive without relying on nuclear weapons; not to assume that nothing can change, thereby ensuring a self-fulfilling prophecy.

The previous approaches of the South Korean and US governments toward the North Korean nuclear issue, particularly after 2009, have been to press the North by maximizing its pain, thereby forcing it to reverse its acquisition of nuclear weapons. These measures have completely failed. Sanctions, diplomatic isolation, and demonstrations of military strength were not sufficient to convince Pyongyang to change its direction. North Korea has only clung more tightly to the idea of "nuclear deterrence." Since the breakdown of the Six-Party Talks in December 2008, the reality is that Pyongyang has enhanced its nuclear and missile capabilities. This outcome serves to illustrate not only the failure of South Korean-US policies toward North Korea but also the need for a new approach.

The core of this new approach is to demonstrate to North Korea that the benefits of discarding its nuclear weapons program are much greater than the costs. In order to achieve this, Seoul and Washington must take an active role in peacefully converting the current armistice regime into a peace regime rather than insisting on the status quo. This sea change requires a perspective of convergence that includes the goal of solving the North Korean nuclear issue within the paradigm of a peaceful regime. This must be a turning point through which true trust-building is realized and the interests of the participating countries are institutionalized.

I began this article by declaring that the South Korean and US governments are too complacent. It would not be too much to say that both governments have all but lost their diplomatic will to resolve the North Korean nuclear issue. The four factors below account for the cause and background behind this complacent attitude.

The first factor is the 'self-fulfilling interpretation' of the last twenty years of history with the North Korean nuclear issue. Today's prevailing belief is that the ultimate purpose of North Korea is to possess nuclear weapons. This historical perception leads to the argument that North Korea will never abandon its nuclear capabilities. However, looking back on the last two decades objectively, the problem is not that simple.

The second factor is the 'wishful thinking' that North Korea will one day collapse on its own. This idea, widespread in ruling circles in the United States, is that the fundamental solution for the North Korean nuclear issue is a sudden change or collapse of the North Korean regime. However, it is important for South Korea and the United States to realize that if they keep to their view that North Korea may collapse, it will further provoke Pyongyang's desire to hold onto nuclear capabilities and the nuclear problem will remain unresolved. One should not dismiss the fact that a contingency plan of attempting unification by absorption, led by the South Korea-US alliance, involves the high risk of a 'colossal mushroom cloud.'

The third factor is the 'subjective conviction' that Pyongyang's "*Byungjin*" (parallel development) policy of 'economic development and nuclear weapons development' will never succeed. This judgment, however, cannot be made so easily. Over the 20 months following the introduction of the *Byungjin* line, North Korean nuclear capability has been considerably enhanced and economic and food conditions in the North have somewhat improved. Bearing in mind that these improvements took place during the incremental sanctions imposed by Seoul and Washington, one should look closely at such improvements in the North.

The fourth factor is the priority accorded to the 'militarism' that tries to deter the nuclear capabilities of North Korea with armed forces. The ROK (Republic of Korea)-US-Japan trilateral cooperation regime, with their linkages such as the ROK-US alliance's 'tailored containment' and missile defense (MD) system, initially aims at the 'containment of the North Korean nuclear threat.' This reliance on military containment means the allies will live with the instability and the danger caused by the nuclear issue until the putative time when the regime in Pyongyang falls. Moreover, the likely arms race on the Korean peninsula precipitated by the arms race between the North Korean nuclear capabilities and the ROK-US alliance's missile defenses, has a high risk of spreading across the whole region. This result follows because in these circumstances it has become difficult to maintain the basis of strategic stability, restrain arms races, and manage crises.

It is unnecessary to take all the aforementioned factors into consideration in this article. There are many well-known articles covering the perception of the nuclear history of North Korea and the views arguing in favor of North Korea's collapse. On the other hand, it is imperative to predict and assess Pyongyang's *Byungjin* parallel-policy that it can survive economically and retain its nuclear weapons; and to address the problems created by reliance on military containment by South Korea and the United States. Captivated with the 'subjective conviction' that the North's parallel-policy will fail and the 'military conviction' that North Korean nuclear capabilities can be contained by armed forces, the odds are favorable that policies toward North Korea will fail and these two governments will face a worsening North Korean situation. Therefore, this article begins with an exploration of the Byungjin parallel-policy and the military containment against North Korean nuclear capabilities.

In the rest of this essay, I will suggest a method to resolve the North Korean nuclear issue. The main point of this article is that South Korea and the United States need to shift the paradigm of their policies toward North Korea in order to manage the crisis, frequently repeated on the peninsula, and to prevent the exacerbation of the situation. The core of the paradigm shift is a conversion from the policies that increase the 'size of the North's pain' into policies that increase the 'size of the North's interests,' which will induce North Korea to make a strategic decision. This article will additionally remark that the security, diplomatic, and economic interests of North Korea coincide with the interests of not only South Korea, but also the whole Northeast Asian region.

What is the *Byungjin* policy?

As mentioned above, the belief of the South Korean and US governments is that North Korea's 'parallel economic and nuclear arms development can never succeed.' President Park Geun-hye has criticized the *Byungjin* policy several times. For instance, during her visit to Germany in March 2014, the president told German broadcaster ARD that *Byungjin* is an 'impossible policy' that will never succeed. president Barack Obama, in a press conference after the US-China summit in 2014 November, said that both leaders had agreed that "North Korea will not succeed in pursuing nuclear weapons and economic development, that it can't have both."

However, Pyongyang had a different idea. In response to Park's comments, North Korea accused Park of making provocative remarks over the *Byungjin* policy and claimed that Park's comments crudely violated a recent inter-Korean deal on halting smear campaign against each other. In response to Obama's denunciation of *Byungjin*, the North also said, "[T] he United States will witness the shining victory of the DPRK's line of simultaneously developing the two fronts before the expiry of the tenure of office of the present administration."

Before assessing the success and failure of the *Byungjin* policy, it is imperative to look at the background and context to this North Korean policy line. With regards to this, I have argued that the Kim Jong-un regime will take a line of 'simultaneously pursuing nuclear armament and economic development' since 2012. The following is an extract from my article in September 2012.

"Ever since Kim Jong-un assumed power, two notable moves have been made in Pyongyang. One was that North Korea's new constitution, revised in 2012, proclaimed its position as a nuclear-armed state, which had been officially recognized as the greatest feat of the former National Defense Commission chairman Kim Jong-il. Another was that North Korea switched its top priority from *Songun*, 'Military First' policy to *Songyoung*, 'Economy First' policy. It is noticeable that these two policies lie in the same context. I can explain that, the *Songun* policy was finalized by the possession of 'nuclear deterrence,' whereas now the nuclear-armed state can focus on economic development. ... We can call this national strategy of the Kim Jong-un era 'a parallel line of nuclear weapons-economic development.'"[1]

In fact, North Korea adopted the "*Byungjin* line of parallel economic and nuclear arms development" in March 2014. What I predicted has turned out to be true, although the order and the expression of words were slightly different. This is not to toot my own horn but to explain that this result was predictable. It was a foreseeable outcome, given the precedents of the other countries that had trouble with their nuclear arms and economic matters and the conditions the North is currently enduring. Although I am not arguing that *Byungjin* policy line is righteous, this shows that Kim Jong-un regime moved in a reasonable way, following the principle of the 'solvency of security.'

A former member of the European Parliament and a specialist on North Korean affairs, Glyn Ford, who has also visited North Korea more than 30 times since 1997, has a similar view. When asked 'Could the *Byungjin* parallel policy of economic and nuclear weapons development possibly work?' he replied that, "(s)ince the North now has nuclear weapons and missile deterrence, wouldn't it be an attempt (by the country) to concentrate its assets on economic development?" Ford also told the interviewer Myung Bok Bae, a correspondent of *Joongang Daily*, that "the simultaneous pursuit of nuclear armament and economic development was a reasonable choice from Pyongyang's perspective."[2]

The core of *Byungjin* parallel-policy is the 'solvency of security.' It is also found in one of North Korea's communiqué. North Korea announced that on March 31, 2013, the March Plenum of the Korean Workers' Party (KWP) Central Committee, the highest decision-making politburo in North Korea, had adopted a "new strategic line on carrying out economic and nuclear construction simultaneously as required given the world order and to meet the lawful prerequisite for revolutionary development." It stressed the strategic line of parallel policy as the, "most revolutionary and people oriented policy for the construction of a powerful socialist nation

---

[1] Wooksik Cheong, September 11, 2012, http://blog.ohmynews.com/wooksik/480284

[2] *Joongang Daily*, March 13, 2014

by consolidating defense capacity through the development of defensive nuclear weapons and economic construction." The proposition was ratified the next day.

Worthy of further note is that North Korea also announced that it would curb its military spending. "The supremacy of the policy is demonstrated by expanding capability in war deterrence and national defense without increasing the defense budget and enabled concentration on economic development and improvement of the lives of the people."

The *Byungjin* policy line reminds us of the 'parallel policy of developing national defenseand economy,' adopted at the plenary meeting of the KWP Central Committee in December 1962. By then, North Korea was confident with its fast-growing and buoyant economy, quickly recovering from the Korean War. At the same time, however, the North was also confronted with a series of changes in the world order such as the Sino-Soviet split, the Cuban missile crisis, the escalation of the Vietnam War, and the potential construction of a ROK-US-Japan trilateral regime. In response to these challenges, Pyongyang adopted the Four-Point Military Guidelines and significantly increased its military expenditure. As a result, the argument for the military adventurism gained more power in Pyongyang, whereas its economic growth slowed down.

Today's *Byungjin* policy line is different from fifty years ago. Priority in the previous parallel line was given to national defense, whilst the present line ranks the economic development as its top priority due to its confidence in its "nuclear deterrence." Furthermore, although the former focused more on the nation's heavy industry, which can be transferred to the defense sector, the latter set its main goal as "innovations in the domains of agriculture and light industry… so as to ensure that the people lead an affluent and happy life."

Eisenhower, Park Chung-hee, Deng Xiaoping, and Kim Jong-un

It is not exceptional that the Kim Jong-un regime adopted the *Byungjin* as its major policy line, which tries to focus on the economic development based on the nation's nuclear power. After WWII, for example, at which time military spending had skyrocketed, Harry S. Truman, who became the first president of a nuclear power, tried to cut US military spending by enhancing its nuclear capability. Nikita Khrushchev, First Secretary of the Communist Party of the Soviet Union, also tried to control military spending by building nuclear weapons at the cost of conventional arms.

In the same way, leaders, such as Dwight D. Eisenhower, Deng Xaoping and Park Chung-hee seriously considered the deep relationship between nuclear armament and economic development. His 'New Look' was summarized by President Eisenhower as motivated by "an unbearable security burden leading to economic disaster." In order to contain defense costs for conventional weapons, the administration shifted from primary reliance on conventional military capability to "air-atomic" capability, emphasizing the role of Strategic Air Command. The Eisenhower administration also adopted the massive retaliation strategy so as to block Communist expansion in Europe and Asia while decreasing the size of conventional capabilities. This shows that the 'New Look' is similar to *Byungjin*, and the massive retaliation strategy to the threat of creating a 'nuclear sea of fire.'

Another similar example is found among the policies of the Park Chung-hee administration, although arguably not to the same degree as the aforementioned comparison. The Park administration faced the difficulty of developing its economy and defense capability in the 1970s as North Korea has done since 1990. Due to its dependence on its patron ally, the United States, the Park administration could not articulate its desire to build nuclear weapons and missiles and instead, tried to build them in secret. Presumably, Park thought that South Korea could improve its economy and defense, by obtaining nuclear capabilities. However Park's dream did not come true due to US intervention.

The most interesting comparison to make with the North Korean *Byungjin* policy is the 'Two Bombs and One Satellite (兩弾一星)' policy line of Deng Xiaoping. He emphasized the importance of science and technology, thanked China's nuclear physicists for building the two bombs and one satellite, and finally said, "[i]f it were not for the atomic bomb, the hydrogen bomb and the satellites we have launched since the 1960s, China would not have its present international standing as a great, influential country." Deng also praised the 'Two Bombs and One Satellite' during the Chinese economic reform, relied on them as assets for military defense, and cut conventional forces at the same time. His successor, Jiang Zemin, also applauded the two bombs and one satellite, asserting that they symbolized the pride and glory of Chinese people and the development of new China. If the speaker's name was hidden, one would hardly know whether the comment came from the leader of China or North Korea.

Can *Byungjin* work?

It is too early to say whether or not the *Byungjin* policy has worked. The appraisal and prospect of the policy line would differ depending on its criterion, either nuclear capability or economy. Judging by the results over the last 20 months, it is hard to say it has failed. Although official data is lacking as to the recent condition of food distribution in North Korea, many visitors to the country say unanimously that it has improved. In addition, figures provided by a few international organizations indicate that, with the improvement in the condition of food distribution of North Korea, the death toll from starvation and the infant mortality rate of the country has decreased considerably.

The argument that the *Byungjin* policy cannot work is based on the judgment that "it is impossible for Pyongyang to normalize its international relations and be provided with humanitarian aid without denuclearization."[3] Furthermore, the North's consistent desire for nuclear capabilities will result in more sanctions imposed by the international society and strengthened military deterrence by the ROK- United States-Japan trilateral alliance. This means that it will be hard for North Korea to achieve its goal of "creating a peaceful environment and easing tensions with the international community for the sake of economic construction."

[3] Jihwan Hwang, "North Korea's Foreign Policy Strategy in Kim Jong-un Era: The Parrllel Line Continuation andChange," *Korean and World Politics* 84(2014): 192, 6

What then is the most plausible scenario? It is most likely that the DPRK will manage to combine 'gradual economic growth' with 'rapid enhancement of nuclear capabilities.' If we suppose that the average annual economic growth is 3 percent and the stockpile of nuclear weapons increases tenfold over the next 10 years in North Korea would the *Byungjin strategy* have succeeded?

In terms of nuclear capability, it would be a 'huge success' whereas economically, the results would be 'average.' But when combined, it would be judged 'comparatively successful.' With the reactors and uranium enrichment facilities in Yongbyon in full operation, North Korea can build 5 to 10 nuclear weapons every year. It will amount to roughly 100 nuclear weapons by the mid-2020s. Additionally, it is highly possible that the North will try to secure various methods of delivery, such as short-, mid- and long-range ballistic missiles, and even advanced ground-to-ground missiles, advanced rocket launchers and submarine-launched ballistic missiles. Eventually, with huge effort, they are likely to be able to gain all of these capabilities.

It is quite predictable that North Korea will reach 3 percent average annual economic growth. The marketization of North Korea, although it had fluctuated in the past, has now settled and has even been spreading since the start of Kim Jong-un's reign. 'Economic Management System in Our Style,' adopted on June 28th in 2012, has passed through its test stage and areas in which this system is applied are expending nationwide. The main aim of this policy is to partially guarantee and progressively increase autonomy and incentives of running farms and factories. Sino-North Korean economic ties are still steadily growing despite a few complications, and Russia-North Korea economic cooperation is gaining traction. From the perspective of *Byungjin* policy, strengthening North Korea's nuclear capabilities can lead to utilizing its internal resources to improve its economy. This means that North Korea can supply themselves with a certain amount of resources for economic development by reducing its security cost.

Taking all the aforementioned points into consideration, it is anticipated that gradual economic growth is feasible for North Korea, although not rapidly, given the antagonistic environment surrounding the country. Admittedly, this anticipation is not definitive. That is because, unlike its nuclear issue, the North Korean economy has variable elements. Take a nuclear test in North Korea for example. It will bring about, as anyone can imagine, increased sanctions and attempts of military containment, considering the international community's condemnation of Pyongyang. These sanctions will affect the North's economy negatively. However, it is implausible that the negative impact will last long afterwards. Pyongyang's ties with Beijing and Moscow may be confronted with a temporary downturn or recession, but even the declining tendency will turn bullish soon enough. Moreover, if North Korea succeeds in miniaturizing its nuclear weapons through additional tests,[4] it will finally be able to focus more on the economic development, without the need for any more tests.

In conclusion, it is most plausible that the North Korean *Byungjin* policy will combine gradual economic growth with rapid enhancement of nuclear capabilities. If this argument is correct, however, the circumstances surrounding the North's nuclear issue will become very complicated. The nuclear threat from North Korea will become remarkably serious, whereas the effect of economic sanctions, that have been believed to be the most effective means to moderate Pyongyang's stance, will diminish.

Although we could speculate about other possible futures, it is less likely that North Korea will fail both in its economic growth and in its enhancement of its nuclear capabilities. Despite the uncertainty of its economy, it is a well-known fact that the North has already reached the level of being able to increase its stockpile in nuclear weapons and enhance them even further. The worst scenario is that Pyongyang massively reinforces its nuclear weapons whilst its economy still treads water. In this instance, which combines an enhanced nuclear capability with a suffering economy, the North Korean regime may turn itself into a truly 'savage beast.'

[4] Since the 21st century, North Korea is the only country to have conducted nuclear test among all nine nuclear-armed states including the North. This fact is often said to blame North Korea. However, the reason why the other nuclear-armed states have not conducted nuclear tests since the 21st century is that they have already succeeded in miniaturizing their nuclear weapons.

Byungjin's policy implications for South Korea

North Korea's "*Byungjin* policy of parallel economic and nuclear weapons development" challenges the South Korean and the US governments, but it can also be an opportunity at the same time. The economic development plan which concentrates on agriculture and light industry is to be welcomed, since it is essential for improving the quality of life North Korean people. It also would be good news if North Korea's conventional military forces were contained or reduced by this policy. Nevertheless, all this is worrying because those seemingly positive moves are based on its nuclear capabilities.

Seoul and Washington have tried to hinder the *Byungjin* policy in a very limited way. The incremental sanctions they have imposed against Pyongyang can disturb its 'economic development' in a minor way. Sanctions have been unable to stop the North's nuclear weapons development in the past and will not do so in the future. In particular, North Korea's recent moves are in independently taking steps to develop its economy, trying to bypass the 'southern route' toward ROK-US-Japan, heading instead toward China and Russia through the 'northern route.'

Considering the Park administration's stance that '*Byungjin* policy shall not work,' no one can expect the administration to lift the May 24 measures, which is one of the biggest obstacles in improving the South-North relationship, although the measure is hurting not only Pyongyang but also Seoul. Indeed, it has been already proven that economically, South Korea has been far more damaged than North Korea by the measures.

Therefore, the alternatives are clear here; a new *Byungjin* (parallel) policy of 'negotiations for denuclearization and economic cooperation' should be adopted in the ROK.

Can the North Korean nuclear threat be contained?

In contrast to its active diplomacy concerning Iranian nuclear proliferation, the posture of the Obama administration dealing with the North Korean nuclear issue has been passive. The empty promises of, "denuclearization of Korean Peninsula through direct US-North Korean dialogue and Six-Party Talks" from his presidential campaign and the former years in the office, have disappeared long ago. The administration's policy toward North Korea is trapped in the ambiguous expression, 'strategic patience,' and no decent negotiations have taken place so far.

There are two reasons for the contrasting responses of Obama administration to Pyongyang and Tehran. First, North Korea is already a *de facto* nuclear state that has conducted three nuclear tests.

Second, the United States sees a more direct threat of nuclear proliferation arising from Iranian acquisition of nuclear weapons than from North Korea. Generally, the United States discounts the possibility that the North's possession of nuclear weapons will result in nuclear armaments in South Korea and Japan.[5] The US government considers that even if public support for nuclear weapons increases in Seoul and Tokyo, it can offset this trend by boosting its alliances in Northeast Asia by increasing the scale of the US forces deployment in the region, providing them with the nuclear umbrella, and reinforcing the US-led missile defense.

This attitude is complacent, arbitrary, and even dangerous. Washington should realize that since North Korea has weaponized its nuclear program, its nuclear threat has become more palpable. This increasing threat should motivate the key players more than ever to return to the negotiating table.

Maintaining this perfunctory stance toward the North Korean nuclear issue will bring about extremely dangerous and on-going instability on the Korean peninsula and in the region, even if either South Korea or Japan does not actually pursue nuclear capabilities.

Strategic stability is unravelling

Strategic instability in Northeast Asia, particularly in regards to North Korean nuclear issues, is a composite of three factors. These are: (1) increasing instability in the armistice regime of the Korean Peninsula (2) escalation of the arms race on the peninsula (3) increasing contention between

[5] *The New York Times*, November 11, 2014.

the four big powers in Northeast Asia. They are deeply related to each other.

The first factor, the instability in the armistice regime of the Korean Peninsula is viewed differently by the parties to the conflict. The US and ROK allies view it as a comfortable rocking chair that provides them with a measure of stability and security. In contrast, North Korea finds the armistice regime to be discomforting to the point that they prefer to reject it altogether than reply upon it. Pyongyang therefore keeps trying to nullify the armistice agreement, offering negotiations or sometimes, giving threats. It seems that the North will attempt to supplant the Armistice in the future by enhancing its "nuclear deterrence." When it does so by increasing its nuclear forces and missiles, the armistice regime will become a source of insecurity and threat to the US-ROK alliance, requiring crisis management as an almost permanent state of affairs rather than a periodic management problem.

The second factor leading to instability is the arms race on the Korean Peninsula, particularly with strategic arms. North Korea is pushing forward to increase the productivity of its nuclear materials, to miniaturize its nuclear warheads, and to secure missile technology. Furthermore, the North also is trying to secure various delivery vehicles for nuclear weapons, developing short-, mid- and long-range ballistic missiles, and even potentially, advanced multiple rocket launcher and submarine-launched ballistic missiles (SLBM). In turn, the South Korea-US alliance adopted 'tailored containment' whereby the United States proclaims that it extends deterrence such as nuclear umbrella, conventional forces, and expansion of missile defense while South Korea is building the Korea Air and Missile Defense system as a defensive measure, and to support its 'kill chain,' a purported preemptive strike capability against a North Korean nuclear attack. All this armament feeds into rather than restraining acquisition of capacities that undermine strategic stability in Korea.

Finally, strategic instability in the region can be explained in three matrices. These are: a) the regional conflict between China and Japan; b) the global conflict between China and the United States; and c) the conflict between the Sino-Russian cooperative regime (a type of "Continental Power") and the US-Japan alliance (primarily combined "Maritime Power.") Each of these conflict relationships has deteriorated because of the North Korean nuclear issue and the riposte of the ROK-US-Japan alliance, attempting to establish missile defenses.

The US-led missile defense system has enabled China and Russia to shift from a formerly bellicose mood to a friendly and cooperative one, and even further, to develop a quasi-military alliance, more or less concurrently with the reinvigoration of the US-Japan alliance and further influenced by their perception from the late 1990s that missile defense was aimed at them, not so much North Korea.

The current situation bears comparison with that which pertained during the Cold War. At that time, the region remained strategically stable in spite of US-Soviet rivalry, ideological struggle, competitive expansion of spheres of influence, and arms races. It was this stability that gave rise to the Cold War's nickname, the 'Long Peace.' Based on the Anti-Ballistic Missile (ABM) Treaty signed in 1972 that banned missile defense systems, it was possible to manage crises and limit arms races—two of the foundations of strategic stability as well as of possibility of bilateral disarmament agreements.

However, the George W. Bush administration abrogated the ABM Treaty after the September 11, 2001 terror attack in New York. Now the treaty has been replaced with the 'shield-making' by the United States, which possesses the world's strongest military capability, and with the 'spear-making' by China and Russia, both of which are trying their best to neutralize the shield. The competition of world powers is about to reach its peak in Northeast Asia. Not only the four countries in the region but also the two Koreas are joining in the clash of ROK-US-Japan versus DPRK-China-Russia. Although once the North Korean nuclear issue united South Korea, the United States, Japan, China and Russia, now the United States is reshuffling the power structure by deploying missile defenses in the region.

Thus, the ABM treaty, which kept the Cold War period in more or less unstable but permanent peace, does not exist anymore. The North Korean nuclear force and missile defenses deployments are racing, influencing the whole region with a potential rise of strategic competition once again between the great powers. Thus, the current international order in Northeast Asia may be less stable and more dangerous than even during the Cold War in some respects. Unless the hostility expressed most directly by North Korean nuclear weapons on the one hand and US-led missile defenses on the other is broken down, regional strategic stability and peace will become as an empty slogan.

Separate to the North Korea and regional nuclear issue, it is critical that a new, twenty first century ABM treaty be signed by the United States, Russia and China. Through this treaty, the world powers could gain momentum for nuclear disarmament, as well as could restore strategic stability by facilitating effective crisis management and limiting arms racing.

The key to resolving the North Korean nuclear issue[6]

Although the North Korean nuclear issue continues unabated and the North's desire to gain further capabilities has no apparent limit, many people have expressed fatigue with the issue. Neither the 'Sunshine Policy,' an engagement policy towards North Korea, nor economic sanctions, diplomatic isolation and military containment have succeeded in halting this dynamic. This perception became stronger after the Kim Jong-un regime came to power. Since then, North Korea proclaimed itself as a nuclear-armed state in the revised constitution, conducted the third nuclear test, legislated the law on consolidating the position of nuclear weapons state, and adopted the policy of 'parallel economic and nuclear weapons development,' all in a consecutive manner. Meanwhile, the specter of regime change in Pyongyang or its outright system collapse drives many to conclude that unification by absorption is the ultimate solution for the North

[6] This section is an edited extract from my report "*the Future Development of the Six-Party Talks in order to denuclearization of Korean Peninsula and establishment of Peace Regime*" (in Korean), December, 2013 to Foreign Affairs and Unification Committee, National Assembly of South Korea.

Korean nuclear issue.

However, one should not dismiss a difference between the fruitful outcomes from previous engagement policies and the unproductive results from hard line policies. Moreover, as much as Pyongyang lacked strategic determination to abandon its nuclear program, Seoul and Washington were equally obdurate, unable to consider shifting their paradigm to achieve a fundamental resolution. For these reasons, now is the time to undertake such a paradigm shift in policies toward North Korea, starting by examining Pyongyang's motive to become a nuclear-armed state in the first place.

North Korea has insisted that its nuclear weapons are "just means for defense as it was compelled to have access to them to cope with the ever-escalating hostile policy of the United States and its nuclear threat," as stated in its 'Law on Consolidating Position of Nuclear Weapons State Adopted,' adopted on April 1, 2013. The goal of the law was stated to be to realize a full-fledged nuclear weapons state capable of beating back any aggressor troops at one strike, firmly defending the socialist system and providing a sure guarantee for the happy life of the people. Even before this law was adopted, Pyongyang announced already on March 31, 2013 that it would try to improve its economy and the people's lives through the Byungjin policy of 'parallel economic and nuclear weapons development,' while enhancing its nuclear "deterrent" at the cost of its conventional military forces.

At a Senate Armed Services Committee on February 11, 2013, James Clapper, Director of US National Intelligence, characterized North Korea's nuclear forces very differently. Said Clapper: "[b]ecause of deficiencies in their conventional military forces, North Korean leaders are focused on deterrence and defense," and "[w]e have long assessed that, in Pyongyang's views, its nuclear capabilities are intended for deterrence, international prestige, and coercive diplomacy."

It is noteworthy that these two hostile countries have parallel arguments and analysis regarding why North Korea acquired nuclear weapons. Both North Korea and the United States highlighted 'deterrence and defense' rather than invasion or preemptive strikes. The United States even suggested that the North's desire for nuclear weapons is motivated by "deficiencies in their conventional military forces."

In my view, the North's desire for nuclear weapons is motivated by four factors. These are: 1) its 'security motive' to cover its deficiencies in conventional military forces whilst enhancing its deterrence; 2) its 'political motive' to protect the North Korean regime and ensure its sovereignty;[7] 3) its 'diplomatic motive' to secure a means to press its demand in a coercive diplomacy; and 4) its 'economic motive' to develop economy and improve its people's lives by controlling its conventional military expenditure.

The important thing in inducing North Korea to permanently abandon its desire for nuclear capabilities is whether South Korea and the United States and other involved countries can provide a 'mutually satisfactory means' corresponding to each and all of the multiple motives mentioned above. The 'mutually satisfactory means' in diplomacy is not a zero sum game but a process in which participants increase mutual benefits through confirming, adjusting and rejecting each other's interests and demands. The interests and demands include agreed terms, matters to be examined, and unacceptable requests. Let me categorize those in three sectors below, with respects to solutions for North Korean nuclear issue.

Firstly, the security issue is most important but also the most sensitive. The conversion from the armistice regime into a peace regime was formerly agreed between the principal parties to the Korean conflict, and is expected to contribute to resolving security issues of not only North Korea but also South Korea, the United States, and China. It is a matter of confirming and practicing what is already agreed as necessary. However, conflicting demands may arise in the actual process of conversion from the armistice into a peace regime. Matters such as cancelling or downsizing the US-South Korean joint military drills, North Korean forward deployed forces and exercises along the DMZ, withdrawing the US nuclear

[7] North Korea has been reluctant to be subordinated by China, and this could have caused a part of desire to obtain nuclearcapabilities. As France and China developed their nuclear weapons to change their reliance on, respectively, the United States and Soviet Union, nuclear weapons signify weapons of self-reliance for North Korea.

umbrella from the Korean Peninsula, reciprocal North Korean and US-ROK disarmament, and resolution of Northern Limit Line issue can all be calibrated during this process. On the other hand, the North's demand for withdrawal of United States Forces in Korea and dissolution of the South Korea-US alliance would not be acceptable and is a non-starter for such a collaborative conflict resolution process.

Second, the political and diplomatic issues must be addressed. Existing agreements already exist to improve ROK-DPRK relations, to normalize DPRK-US relations and DPRK-Japan relations. The September 19, 2005 Joint Statement presents the "spirit of mutual respect and equality." In compliance with the latter statement, three main points should be considered for North Korea; the right to peaceful uses of nuclear energy, the right to satellite launch, and the human rights issue. It is unacceptable that Pyongyang rejected questions and demands from the international community about its human rights record, claiming the country's sovereignty disallows interference in its domestic affairs. Nevertheless, the United Nation's resolutions calling for the North Korean leader to be referred to the International Criminal Court over alleged crimes against humanity is ineffective but intervenes in its sovereignty causing setbacks in strategic dialogue. If the latter is initiated in good faith, then the North Korean human rights issues can be resolved via dialogue and cooperation with the North. I will come back to the issues regarding peaceful uses of nuclear energy and satellites by North Korea.

Lastly, the economic issues have also been attended to in the past, including substantial food aid and energy assistance to North Korea. Each country's unilateral sanctions against the North should be solved in the context of improving bilateral inter-state relations, and sanctions by the United Nations Security Council may be eased, suspended, and lifted, depending on the North's behavior, especially reciprocal steps to implement its denuclearization promises and obligations.

In conclusion, South Korea and the United States hould be able to judge what the gains and losses are from North Korea's abandonment of nuclear weapons and demonstrate acumen on the negotiating table. To date, the putative gains from abandoning its nuclear weapons have been too uncertain and unlikely to be sustained to be meaningful to the North's leadership. At the same time, the losses from possessing them were not critical enough to induce them to abandon such weapons. Thus, a new approach is needed to shift the DPRK's decision-making calculus. In addition, the benefit has to be sustainable and irreversible once the DPRK implements its nuclear disarmament over time. To make progress on these key issues, it is essential to build trust and institutionalize the outcomes.

North Korea's return to the Nonproliferation Treaty and the signing of a peace treaty

So long as the North has nuclear weapons, it is unlikely that it can be pressured by sanctions into abandoning them, or that the United States will take initiatives to improve relations with the North by signing a peace treaty or lifting sanctions. Nor will Seoul move forward independently. The North's obsession with nuclear weapons and the United States and South Korea's negative views on the adoption of a peace system leave the Armistice in place as the basis for avoiding war.

To avoid a catastrophic outcome from the possible failure of the armistice regime, the South Korean and US governments need to shift their paradigm as to policles toward North Korea.The fundamental reorientation is to move toward 'peaceful efforts to change the status quo.'

In this context, I suggest the combination: 'North Korea's return to the NPT in return for which four-parties to the Korean conflict sign a peace treaty.' On one side, Seoul and Washington are highly suspicious about North Korea's will for denuclearization. On the other side, Pyongyang doubts that the South Korean and US governments would ever withdraw their hostile policies toward the North. This is why it is essential to find a way to change the vicious circle of mistrust into a virtuous circle of trust. Both governments need to find a way to visibly and simultaneously implement the outcome sought by the other side in order to build trust. In other words, they need an 'exchange of sincerity in the highest degree' between the South Korea-US alliance and North Korea. North Korea's return to the NPT would prove Pyongyang's will for denuclearization. Likewise, four-parties' signing of a peace treaty would confirm the alliance's will for peaceful co-existence. This exchange could be an 'inflection point' at which the relations of hostility and mistrust are converted into the relations of peace and trust between the ROK-US alliance and the DPRK.

At his entry into office, President Obama said that he is would consider economic aid, a peace treaty, and normalization of relations with the North as long as North Korea is prepared to discard its nuclear program. North Korea's return to the NPT and inclusion of an article about denuclearization in the peace treaty would be one necessary step forward to resolve the core conflict by the North. Pyongyang has consistently argued that the nuclear issue will be solved only if the United States' hostile policies toward the North and US treats to its sovereignty and survival are removed. The US cessation would include a peace treaty, normalization of the DPRK-US relations, and lifting of economic sanctions against North Korea. North Korea's return to the NPT and four-parties' signing of a peace treaty would meet both sides' demands.

Signing a peace treaty in exchange for the North's return to the NPT has a significant meaning to formally ensure interests, in other words, to institutionalize them. The North's return to the NPT could give momentum to the process of solving the North Korean nuclear issue in a formal manner. North Korea is the only country in history, to withdraw from the NPT and build nuclear weapons. Thus, if North Korea returns to the treaty and abolishes its nuclear weapons program, it will significantly contribute restoring the nuclear nonproliferation system. This will be beneficial not only for the United States but also for the whole international community that pursues enhancing the NPT in an official way.

This plan of exchange entails delicate sequencing. The apparent gridlock over which should come first, a peace regime or denuclearization, is formed in a conflict structure. I will come back to how this conflict structure could be solved and the sequencing achieved. In addition, it is contentious whether the UNSC should end its resolutions of pressing North Korea with sanctions. Since the resolutions by the UNSC kept demanding that North Korea return to the NPT, the North's return to the NPT could be the basis to begin negotiations as one of the conditions to lift the sanctions in return. The proposed resolutions would also include provision for peaceful uses of nuclear energy, and stringent verification of North Korean nuclear program, which can effectively handle 'hot potatoes' that have been troublesome in the negotiations with Pyongyang for the last twenty years.

This plan requires two fresh approaches in order to improve the feasibility and effectiveness in the actual process. The first approach is to blend the nuclear issue on the Korean Peninsula with the establishment of a peace regime. It has been controversial about 'which comes first' since the views on denuclearizing the Korean Peninsula and on establishing a peace regime have been separated in the past, for example, as on the September 19 Joint Statement from the Fourth Round of the Six-Party Talks in 2005. Therefore, I suggest convergence replace separation, including the denuclearization (or a Nuclear Weapons Free Zone) issue in the concept and the ultimate goal of establishing a peace regime.

Second is to develop the idea of denuclearization of the Korea Peninsula into the idea of creating a Nuclear Weapons Free Zone (NWFZ). Although the basic goals to solve the nuclear issue on the Korean Peninsula are embodied in the Joint Declaration of South and North Korea on the Denuclearization of the Korean Peninsula (1991) and in the Joint Statement of the Fourth Round of the Six-Party Talks (2005), neither the former nor the latter entails obligations be undertaken by nuclear-armed states, as would a NWFZ. This approach is also consistent with the Obama administration's advocacy of 'a world free of nuclear weapons' whilst the international civil society is calling for a NWFZ in Northeast Asia, not just in Korea.

Given the reality and the prevailing opinions, I argue that solving the nuclear issue on the Korean Peninsula include stated obligations for nuclear-armed states, while solving the North's nuclear issue and keeping the South's promise of denuclearization, and the United States' negative security assurance toward North Korea. Further concrete steps could include negative security assurances by other nuclear-armed states toward the Korean Peninsula,[8] a ban on nuclear weapons deployed on or passing through the peninsula, and withdrawal of the US nuclear umbrella, and the creation of a regional NWFZ. These approaches can fundamentally resolve the nuclear issues on the Korean Peninsula, revitalize the peace and security regime in the Northeast Asia, and finally advance the 'nuclear weapons-free world.'

The North's return to the NPT and the signing of a peace treaty

The core and details of this plan consists of three parts; 1) the North's return to the NPT, 2) Four-Parties' (ROK, DPRK, China, and the United States) signing of a peace treaty, 3) the UNSC's lifting of sanctions against North Korea. It is very important to simultaneously implement these detailed plans in a perspective of convergence.

North Korea needs to pledge to abolish its nuclear program and to return to the NPT and a safeguards agreement with the International Atomic Energy Agency (IAEA) on a 'transitional status.' The transitional status means that although at a time of the return to the NPT the North has not yet completed the abandonment of its nuclear weapons, it affirms its goal and status of a non-nuclear-armed state. This can show the North Korea's sincerity to discard all nuclear weapons program in the highest degree.

It is not obligatory for the North to thoroughly abandon its nuclear weapons and existing program in advance before returning to the NPT. Not only is there no such demand in the NPT, but also countries such as Ukraine, Kazakhstan and Belarus joined the NPT on a transitional status while only promising to abandon its nuclear weapons. They became nuclear-armed states as the Soviet Union collapsed in December 1991. It took roughly three years from joining the NPT to completing the abandonment in those countries.

In North Korea's case, it would be realistic to take the action step by

[8] In order to expand the NWFZ through Northeast Asia, the negative security assurance is also required for Japan.

step, on the premises of a comprehensive agreement. At the first stage, the goal could be a 'permanent freezing' of its nuclear weapons. The specific objects to be frozen are graphite moderated reactors (GMR) and nuclear reprocessing facilities that have been used to produce nuclear materials. These facilities must be dismantled, not just disabled. In order to decide whether to retain experimental light water reactors and uranium enrichment facilities, which can be used to produce nuclear materials, we need to find a 'mutually satisfactory means' with respect to both the North's peaceful uses of nuclear energy and alternative efforts for denuclearization. Until alternative options are available, these facilities need to be shut down under the observation of the IAEA. Moreover, with regards to the possible presence of secret uranium facilities in North Korea, it would be more realistic to take gradual progress to find a solution and build trust, instead of inspecting everything at once.

The next step is to block any potential improvements in Pyongyang's nuclear capabilities. The core of this stage is to shut down nuclear test sites and nuclear-research and manufacturing facilities for nuclear materials. It is also required to secure suspensions on test-launches of all types of ballistic missiles in North Korea.

The final step is to discard all nuclear materials and existing nuclear weapons in the North. The options can vary from discarding them in a yearly consecutive order to discarding them *en bloc* within a certain limit of time period. In the actual steps to discard them, the North's nuclear materials and weapons should be transported to Russia. This is because Russia has: 1) experience and know-how in discarding nuclear weapons and materials, 2) shared borders with North Korea which give it accessibility, and 3) friendly relations with involved countries as well as a neutral status in the Six-Party Talks. Russia is the least cost, fastest, and most irreversible pathway to dismantle North Korean nuclear materials and weapons.

In regards to the time limit to discard the North's nuclear weapons, we need to consider agreements, implementation, and trust-building thoroughly. We could expect the nuclear weapons to be discarded 'within five years' after the North's return to the NPT simultaneously with Four-

Parties' signing of a peace treaty. A five-year period is considered to give enough time to build concrete trust among involved countries through implementing all the agreed steps faithfully.

2) South Korea, North Korea, the United States and China need to sign a peace treaty to replace the existing armistice agreement. In regards to the North Korean nuclear issue, the peace treaty needs to clearly state what to, how to, and when to discard existing nuclear materials ad weapons in the North.[9] Signing a peace treaty is a crucial turning point, because the treaty is a legal basis to move from the current armistice regime to a peace regime. By signing the peace treaty, South Korea and the United States can truly show that they have no hostile intention toward North Korea, and also gain momentum to resolve the nuclear issue on the Korean Peninsula and military crisis. In the same context, it is crucial to banish away the idea that signing a peace treaty is capitulation to North Korea's threats or a free gift.

The peace treaty should consist of 'a basic treaty and an additional protocol,' which is the format used in many international treaties including the inter-Korean Basic Treaty (1991). The basic treaty should include articles that state mutual respect on sovereignty, an official end to Korean War, mutual non-aggression, the resolutions of nuclear issues on the Korean Peninsula, and measures to build military trust. The additional protocol should include a deal with more detailed and complex contents such as the Northern Limit Line issue,[10] the United Nations Command issue, the USFK issue, disarmament, and the establishment and operation of a management agency for the peace regime. In this way, the speed and feasibility of solving various issues could be accelerated. Furthermore, it also should be considered to include other five nuclear-armed states in signing

---

[9] Since this includes not only the basic contents of the peace treaty but also of the NWFZ, the title could be 'Treaty (Agreement) of denuclearization and a peace regime of the Korean Peninsula.'

[10] The Nothern Limit Line (NLL) issue, which will be the trickiest one in the discussion of a peace treaty, should be examined with the 'principle of reservation,' applied with the specificity of the South-North relations. Both the North and the South need to agree that, "(s)ince the NLL issue is an unusual problem that has happened in a process of reunification, the ultimate resolution is in unification. Thus, the NLL issue would be handled in a way to contribute to a common security and prosperity."

another additional protocol, and to adopt the UNSC's resolutions.

This proposal is not only to follow one of the intents of the 'declaration of an end to the Korean War' from the second inter-Korean Summit in 2007,[11] but also to overcome the limitations of the declaration in a future-oriented way. At the time of the summit, it was considered that ground-breaking measures in military assurance were needed to induce North Korea to abandon its nuclear weapons whilst an agreement on a peace treaty would take considerable time. That was how the idea of the 'declaration of an end to the Korean War' firstly came out, in order to solve the North's nuclear issues while creating only a preliminary design of a peace regime.

The 'declaration of an end to the Korean War,' however, carries a few limitations. First, the United States' government, one key player of the armistice agreement, considers a declaration of an end to the Korean War as an agreement to a peace treaty. Second, given the fact that the core of a peace treaty is a declaration of an end to the Korean War, it might create confusion in understanding of the declaration, perceiving it as a preliminary process. Lastly, the declaration is not clear about what will be offered to North Korea since the declaration itself is an ambiguous and abstract concept. The suggested proposal with 'a basic treaty and an additional protocol,' however, embodies the intent of a declaration of an end to the war, as well as takes complementary measures.

3) The UNSC needs to lift sanctions against North Korea and seek for a mutually satisfactory means to handle the rocket-launching issues of North Korea. As long as South Korea and the United States view the sanctions as a goal and the North as the core of their hostile policies, it is hard to expect to reopen dialogues or make any progress through possible talks. However, this stance also means that it is vital to resolve the conflicts surrounding sanctions, in order to gain momentum in trust-building and denuclearization. Additionally, the primary reason that the issues on the

---

[11] The agreement reached at inter-Korean summit says, "The South and the North both recognize the need to end the current armistice regime and build a permanent peace regime. The South and the North have also agreed to work together to advance the matter of having the leaders of the three or four parties directly concerned to convene on the Peninsula and declare an end to the war."

Korean Peninsula became troublesome after 2009 were rocket launches in North Korea and the UNSC's riposte. This is why a parallel solution for sanctions and rocket-launching issues is required.

The resolutions by the UNSC state that it "affirms that it is prepared to lift the measures." The aforementioned actions, expected to be taken by North Korea, would be compliant with the condition from the UNSC's resolutions, for example, the North's returning to the NPT, promising to discard its nuclear weapons, and stating objects, methods, periods of the abandonment in a peace treaty. In regards to the rocket-launching issues of North Korea, here are three suggested stages. The first stage is to suspend all types of launches in the North, including satellites using the ballistic missiles technology. This commitment also needs to be included in an agreement once the Six-Party Talks reopen or North Korea and the United States restart dialogues in the improved process from the failed February 29 Agreement. At the second stage, a third country could launch rockets for North Korea, from the period the North returns to the NPT and promises to denuclearize, to the period it completes discarding its nuclear weapons. This step was almost agreed in the negotiations between North Korea and the United States in 2000 and should be resurrected. The third stage is the North exercises its right to launch satellites, after it completes discarding its nuclear weapons, in compliance with transparency in the international community.

How should it begin?

If the aforementioned proposal is a 'turning point' toward resolving the issues on the Korean Peninsula,[12] it is crucial to find a 'starting point' for the journey. The current situation, however, is that South Korea and the United States are demanding the North's sincere steps for denuclearization, and in return, the North are calling for the reopening of dialogues without pre-conditions.

It seems feasible for both parties to compromise with an agreement

[12] A new agreement for the Six-Party Talks is in the appendix.

to the February 29 plus side agreements in the North Korea-US high-level talks or the Six-Party Talks. This agreement would mean that South Korea and the United States open the Six-Party Talks while North Korea takes measures in compliance with February 29 Agreement and further. There were four promises in the agreement, *viz*: the North's suspension of nuclear tests, long-range missile launches and uranium enrichments; and the IAEA inspectors' returns to Yongbyun. Further steps would include suspension of launching rockets, disabling the 5 MW graphite moderated reactor and nuclear reprocessing facilities, and a moratorium on operating experimental light water reactors.

In response, the proposed agreement of an expanded February 29 Agreement should include food aid and reopening of the DPRK-US high-level talks as promised by the United States in the February 29 Agreement. Most of all, what is required is the opening of peace talks by the four parties to the Korean conflict, in order to replace Armistice Agreement with a peace agreement. South Korea, the United States, or the UNSC could consider lifting some of its own sanctions against North Korea.

Conclusion

As the old proverb said, "nothing is complete unless you put it in final shape." Good policies and ideas will be of no use unless support exists along with the will to put them into action. Most of all, policy makers must lead. It is required for them to have a positive attitude, based on trust and strong ties with other parties, and work to bring about constructive change.

It is truly sad that, although South Korea and the United States need to solve issues through dialogues both have set pre-conditions to even entering upon a dialogue. Furthermore, a significant amount of time and energy have not been spent on dialogues but been wasted on isolating, sanctioning, and blocking North Korea.

In the conclusion, I want to emphasize that there is no substitute for contact between top leaders and officials. South Korea and Japan have held summit talks with North Korea in the past, but never the United

States. Thus, future diplomacy with North Korea should aim at achieving direct talks with the leader of North Korea, Kim Jong-un, and establishing direct personal bonds with him. Former President of the United States, Ronald Reagan, and Mikhail Gorbachev, General Secretary of the Communist Party of the Soviet Union, brought the non-violent end of Cold War, only three years after they had met for the first time. The following is the conversation between them taking a walk in the Kremlin.

"Mr. President, do you still believe that the Soviet Union is an evil empire?"

"No, I no longer think so."

Reagan wrote in his memoir, that Gorbachev and himself must have sensed a personal connection. Gorbachev also told Nancy Reagan that it seems that Reagan and he made a certain chemical reaction. The summit of Regan and Gorbachev is an example to show that a 'human touch' can change the reality of the international politics. I expect this will come true on the Korean Peninsula one day.

[Appendix]

Comprehensive Plans for the Implementation of the September 19 Joint Statement

For the cause of peace and stability on the Korean Peninsula and in Northeast Asia at large through denuclearization and the establishment on the Korean Peninsula, and normalization of DPRK-US relations and of DPRK-Japan relations, the six parties agreed to achieve the goal within six years and take coordinated steps as following:

1. Denuclearization of the Korean Peninsula

- The DPRK committed to transferring all nuclear weapons and existing nuclear materials to Russia, abandoning them in the country, and stating the aforementioned fact on the basic peace treaty of the Korean Peninsula. To achieve this, the DPRK returns within a year to the NPT and IAEA safeguards on a 'transitional status.' The other parties welcomed the commitment of the DPRK and agreed to consider that the time of completion of abandoning all nuclear programs of the DPRK is when all nuclear weapons and existing nuclear materials are transferred to Russia.

- The DPRK agreed to the 'eventual abandonment' of the Yongbyon nuclear facility as described in the 10.3 Agreement within one year after signing the peace treaty. The DPRK will also abandon nuclear facilities, including nuclear test sites, research and manufacturing facilities for nuclear materials, within three years after signing the peace treaty.

- The United States affirmed that is has no nuclear weapons on the Korean Peninsula and has no intention to attack or invade the DPRK with nuclear or conventional weapons. The United States will state the aforementioned fact on the basic peace treaty of the Korean Peninsula.

- The ROK and the United States will undertake discussing the subject of the withdrawal of the United States's nuclear umbrella over ROK, and will officially withdraw it at a time of completion of abandonment of the DPRK's nuclear weapons.

- The steps of denuclearization of the Korean Peninsula have to be verifiable. For this, the DPRK in return to the NPT and IAEA, agreed to the investigation in accordance with the international standards. Six-Parties, coordinated with the IAEA, will adopt an investigation protocol that can verify the DPRK's nuclear program, including all nuclear programs in the past, uranium enrichment. The ROK and the United States will accept investigations, in case of the DPRK's demands, in order to verify absence of nuclear weapons within ROK's territory.

- The DPRK will ratify the additional protocol of the IAEA, within three years after signing the peace treaty in order to cooperate with the continuous investigation.

- For the purpose of permanent security assurance of the denuclearized Korean Peninsula, the United States, China and Russia will provide the ROK and the DPRK with negative security assurance, will not deploy nuclear weapons or nuclear bombers over the Korean Peninsula, and will not pass through the territorial land, waters and sky of the ROK and DPRK with such weapons. In order to regulate the aforementioned fact as the obligation of the five nuclear-armed countries, including the United Kingdom and France, the United States, China and Russia agreed to promote adopting an additional protocol of nuclear-armed countries or a UNSC resolution.

- The DPRK expressed that it has the right to peaceful uses of nuclear energy, and the other parties expressed their respect to the right. At the same time, Six-Parties agreed to promote cooperation to solve the DPRK's energy scarcity without relying on the nuclear energy.

- The Six-Parties agreed to the joint research for the provision of non-nuclear energy to the DPRK, as an alternative to the light water reactor business of the DPRK, including its own experimental 30 MW light water reactor in construction.

- The Six-Parties agreed to the transfer of the DPRK's uranium enrichment facilities to the International Fuel Bank, and to the joint research for the commercial use of it.

-The Six-Parties agreed to the research for the application of the US-led CTR (Cooperative Threat Reduction) program, for the purpose of the transition of the DPRK's nuclear facilities to non-nuclear facilities, and of the career move of the involved staffs.

- The ROK and the DPRK agreed to abide by the Joint Declaration of South and North Korea on the Denuclearization of the Korean Peninsula.

- The ROK and the DPRK agreed to discuss a joint construction of high-level nuclear waste facilities and a joint research for it, such as a transit of Punggye-ri Nuclear Test Site.

2. A Peace Regime of the Korean Peninsula

- The Six-Parties committed to joint efforts for the establishment of a permanent peace regime on the Korean Peninsula, expressing their respect that the existence of the regime on the peninsula would promote denuclearization of the peninsula and be essential to enhance peace and stability on the Korean Peninsula and in north-east Asia at large, and committed to joint efforts for the regime.

- The ROK, the DPRK, the United States and China agreed to sign a basic peace treaty to replace the existing armistice agreement, within a year after this agreement. The four parties will sign the basic peace treaty as the

DPRK submit its application to the NPT and ratification to an entrusted country. The peace treaty will be signed by the leaders of the countries at a summit. The four parties will discuss an additional protocol to secure the completion and continuity of the basic peace treaty of the Korean Peninsula.

- The ROK, the DPRK, and the United States will take cooperative steps to build political and military trust, which will create a favorable environment to a peace regime, easing the tension on the Korean Peninsula. The three parties reaffirmed the willingness to abide by the armistice agreement until signing the peace treaty of the Korean Peninsula. The ROK and the United States will stop the joint military drills such as 'Key Resolve / Foal Eagle.'

3. Normalization of Relations.

- The DPRK and the United States agreed to undertake to take steps to normalize their entire relations. Within two years, both parties will open liaison offices in the capital of each country. Within three years, both parties will establish full diplomatic ties.

- The DPRK and Japan agreed to undertake to takesteps to normalize their entire relations in accordance with the (2002) Pyongyang Declaration, within three years.

4. A Peace and Security Regime of Northeast Asia

- The Six-Parties reaffirmed the need to develop the Six-Party Talks into a peace and security regime of Northeast Asia, for the common prosperity and peace.

- The Six-Parties agreed to hold ministerial talks of foreign affairs, within a year.

- The Six-Parties agreed to discuss a Nuclear Weapons Free Zone (NWFZ) of Northeast Asia, in order to contribute the denuclearization of the Korean Peninsula to solving the world nuclear issues. The discussion will be held in the conference of the peace and security regime of Northeast Asia, one of the five working groups of Six-Party Talks.

5. The Six-Party Talks on a Regular Basis, and The Resolution of Conflict

- To implement the aforementioned agreements effectively, the Six-Parties expressed their respect and agreed to hold the Six-Party Talks on a regular basis. Regular meetings will be held once every half of the year, and delegation meetings and five working groups' meetings will be held frequently.

- The Six-Parties agreed to, in case of an impasse, immediately hold the Six-Party Talks and break it in a peaceful manner. The other parties agreed that China, the chair country, has the right to call meetings, and to accede to a call.

CHAPTER 9

ARE THE SIX-PARTY TALKS DEAD?

Taeho Kang

The Past 20 Years' Policy toward North Korea's Nuclear Program Has Been a Failure

The United States and North Korea agreed upon the US-DPRK Agreed Framework (hereafter Geneva Agreement) in October 1994, exactly 20 years ago. Robert Gallucci, the chief US negotiator of the Geneva Agreement, delivered a speech in Seoul on October 10, 2014. He announced that "the policies of US and South Korea to solve the (nuclear) threat of North Korea have failed." In view of DPRK's nuclear issues that confront us today, it is hard to object to his conclusion. Why did it fail? What can we do to overcome those failures? To seek an answer for these questions, the past 20 years' North Korean nuclear issues will be reviewed.

The Path of the North Korean Nuclear Crisis and Some Events for Reversing a Situation

It was 12 March 1993 that North Korea declared the withdrawal from the Nuclear Non-Proliferation Treaty (NPT). This occurred one day after the President Kim Young-sam administration repatriated the unconverted long-term political prisoner In-mo Lee whom North Korea consistently requested be repatriated. The North Korean nuclear issue began to emerge in the late 1980s, and were apparently resolved by the South-North Joint Declaration on the Denuclearization of the Korean Peninsula and Inter-

Korean Basic Agreement, both signed in 1992. Nevertheless, because the South-North Joint Nuclear Control Commission (JNCC) for the Denuclearization on the Korean Peninsula struggled with the issue of short-notice inspections, and also because the US-ROK military authorities announced a resumption of the Team Spirit exercise by 1993 in December 1992, North Korea eventually withdrew from the NPT a month after IAEA had passed a resolution on a special inspection in February 1993. This was the origin of the first nuclear crisis. The Korean peninsula was confronted by catastrophe, pushed to the brink of war, when nuclear negotiations between North Korea and the United States came to a deadlock in May 1994. But negotiation between the former US President Jimmy Carter and Kim Il-sung became an opportunity of reversing the situation, and in spite of the sudden death of Kim Il-sung in July that year, the United States and North Korea agreed upon the Geneva Agreement in October 1994 via high-level talks.

However, in 1998, the Geneva Agreement went downhill due to the confrontation over implementation processes, and was confronted with considerable challenges after North Korea launched a three-stage rocket (Taepo Dong-1) and suspicions erupted over the Geumchang-ri underground "nuclear facility." Then, Kim Dae-jung administration's 'Sunshine Policy' and the Clinton administration's 'Perry Process' transcended such crisis and initiated negotiations– the so called 'the Korean Peninsula Peace Process.' Starting with the historic first inter-Korean summit talks in June 2000, the United States and North Korea were engaged deeply in an attempt to overcome the nuclear issue once and for all. They agreed on the 'US-DPRK Joint Communiqué' through mutual visits to Washington and Pyongyang by the Secretary of State Madeleine Albright and Vice-Marshal Myong-rok Cho respectively, prefiguring a proposed visit by US President Clinton to North Korea to conclude the US-DPRK missile negotiations in line with the completion of his presidency. It seemed that the Korean Peninsula Peace Process drove a final stage of conflict settlement by overcoming the limits of the Geneva Agreement through a division of labor with President Kim Dae-jung in the driver's seat and President Clinton in the passenger seat.

However, when Republican President George W. Bush won the disputed US presidential election over the Democratic presidential candidate Al Gore in November 2000, all of the foregoing agreements were endangered. President Bush denied all the Clinton administration's policies, for instance, the US-DPRK's missile negotiation, for the purpose of abolishing the Anti-Ballistic Missile (AMB) treaty which stood against US Missile Defense (MD) system. Subsequently, he stigmatized North Korea as a part of the 'Axis of Evil' in his State of the Nation Address on 2001. In October 2002, James Kelly, Assistant Secretary of State and President Bush's point man on North Korea, and his team strongly pushed North Korea into a corner by affirming that "we secured evidence that North Korea secretly operated a uranium enrichment program." North Korea countered this with the announcement that "we had more than that." The Geneva Agreement collapsed within 3 months, from October of that year to January 2003, starting from the suspension of heavy fuel oil to the North under the Geneva Agreement. As a result, North Korea ultimately withdrew from the NPT and commenced reprocessing of a nuclear fuel rods. This event marked the second nuclear crisis. The United States and North Korea clashed head on as they had in the first nuclear crisis. As it became obvious that the Bush Administration would invade Iraq in March 2003, North Korea retained their nuclear armament option by accelerating plutonium reprocessing, and the United States chose a militaristic response, considering a bombing campaign against the North. As had been the case in 1994, the Korean Peninsula was once again on the verge of a war.

At that moment, China actively took an initiative in arbitration. As the Chinese President Hu Jintao's special envoy, Vice Premier Qian Qichen flew to Samjiyon, near Mt. Paektu, via a special plane and engaged in direct negotiations with the North Korean leader Kim Jong-il. Eventually, the Six-Party Talks, in which North and South Korea, the United States, China, Russia and Japan participated, took place in August 2003, as a result of the US-China-North Korea's Beijing trialogue. Overcoming the crisis of North Korea's declaration on its nuclear capability in February 2005, the Six-Party Talks finally achieved the 'September 19 Joint Statement' at its fourth round in September, after 3 years of difficult negotiations. However, the US Treasury Department immediately revealed allegations on North Korea's illicit financial trade via Banco Delta Asia (BDA) and production of the 'Super Note,' the North's so-called super-precision counterfeit US dollars. Washington's financial sanctions dealt a severe blow to North Korea's foreign currency trade and, resultantly, North Korea pushed back by refusing to participate in the Six-Party Talks as well as strong show of force. The North launched a three-stage variant of its Taepodong-2 rocket, which was aimed towards the mainland of the United States in July 2006, and conducted an underground nuclear test near the village of Punggye on October 9 as the United States tightened its financial sanctions against North Korea. The Korean peninsula was once again on a downward spiral as a result of the US-led United Nations Security Council Resolution 1718 on North Korea.

Nonetheless, circumstances turned around again. President Roh Moo-hyun persuaded the Secretary of State Condoleezza Rice during her visit to Seoul of the efficacy of engagement, while China's special envoy Tang Jiaxuan visited Pyongyang and persuaded the North Korean leader Kim Jong-il. President Bush approved the US-DPRK bilateral dialogue with high expectations of China playing a pivotal role. On the basis of such efforts, the participating states adopted the February 13 Agreement (Initial Actions for the Implementation of the Joint Statement) at the fifth round of the Six-Party Talks on February 2007. Then, a second agreement on disabling North Korea's nuclear project was agreed on by October 3, 2007 as the Initial Actions finalized: 1) shutdown and sealing of Yongbyon nuclear facility; 2) IAEA inspection team's visit to North Korea and resumption of investigation activities; and 3) negotiations on the list of all nuclear programs. A virtuous cycle of resolving the matter of North Korea's nuclear issues and improving inter-Korean relations was made possible because North and South Korea both agreed on the second summit talks in fulfilling the initial actions.

The 'Declaration on the Advancement of South-North Korean Relations, Peace and Prosperity (October 4 Declaration)' was approved at the second inter-Korea summit talks held right after an agreement of the second level of disablement of nuclear program. This declaration ended the Korean war as a precondition demanded by North Korea before proceeding with the third stage of disablement of nuclear program. That is, denuclearization was to be concurrent with creation of a "peace regime" on the Korean Peninsula. This approach prefigured a final solution to North Korea's nuclear issue, similar to that taken in the inter-Korean summit talks and the US-DPRK Joint Communiqué in 2000.

The presidential election of South Korea imperiled the agreement in 2007 in the same way that the US presidential election had done in 2000. The October 4 Declaration was buried by the President Lee Myung-bak government just like the US-DPRK Joint Communiqué was abandoned by the Bush administration. The crisis triggered by the launching of a long-range satellite launching rocket in April 2009 led to North Korea's second nuclear test in May, and the Six-Party Talks were rendered moribund. According to Yang Xiyu, a senior research fellow at the China Institute of International Studies (CIIS), China issued an announcement of statement in a firm tone regarding the second nuclear test with the exceptional expression of 'arbitrarily.' This word only had been applied for 7 times in the Chinese history to condemn an invasion of Chinese sovereignty or other events related to a violation of international law, and North Korea was the seventh case. China then voted in favor of sanctions against North Korea drawn up by the UN Security Council. North Korea's launching of a satellite for the second time in April and December of 2012 was followed by the robust UN Security Council Resolution 1874 on North Korea. In January 2013, after blaming failure of the Six-Party Talks and the September 19 Joint Statement, North Korea conducted its third nuclear test on February 12.

Such incidents are indicative of the 'inter-decadal theory' in that the first nuclear crisis of 1993 led to the second crisis in 2003, which in turn to the third nuclear crisis in 2013 after a further ten years. Coincidentally, the nuclear crisis approached a tipping point during February and March, the period marked by the inauguration of a new South Korean government, for instance, the Kim Young-sam administration in 1993, the Roh Moo-hyun administration in 2003, and the Park Geun-hye administration in 2013. That is, the argument goes, the DPRK uses the period of time when a new government settles in to drive the situation of the Korean peninsula into a crisis. How should we interpret this argument? Is there evidence that this pattern may recur? From the temporal perspective, cumulative frictions and confrontations precipitated a phase of frontal confrontations prior to US-ROK joint military exercises such as Team Spirit and Key Resolve. Furthermore, a policy switch due to the advent of a new administration increases pre-existing conflict. The policy disconnect between South Korean administrations led to the collapse of these agreements with the North. It is clear that the transition of governments resulting from the US presidential election in 2000 and the South Korea's presidential election in 2007 and resulting lack of consistency and continuity of policies contributed directly and significantly to the collapse of the agreements already struck with the North to resolve the nuclear issue, no less than the confrontations between US-ROK and North Korea in the course of carrying out those agreements.

A Death of Kim Il-sung and Kim Jong-il, and Uncertainty of the Situation

As soon as new administrations were elected in the United States and South Korea, the deaths of two North Korean leaders brought about dramatic transitions or reversals of the situation on the Korean peninsula. This could be considered as a power succession or hereditary succession rather than a change of government, yet it could be also interpreted as another type of regime change in a broad sense.

The death of two North Korean leaders occurred in a dramatic fashion that no one could have anticipated. The demise of an unrivaled chief and another supreme leader who succeeded his father's supreme power was not only shocking *per se*, but their aftermath was not only limited in North Korea. It also led to a phase of dialogues and negotiations that culminated in confrontation and crisis. The death of Kim Il-sung on July 7, 1994 was just two weeks ahead of the inter-Korean submit talks. The first-ever inter-Korean submit talks foundered owing to internal conflicts within South Korea on condolence issues. Eventually, a scare campaign in the South made summit talks impossible to convene. In contrast, the negotiations between North Korea and the United States were not interrupted after Kim Il-sung's death and led to the Geneva Agreement ('Agreed Framework between the United States of America and the Democratic People's Republic of Korea'.) Conversely, the absence of inter-Korean talks and conflict within both Koreas lingered for some time even throughout the Kim Young-sam administration, and these confrontations worked as a factor to spoil the Geneva Agreement.

The sudden death of the North Korean leader Kim Jong-il also became a watershed moment for the reversal of the situation and has affected North Korean nuclear issues since 2013. As a combined result of the Cheonan incident in March 2010, the ensuing May 24 sanctions, and the North Korean attack on Yeonpyeong Island in November 2010, the military confrontations between North and South Korea were severe. Kim Jong-il's visits to China three times improved the China-North Korean relationship. Due to the gap between the US-South Korea relations and the China-North Korea relations, conflicts and confrontations between North and South Korea drove the Korean peninsula into their most critical situation by the end of 2010. The inter-Korean confrontation overlapped those between the United States and China on the matter of deploying a US Aircraft carrier to a joint US-ROK exercise on the West Coast.

The turning point away from such a confrontational atmosphere was the US-China presidential talks on January 19, 2011. Using President Hu's visit to the United States as a momentum, China announced a transition of relationship with the United States from checks and confrontations to dialogues and cooperation. Chinese Foreign Minister Yang Jiechi, concerning US-China relations, emphasized that 'it should be cooperative and a win-win game, not a zero-sum game,' in his interview about the issue of Diaoyudao Islands (in Japanese, Senkaku)' with Chinese media, on December 12, 2010, in Beijing. Additionally, Zbigniew Brzezinski, the former

US National Security Advisor, commented on President Hu's visit to the United States in his column of *International Herald Tribune* on January 3, 2011 that "it will be the most important diplomatic event in US-China relations in almost 30 years since President Deng Xiaoping's visit, and the two countries must freely admit their differences and solve the issues in recognition of mutual needs, despite some conflicting views on several issues remain."

A tough response from South Korea, which included an artillery exercise on Yeonpyeong Island in December 2010 and the start of powerful military retaliation against North Korea, led to stress between the United States and China over their common interest in securing stability and peace on the Korean Peninsula. The telephone call between President Hu and President Obama on December 5 became a watershed moment toward the cooperative US-China relations since the North Korean attack on Yeonpyeong Island. While seeking a mutual response through US-Japan-South Korea trilateral Foreign Minister Talks on December 7, the United States concurrently made a firm response by dispatching Mike Mullen, the chairman of the Joint Chiefs of Staff, to South Korea on the 8th. Mullen's visit to South Korea had an ulterior purpose to ease South Korea's adventurous and dangerous use of the right to self-defense, for instance, the necessity of preventing the possibility of escalation into war which originated from the new Minister of Defense Kwan-jin Kim's claim to mobilize aircraft.

China solicited an agreement on December 9 through a meeting with the North Korean leader Kim Jong-il. This agreement aimed to suppress North Korea's additional provocation toward an artillery exercise on Yeonpyeong Island, by sending State Councilor Dai Bingguo to North Korea. North Korea simultaneously sent a signal as regards the acceptance of the investigation team from IAEA and the resumption of the Six-Party Talks without any preconditions.

Based on such efforts, the United States continued to work towards US-China summit talks as James Steinberg, Deputy Secretary of State, and Jeffrey Bader, the Senior Director for Asian affairs on the NSC, visited China. And China, in response, agreed with Defense Secretary Robert Gates' visit to China, which they had declined since the Cheonan incident, and consented to a mutual exchange for US-China military cooperation. At this point, it was made clear that US-China summit talks in Washington could only take place if they were based on the awareness that US-China cooperation is possible including joint efforts for peace and stability on the Korean peninsula.

Nonetheless, the Lee Myung-bak government carried out a live ammunition exercise on Yeonpyeong Island on December 20, in order to punish North Korea. President Lee said that "as a sovereign state, it is a matter of certainty that we conduct a military exercise as a way of defending our territory under the circumstance of an armed confrontation in a divided country." And he added: "no one can interrupt on this matter." This event occurred right after the Chinese Vice Minister of Foreign Affairs Zhang Zhijun made a statement on December 18, and proclaimed a strong opposition against the naval firing exercise on Yeonpyeong Island. China publicly opposed President Lee's comments. On December 20, Vice Minister of Foreign Affairs Cui Tiankai mentioned that "no one had a right to draw blood from the people on the Korean Peninsula."

How did the United States respond to these developments? The *Washington Post* pointed out on December 21 that "the difficulty of what South Korean President Lee encountered is a second factor that increases tension on the peninsula." Even before then, on December 12, Dennis Blair, the former US Director of National Intelligence, warned that the South Korean government might take military actions against North Korea, stating that "South Korea is now losing their patience with North Korea."

Both the United States and China – each with a difficult counterpart to deal with, that is North and South Korea respectively – started to become involved in the issues concerning the Korean Peninsula from the standpoint of mutual interest for peace and stability on the peninsula, beyond the "alliance trap." President Obama and Hu Jintao agreed to initiate negotiations on the basis of a mutual interest on the resumption of the Six-Party Talks through inter-Korean dialogue, as well as mutual concerns on the

North Korea's uranium enrichment program. That was only possible since the United States respected Chinese national interests instead of hampering them, and China expressed their intention to never challenge US national interests in the ROK. In this respect, then US Secretary of State Hillary Clinton formulated a three-step process to the Six-Party Talks – 1) South-North dialogue; 2) US-North dialogue; and 3) the Six-Party Talks – on the occasion of her visit to South Korea on April 17, 2011.

The high-level talks between North Korea and the United States that commenced with the inter-Korean talks of chief delegates to the Six-Party Talks at the ASEAN Regional Forum (ARF) in July 2011 was a result. Within 1 year and 2 months after implementing the May 24 sanctions, the Korean Peninsula was finally returning to an atmosphere for dialogue in relation to the resumption of the Six-Party Talks. At that time, the Minister of Unification Woo-ik Yu modified his attitude to prepare a dialogue through an effective inter-Korean channel. However, North and South Korea eventually failed to start a conversation, being tied up with the May 24 sanctions, and dialogues could become feasible only with the United States and China at the center.

Most of all, China consistently claimed that US-China cooperation was vital to the resumption of the Six-Party Talks. North Korean leader Kim Jong-il received confirmation from China that it wished to reinforce their partnership and would provide unwavering support for his successor provided the North agree to the Chinese claim for the resumption of the Six-Party Talks during his visit to China for three times in his last year, from May 2010 to May 2011. China pronounced itself as sincerely supportive of Pyongyang. Accordingly, China opposed to referring the uranium enrichment issue back to the UN Security Council. Moreover they announced that the North's peaceful nuclear power program should be respected. China exhibited a special relationship with North Korea with a firm posture against the opposition of the United States and South Korea on the issue of repatriation of North Korean defectors.

North Korea and the United States had negotiated in the second Geneva talks in October 2011 after the first New York talks, which was a kind of a reconnoitering skirmish. They both acted in the third talks according to a strategic agreement that they would arrive at a conclusion for the resumption of the Six-Party Talks. In particular, North Korea made a breakthrough as they showed clear willingness to negotiate on suspension of uranium enrichment at the Geneva talks. Based on such results Glyn Davies, the US Special Representative for North Korea Policy, shared an opinion during his visit to South Korea, Japan and China from December 8 to 15, and Robert King, the Special Envoy for North Korean Human Rights Issues, and Gun Ri, the DPRK's Director General of North Korea American Affairs Bureau, concluded agreements on humanitarian assistance, such as monitoring on food support program, on December 15 and 16, in Beijing. As a result, the third US-DPRK talks was just a few days away and, on December 19, 2011, the US Secretary of State Hilary Clinton was about to announce that the third US-North Korea talks would be held on December 22. However, on that very day, North Korea announced the death of the North Korean leader Kim Jong-il on December 17. Everything was suspended and became unclear, yet again. In addition, the statement of the National Defense Commission on December 30, 2011 labeled the measures taken by President Lee's administration during the periods of mourning as an 'anti-national high treason,' and swore revenge to the very last.

In contrast, the North Korean leadership surprisingly chose to resume conversations with the United States after resolving the funeral details, led by Kim Jong-un, even though the nation was faced with important procedures for the succession of leadership, such as the Party Representative Assembly, which was to be held in early April 2012. This was directly against the expectation that North Korea might take provocative actions in response to the US-South Korea's joint military exercise. The reason for the DPRK's flexibility may be found in the fact that they needed to secure a strong alliance, such as with Russia and China, including food aid from China as well as the United States. China actively supported the third US-DPRK talks. There was more to the meeting between North Korea and the United States than the third US-DPRK talks, which was held in December

2011 to deal with the issue of food aid in Beijing. China affirmed an expansion of food aid, sending Vice Minister for Foreign Affairs Fu Ying to Pyongyang in advance of the third meeting.

As Masao Okonogi, a professor at Keio University, pointed out, the third US-DPRK high-level talks in Beijing on February 24-25 had been already planned with expectations for some progress, and it had been only postponed for two months due to the death of the North Korean leader Kim Jong-il. In this third meeting, the United States confirmed US food aid to North Korea, and North Korea affirmed that they would stand down from a nuclear test, a long-range rocket launch, nuclear activities in Yongbyon including uranium enrichment, and averred that they would bring nuclear activities in Yongbyon under IAEA's surveillance (the so-called 3+1). The February 29 Agreement was evaluated for the fact that the political system of North Korea continued its existing policy, which had been handed over dynamically in spite of the Supreme leader's death. The United States and North Korea jointly announced these agreements in Washington and Pyongyang on February 29. This became known as the Leap Day Deal (or February 29 Deal.) The United States and North Korea, however, did not promulgate this understanding as an official act of state based on a mutual agreement, and even expressed it as a 'deal,' not an 'agreement.' In this regard, they simply ended up with sharing a lower level of opinion rather than an agreement. However the Leap Day Deal between the United States and North Korea became a milestone towards the resumption of the Six-Party Talks for the Obama administration. Leon Sigal, the North-South Korea expert at the Social Science Research Council (SSRC) commented that: "even if it was just a venue for dialogue with unilateral demands by North Korea for the US, now it has become a cooperative relationship with some give and take."

Kim Jong-il's Deathbed Instructions and the Satellite Launching

Nonetheless, the Leap Day Deal collapsed as soon as North Korea launched the satellite, Kwangmyongsong-3, loaded on the Unha-3 long-range rocket since the middle of April. How can such actions by North

Korea be interpreted? Apparently, they did not expect negotiations with the United States to occur as their launch contradicted the Leap Day Deal that (from the American account) specified the suspension of a long-range missile launch.

On December 28, 2011, *Rodong Sinmun* referred to nuclear and missiles as the greatest legacy of Kim Jong-il, and pointed out that thanks to his bequest, "the weak group, caught in the middle of super powers, could triumphantly look to the world with our chest thrown out." It said that nuclear and missiles developments were the deathbed instructions of Kim Jong-il, so, in this regard, Kwangmyongsong-3 had been planned for a long time. According to Okonogi's analysis, the normalization of relationship with the United States was also a central part of the deathbed instructions of Kim Jong-il, and those two were not in a necessary contradiction.[1] This is because Kim Jong-il's fundamental strategy was the use of nuclear weapon and missiles as means of containment and diplomacy in order to achieve normalization of relationship with the United States, not to fight it. In that sense, they contended that the temporary freezing of North Korea's activities in uranium enrichment facilities, the Leap Day Deal, which stipulates that such activities be placed under the IAEA's control, and the satellite launch can all be compatible.

Yang Xiyu, a senior research fellow at the CIIS, indicated a flaw in this agreement, underlining that it was very unstable position and could be derailed by a nudge when different views and unexpected incidents occurred, due to the strategic distrusts between the United States and North Korea, and North and South Korea. Professor Okonogi emphasized that, as the Secretary of State Hillary Clinton pointed out, this US-DPRK agreement was no more than just 'a first move towards a right direction,' and added that North Korea still prevented dialogues with the Lee administration, even after the Leap Day Deal.

[1] Masao Okonogi, "Exploring Major Powers' Policy on North Korea under Kim Jong Un's Leadership- A Japanese perspective"(paper presented at the International Conference on the Peace of the Korean Peninsular, Seoul, Korea, March 12, 2012)

The Leap Day Deal was the only agreement with North Korea during the past four years for the Obama administration, which occurred prior to the 2012 presidential election. Thus, the Obama administration attempted a dialogue with North Korea by dispatching intelligence officials to North Korea in secrecy, but North Korea declined and pressed ahead with its rocket launch.

In fact, those in the Obama Administration who favored negotiation and dialogue with North Korea lost their footing after the failure of the Leap Day Deal. In addition, the young North Korean leader Kim Jong-un specified the status of a nuclear power state in their constitution, launched the satellite, and even conducted the third nuclear test in March 2013. As a result, the theory of uselessness, which argued that cooperation with North Korea only gave them time to proliferate and that any agreement was meaningless, gained strength. But the most important fact to consider is that the young leader Kim Jong-un chose to directly confront the United States.

Warning of Full-spectrum Confrontations

On August 8, 2012, a military aircraft headed to Pyongyang from a US military base in Guam. That aircraft carried Joseph DeTrani, the Director of the National Counter-proliferation Center (NCPC) of DNI, and Sydney Seiler, President Obama's senior adviser on Korean affairs. DeTrani was an expert on North Korean issues who had served as a senior advisor in the Office of Weapon of Mass Destruction Issues in DNI, and Seiler was an expert, fluent in Korean, to assist Glyn Davies, the US Special Representative for North Korea Policy. It was later revealed that they met the Vice-chairman of the National Defense Commission Song-taek Jang and others, and discussed pending issues between the United States and North Korea after the death of Kim Jong-il.

The *Los Angeles Times* revealed that DeTrani and Seiler both urged the new leadership of North Korea to take a comprehensive foreign policy after the death of Kim Jong-il. DeTrani said that "I persuaded them not to launch a long-range missile but they objected to it. At first, myself and other experts believed that Kim Jong-un would take a more moderate path than that of his father as he had appointed moderate people, but it was not long before we lost hope."

Prior to this, two experts visited North Korea on April 12 before North Korea launched Kwangmyongsong-3 satellite (the Unha-3 long-range rocket). DeTrani emphasized that "from the US point of view, an attempt to open dialogues with the North Korean officials was surely pertinent after the death of Kim Jong-il."

What they were discussing during their secretive visit to North Korea is still veiled, but the *Choson Sinbo*, an official newspaper of the pro-Pyongyang federation of Korean residents in Japan (Jochongnyeon,) revealed some part of it on 21 January 2013. It argued that "North Korea of Kim Jong-un's era unified the history of US-DPRK relations, and from this, delivered an ultimatum on the nuclear issues through officials from NSC and CIA." The ultimatum was: "unless the United States draws back from its hostile policy against North Korea, it will be inevitable for North Korea to extend nuclear programs, and conversation on the issue of denuclearization cannot help but be halted." This fact was reconfirmed by Joel Wit, former US State Department official. Wit was a leading US expert on North Korean issues, and he was delivered a message from Sun-hee Choi, the Deputy Director General of North Korea's foreign ministry, Sung-ryul Han, the North Korean Deputy Ambassador to the UN, and others at the closed two-track meeting in Singapore, July 2012:

"North Korea urges United States to take the first action as proof of their authenticity, and if this does not happen, North Korea will discard the principle of the 'concurrent action' in the September 19 Agreement of 2005 by reinforcing nuclear deterrence and developing additional missiles."

Wit delivered this message to the Obama administration after the meeting, and he warned that the first crisis of the Obama administration will be North Korea. This turned out to be true in 2013. The Obama administration, however, ignored his advice at that time.

The DPRK's Ministry of Foreign Affairs intended to send their message both openly and officially through a memorandum. This memorandum, disclosed by the North Korean Central News on August 31, 2012, was included in an official document of the UN Security Council in October. The memorandum was not distinctively different from the aforementioned final ultimatum, but included more details. At first, it brought the case that – as a typical example of the US hostile policies against North Korea – the United States tried to restrain North Korea with the Security Council Resolution on DPRK's satellite launch. They argued that such policy stemmed from an adversarial viewpoint, which depicts North Korea as an enemy.

Next, the memorandum inquired in a logical manner on what came first between DPRK's nuclear and the American hostile policy. They had to inevitably own nuclear weapons because of the US hostile policies, and not due to domestic reasons. Thus, if the United States does not withdraw its hostile policy against North Korea, there will be no space to resolve DPRK's nuclear program. This argument suggested that North Korea was willing to abandon its nuclear program on condition that the United States abolished its hostile policies. The memorandum demanded a decision by the United States on whether the nation will nurture peace and stability on the Korean Peninsula by abandoning its hostile policy, or await the situation in which North Korea's nuclear armory continue to expand and strengthen.

It is likely that North Korea had already signaled its intention to conduct its third nuclear test on February 12, 2013 since the summer of 2012, as they had launched the Unha-3 long-range rocket on December 12. Even if this memorandum had failed to garner much attention, it was not an empty talk in view of their statement – "procuring nuclear power is inevitably time-consuming, and our nuclear deterrence will be upgraded and modernized beyond the imagination of the US."

North Korea again urged the United States to make its decision in the spokesperson's presentation of the Ministry of Foreign Affairs on February 12, 2013, after its third nuclear test: "The United States must choose between a peaceful and stable state, which respects our rights to launch a satellite, and an erroneous path towards explosion, which occurs in pursuit of its hostile policy against North Korea."

What exactly was the abandonment of hostile policies that North Korea was demanding? Immediately after President Obama's reelection, North Korea mentioned the DPRK's requirements by releasing an editorial of an individual writer in the *Chosun Sinbo* on November 10, 2012 and the *Rodong Sinmun* on November 12. The DPRK sought "a direct negotiation to find a final solution and to normalize the history of US-DPRK negotiations that cannot carry out the agreements over the past 20 years." There were two general agreements in the past. First, the editorial reminded that "The United States affirmed the non-use of nuclear weapons; respect of sovereignty; non-interference in domestic affairs; and support for the peaceful unification of the two Koreas in the US-DPRK Joint Declaration 20 years ago (the first US-DPRK high-level talks)" The DPRK also refers to the first meeting prior to the third US-DPRK high-level talks in 1994, as well as the missile negotiation and the US-DPRK Joint Communiqué, which President Clinton aimed to finalize during his visit to North Korea in 2000.

It also reminded that "the two leaders of the two Koreas in the past agreed to resolve the issue through a declaration to end the war by 3 or 4 heads of states concerned," in 2013, which was the year commemorating the 60th anniversary of the armistice agreement. This refers to the October 4 North-South Declaration (Declaration on the Advancement of South-North Korean Relations, Peace and Prosperity.) It added that if the Obama administration does not take the appropriate actions to honor its commitments inherited from the Clinton and Bush administrations, then the dialogue between the United States and North Korea, which has lasted for over 20 years, would end.

What North Korea demanded from the United States, to materialize a final negotiation, was a dangerous and reckless gamble, given that Obama's second term had just begun. North Korea stressed that "if the second Obama administration makes a resolute decision to put an end to the longest war in US history, North Korea will be ready to welcome it willingly." Quoting the *Chosun Shinbo's* words, it meant that "it is a time for the final judgment, thus come forward for peace talks to prevent war."

Joel Wit, a former US State Department official on North Korea issues, mentioned that "North Korean officials clarified their intention to abolish the 'mutual action principle' in the September 19 Joint Statement of 2005, and wanted to take the first action in order to demonstrate their authenticity," in the interview with the *Hankyoreh* in February 2013. Furthermore, he emphasized that "this shows that North Korea will go further and strive to develop their nuclear deterrence." Taking into account the fact that the United States had demanded North Korea to renounce its nuclear weapons first, demanding US actions to improve the US-DPRK relations implied that North Korea would no longer pay attention to unfavorable outcomes arising from the lack of enagement and agreement with the United States.

Indeed, the DPRK's third nuclear test supported the idea that nuclear renunciation through cooperation was not possible anymore. North Korea had empowered its nuclear armament to become a tool exacting a military as well as political response by the United States, its allies, and its strategic partners such as China and Russia. The North's actions solidified the theory of the Uselessness of Negotiations, demonstrating that they will never relinquish nuclear armament so long as it needed them to maintain its regime. The Obama administration perceived such either-or demand as a full-frontal confrontation and responded in kind.

2013 Spring's Full-frontal Confrontation toward the End of the War, and Playbook

In 2013, the Korean Peninsula was under the shadow of a serious war, perhaps more so than any time since the mid seventies. North Korea exercised No.1 combat readiness posture on March 26 after its third nuclear test on February 12, and a statement of the DPRK's supreme command announced that "all field armies, including the Strategic Rocket Force and long-range artillery corps will carry out No.1 combat readiness posture from this moment forward." Declaration of the No.1 combat readiness posture meant that the Supreme Commander Kim Jong-un had ultimately approved of the Strategic Rocket Force's attack on US military bases located in the US mainland, Guam and Japan. In reality, North Korea was on a standby to launch a missile by deploying a mid-range missile, presumably with a range of 4,000km, to Musudan on the east coast. According to the *Chosun Shinbo's* reports, it was a frontal confrontation by North Korea in response to UN Security Council's resolution on December 12, 2012 that denounced the satellite launch as illegal.

On the contrary, the *Wall Street Journal* defined the US response as by the 'Playbook.' The origin of the playbook, as a lower level of an operational plan, is a tactical manual prepared by the US Pacific Command to counter DPRK's military threats during December 2012. Its purpose was to deter further provocations of North Korea through its armed protests, as well as to suppress South Korea's excessive military response against them.

As a result, the United States and DPRK conducted a simulated all-out war, starting with the Key Resolve exercise on March 11, but in which actual weapons were employed. The United States ordered the deployment of the B-52 strategic bombers three times in March alone, placing them on the Korean peninsula on March 19. In addition, the US released publicly the fact that nuclear attack submarine, the USS Cheyenne, was sent to an exercise. In response, North Korea declared a military confrontation if the B-52 bombers made a sortie, and that it would exercise No.1 combat readiness posture for the Strategic Rocket Force and long-range artillery corps. In response, the United States ordered the nuclear-certified B-2 stealth bomber to fly over from the continental United States. Faced with this threat display, North Korea never yielded an inch. On the 29th, Kim Jong-un called an operational emergency meeting on a bombing mission of the Strategic Rocket Force and instructed his forces to adopt a 'ready position.' North Korea also revealed this meeting to the media and the United States disregarded it by dispatching its latest F-22 Raptors to the Korean Peninsula.

Suspension of the Musudan Missile – Signs for Transition to a Dialogue Phase

On April 21, North Korea demonstrated its intention to suspend the activities of the Musudan missile launch by amending the order to close their embassies abroad on the grounds of a possible war. It was its first attempt to avert a full-frontal confrontation. The CNN reported that North Korea brought the Musudan missile down from launch preparations, quoting US military sources. Prior to this event, the *Wall Street Journal* said that the United States had begun adjusting their exercise tempo due to concerns over the playbook strategy. On April 3, the Secretary of Defense Chuck Hagel unexpectedly suspended the test of the Minuteman III (latest ICBM), stating that "we do not want to worsen a 'complicated and combustible situation'." The United States had also taken measures to adjourn the ROK-US Military Committee Meeting (MCM) and Secretary Hagel explained that "it was because of the increased tension on the peninsula and the possibility of misjudgment by North Korea."

On April 12, 2013 North Korea implemented a no-launch condition and Secretary John Kerry joined the foreign minister talks with South Korea. At a press conference after the meeting, he announced that "we want a dialogue with North Korea." At the same time he enunciated the conditions and goals of the dialogue as 'denuclearization of the peninsula.' This remark followed President Park comment the previous day that the ROK "will communicate with North Korea." That is, the United States and South Korea jointly sent a message seeking dialogue with Pyongyang. In addition, Secretary Kerry emphasized that "President Obama contributed to ease the tension in the region by reconfiguring several military exercises," referring to Obama's action to delay the ICBM test. He said that "now the choice is up to Kim Jong-un, he must exert responsible leadership," and urged his decision. North Korea responded to this overture via China – the Director of the DPRK's General Political Bureau Ryong-hae Choe visited China with the title of 'special envoy' on May 22 who affirmed their policy shift from a full-frontal confrontation. The DPRK now sought: 'A dialogue policy with concerned parties of the Six-Party Talks.' Mr. Choe announced in his meeting with Chinese President Xi Jinping that included an offer for a ROK-DPRK inter-government talks on June 6, and another one for US-DPRK's high-level talks through a statement by the National Defense Commission on June 16.

A war had been avoided again, but it was not a resumption of negotiation, rather just entertaining the possibility. North Korea and the United States had struggled regarding the resumption of the Six-Party Talks in spite of Chinese active intervention. In addition, although North and South Korea continued their respective efforts to resolve the issue of the motionless Geaseong Industrial Complex, the outcome was limited to only a recovery.

China's New Approach – Rebalancing Policy on the Korean peninsula

About the time that the military collision, which originated from the DPRK's frontal confrontation tirade, was averted, the first US-ROK summit talks since the inauguration of the Park administration were held on May 7, 2013 in Washington. The message to North Korea in the meeting was about 'the Trust-Building Process on the Korean Peninsula' and 'Burma.' It was intended that North Korea must lay down its nuclear weapons and look for a peaceful and progressive path by accepting the Trust-Building Process on the Korean Peninsula, and after then the normalization of relationship with United States could be possible, as have been so for Burma.

Unexpectedly, the Bank of China, one of the four national commercial banks in China, closed down an account of the Foreign Trade Bank of North Korea, as if it was responding to the US-ROK presidential talks. It was an answer to President Park's demand that "China should exert more influence over North Korea in order for North Korea to take a right direction," in her interview with *Washington Post* on May 7. Such a Chinese measure was a result of an interchange of ideas with the United States. Previously, President Obama made an appearance in the 'Good Morning America' TV show on March 13, and stated that "there was a sign from the Chinese in reconsidering its policy toward North Korea."

The leadership in the Xi Jinping government, since its 2013 inauguration, has been actively engaged in North Korea's nuclear affairs, perhaps more than any time since the end of the Korean War, professing to apply diplomatic and economic pressure together with UN sanctions on North Korea. It was a new approach that considered the denuclearization of North Korea, insecurity, and inter-Korean relations all together. Chun-bok Lee of the Sungkyun Institute of Chinese Studies appropriately named it as the Chinese 'Rebalancing Policy on the Korean Peninsula.' The rationale for this policy is based on the consideration that North Korean issues should not be utilized as a tool of the US-ROK-Japan's trilateral containment strategy against China, and that the United States and China need to cooperate in dealing with the North Korean nuclear issue with regards to carrying forward the new type of great power relations between the United States and China. To elaborate, Wang Yi, China's Foreign Minister, clarified that "we are confident about deducing an agreement on how the Six-Party Talks should be resumed," after a meeting with John Kerry, the US Secretary of State. He also delivered a speech on North Korea's willingness to return to the February 29 US-DPRK agreement. This is how China amended North Korea's position that it had denied the Six-Party Talks and the September 19 Joint Statement. In reality, North Korea's First Vice Foreign Minister Kye-gwan Kim reconfirmed Wang Yi's statement in the Seminar that commemorated the 10th Anniversary of the Six-Party Talks on September 18 in Beijing. He affirmed that denuclearization is a policy goal of North Korea, with a particular stress on the importance of denuclearization on the Korean peninsula, as it was a deathbed message of Kim Il-sung and Kim Jong-il. Additionally, he delivered a speech regarding the resumption of the Six-Party Talks, without any preconditions, as well as fulfilling the September 19 Joint Statement.

This statement prompted the Secretary of State Kerry's remarks on October 3, 2013: "we are ready to sign a nonaggression treaty if North Korea is determined on denuclearization towards a sincere negotiation." The talks between North Korea and the United States, however, failed to come about. According to Professor Chung-in Moon of the Yonsei University, participants from the United States and South Korea demanded investigation as two why February 29 Leap Year Agreement and additional actions to North Korea were treated as rigid prerequisites for the Six-Party Talks. These demands show that the arbitration of China failed to resolve such gaps, as North Korea contradicted them immediately with its own proposal. The National Defense Commission October 12, 2013 statement expressed its refusal of the US negotiation packages, stating that "it was just the sly maneuver of inspiring with seductive language that 'there will be talks and improvement of relations if North Korea lays down its nuclear weapons." Soon after, the United States and North Korea indulged in mutual slanders.

The United States and North Korea confront each other with an alternative approach

North Korea demanded negotiations for the joint resolution of the nuclear issue and the abolition of hostile policies toward North Korea, but pretalks about talks simply became the grounds for the justification of the tough US responses to the effect that 'there is no talk without denuclearization.' Secretary Kerry, at the US House of Representatives committee hearing in April 2013 stated that the United States will no longer communicate with North Korea concerning the issues of economic aid and peaceful regime without the denuclearization precondition. The approach to nuclear issues taken by North Korea, underlying a statement of the National Defense Commission in June 2013, was also a rejection of the methods stipulated in the Geneva Agreement 1994, as well as the September 19 Mutual Statement of 2005. For instance, an editorial in late March 2013 of the *Rodong Sinmun* declared that "the era in which the United States hindered economic development by threatening us with nuclear weapons is already gone," immediately after adopting its dual track strategy. It meant that North Korea should be properly recognized as the nuclear armed state that it had already become, and in particular, it wanted to consider negotiations on an equal footing with the United States. Professor Chung-in Moon explained the positions of the US and DPRK as follows: "as nuclear weapons are DPRK's last resort, just like insurance, it cannot be given up. Thus, North Korea cannot accept such demands that require denuclearization, unless there are assurances about their regime." Indeed, the United States perceives DPRK's intention to refuse denuclearization as a deception. Even Secretary Kerry, who is forward-looking, forecasts that the problem cannot be resolved without such premise.

One likely reason behind the American rejection of a denuclearization meeting by North Korea originates from the fact that it does not agree with the need to adhere to any suggestion that energy aid to the DPRK as part of a denuclearization package might include support for the construction of a light water reactor. Additionally, North Korea clarified that such a light water reactor remains at the core of its policy, stating that "the dual track of North Korea Korean Party not only empowers nuclear capability based on a self-reliant nuclear industry, but also resolves issues of electricity."

In this regard, China's unprecedented positive intervention could not help, but only revealed its limits. "The United States did not negotiate, it rather exacted obedience," Yu Shaohua of the China Institute of International Studies stated in a critical comment. She also added that the United States maintained a flexible posture towards DPRK's nuclear weapons, which stems from the evaluation that regards the actual use of those weapons as quite unlikely, compared with the the dangers accruing from the proliferation of DPRK's nuclear weapons. Moroever, in view of the US efforts to strengthen containment of China by enhancing military cooperation with South Korea and Japan, it is quite unlikely that the United States actually intends to resolve DPRK's nuclear issue. Rather, it relies on China and South Korea to control or suppress the DPRK. Yu emphasized that such attitude of the United States will bring a negative impact on the denuclearization of the peninsula in the long-term. Yu states: "The DPRK's interest in economic development is rooted in its confidence that they have already become nuclear power. In this light, forcing denuclearization without any alternatives is far from negotiation."

Theory of the Uselessness of Negotiations and the Absence of Alternatives

Twelve years ago, the first Six-Party Talks were held in April 2003. There were two kinds of opinions surrounding the Six-Party Talks: one is the 'theory of uselessness of the Six-Party Talks.' Another is the 'theory of adherence to cooperation' due to lack of alternatives. To illustrate, the theory of adherence to cooperation criticizes the theory of uselessness on the basis that it is nothing more than doing nothing – it cannot be an option in resolving the nuclear issues because if there is no cooperation, the only things left to do are to wage war or respond to the collapse of North Korea. Thus, it argues that the theory of uselessness is irresponsible.

Nonetheless, after the collapse of the February 29 Deal, it became increasingly difficult to find proponents of dialogue with the DPRK. The theory of uselessness of cooperation gained strength. The idea that 'because North Korea never relinquished its nuclear weapons, solving the problem through cooperation is unachievable,' lies at the bottom of such recognition. This kind of general opinion was stimulated by the skepticism surrounding the opposition to convening another round of the Six-Party Talks or demanding a substantive prerequisite – even if the Six-Party Talks resume, these may serve as an excuse for North Korea to ignore it and continue its nuclear development.

Joon-kook Hwang, the Special Representative for the Korean Peninsula Peace and Security Affairs, participated at a seminar commemorating the 20th anniversary of the Geneva Agreement next to Robert Gallucci, the former Ambassador-at-Large. Hwang retold the story from the US negotiators to the 1994 Geneva Agreement when he was a low-ranking officer in the Ministry of Foreign Affairs.

> "At this moment, North Korea keeps producing nuclear materials, in addition to missile and nuclear weapons technologies. It is very important to grasp how the crisis we are facing can be resolved. If the wishful thinking that undermined DPRK's will to develop nuclear weapons had been a problem in the 1990s, one that overshadows today's problem is the pessimism on nuclear

issues. Meanwhile, we have tried our best to resolve this issue, but skepticism has been dominant as all attempts had ended in failures."

This skepticism – that it is difficult to have North Korea give up its nuclear weapons – permeated American public opinion, including the Obama administration and other experts. For instance, President Barack Obama never mentioned North Korea during his keynote speech at the United Nations General Assembly in September 2014, in spite of the many other external issues that he listed. This meant that the United States adhered to the so-called 'pre-action, post-dialogue' principle, which emphasizes the authenticity of DPRK's measures for denuclearization in order to initiate negotiations, and which underlines that there will be no more engagements in the matter before a change of North Korea's posture. This posture verged on strategic ignorance rather than strategic endurance. In addition, Secretary Kerry concentrated all his efforts on the Middle East issues and the Ukrainian turmoil.

Reforms in Strategic Forces and the Minimum Deterrence Strategy

Given this gridlock, we must critically review the situation in accordance with 'what constitutes a gain and a loss' in that the Six-Party Talks, already widely declared as dead, are meaningless if North Korea does not denuclearize before resumption. Does this standoff mean that North Korea losing its game? So far, it appears to be not so. Rather, North Korea has successfully increased its nuclear arsenal. The United States received support from China only in the form of political pressure on DPRK, but failed to prevent the North's nuclear armament. North Korea continued with two more nuclear tests, in May 2009 and February 2013, and placed a satellite in orbit in December 2012. This made North Korea the eighth country in the world in terms of nuclear tests and the tenth member of the 'Space Club' as it had launched its own satellite, with its own rocket, from its own territory.

Of course, the development and possession of nuclear materials and delivery systems do not guarantee North Korea the status of a nuclear weapons state. Apart from developing nuclear materials and owning its delivery system, an actual nuclear power state should have a nuclear doctrine and a command and control system for nuclear missiles. However, as we shall see, North Korea has demonstrated to have fulfilled to those requirements – in 2013, the Supreme People's Assembly adopted the 'Law on Consolidating Position of Nuclear Weapons State,' and initiated the KPA Strategic Rocket Force Command in April 2014.

Under the Law on Consolidating Position of Nuclear Weapons State, North Korea announced ten items of a nuclear doctrine: 1) Purpose of possessing nuclear weapons; 2) Use of nuclear weapons; 3) Reinforcement of nuclear deterrence; 4) Use of nuclear weapons by a supreme commander; 5) Ban on nuclear arms against a non-nuclear power state; 6) Assurances of possessing nuclear weapons and experiment safety; 7) Control over illegal leakage of nuclear technology and material; 8) Participation in the international nonproliferation agenda; 9) Support for international nuclear disarmament; and 10) Actual plan for law enforcement. North Korea repeated the launches of a short-range missile and long-range artillery in 2014. They also launched 111 short and long-range projectiles, 19 times from February 21 to September 6, including the latest tactical missiles with ranges up to 500 km, 300 mm new launcher, Rodong missile, and FROG rocket. This record of deployment was more than 10-fold to that in 2013. They additionally expanded missile launch points from Wonsan of Kangwon province to North Pyongan Province (Myohyangsan), Pyongsan of Hwanghae Province, Gaeseong, and even Chagang Province which borders China.

Along with the establishment of the strategic force, the short range missile launches attempted to establish and operate the command system of nuclear missiles for the sake of acquiring a second-strike capability, as the nation strived to secure its survivability. Intelligence authorities observed that the establishment of the strategic force signified a reform of the system so as to fulfill Kim Jong-un's orders to shoot more efficiently by means of an automated launching system. An intelligence source proved that "the reason for establishing the strategic force was to automate the missile launching system and to unify the command system." Another source evaluated that "originally, Rodong/Scud/Musudan missile brigades belonged to the existing Strategic Rocket Forces subordinate, yet the new strategic force merged those brigades," and added that "this tells us that Kim Jong-un seized the initiative of supreme power over missile capability, and, as a result, the rate of response could be improved."

The Soviet Union founded its Strategic Rocket Force 10 years after the first nuclear test, and China established the Second Artillery Corps two years after its first nuclear test. North Korea mobilized its Strategic Rocket Force in 2012, which was 16 years after its first nuclear test. The Soviet Union and North Korea established the Strategic Rocket Force after ballistic missile tests, yet China had the Second Artillery Corps prior to the test.

The Strategic Rocket Forces of the Soviet Union and China are considered as a separate group from the Army, Navy and Air force, and these are under control of the State leadership. DPRK's Strategic Rocket Force is more close to the Soviet's case in terms of its name and the time of foundation. The Soviet Union and China founded the Strategic Rocket Force and Second Artillery Corps at the stage of the so-called 'minimum deterrence strategy,' which possesses a nuclear warhead with long-range target capability. If so, apart from the US noncommittal evaluation of the miniaturization of DPRK's nuclear warhead, North Korea revealed itself as capable of the minimum deterrence strategy.

In order for North Korea to meet the standards of the minimum deterrence strategy, it must demonstrate two required techniques. Most of all, North Korea is considered to have no re-entry techniques into an atmosphere thus far, which is a core competency of the long-range target capability. Through several attempts of satellite rocket and long-range missile tests, North Korea eventually succeeded in placing Kwanmyongsong-3 and 2 in orbit. This rocket should have been able to re-enter the atmosphere but North Korea had failed to prove this technique. Nonetheless, there was news that it is only a matter of time before North Korea secures such technology, since re-entry techniques into the atmosphere were developed 50 or 60 years ago.

In relation to this, James Clapper, the Director of US National Intelligence, announced at the Senate Intelligence Committee, January 2014 that North Korea expanded its uranium enrichment facility, reactivated the plutonium reactor and took the initial measure to arrange KN-08 (Hawsung-13), the mobile ICBM. The recently retired Commander of the Pacific Forces, Samuel Locklear, elaborated in his interview with the media that North Korea has the capability to directly strike US territory, and is taking steps to deploy its mobile ICBM.

South Korean Defense Minister Min-goo Han also announced at the National Assembly Defense Committee's inspection on December 27 that "it can be said that the DPRK's technological standard has been improving, considering that even North Korea publicized its achievements of a significant level attained from three nuclear tests." The USFK Commander Scaparrotti shared his view on DPRK in his visit to Washington for the ROK-US Security Consultative Meeting (SCM) on October 24, stating that he believed that North Korea is capable of miniaturizing nuclear weapons. Generally, manufacturing a nuclear bomb with a 1,000 kg warhead with 90 cm in diameter is a standard for miniaturization. This weight and size can be delivered by DPRK's SCUD-B missile, and this missile, with a range of 300 km, can reach most of the southern parts of the Korean Peninsula.

Ceaseless Weapons Buildup of Great powers – Security Dilemma

Even if some claim that the Six-Party Talks and the September 19 Mutual Declaration have failed to suppress the nuclear development by North Korea, three nuclear tests in 2006, 2009 and 2013 were conducted under the circumstance when all channels of communication had been cut off. Moreover, it is only plausible to assert that any policies and strategies that had replaced the Six-Party Talks have failed to weaken or deter nuclear threats by North Korea.

Instead of negotiations and meetings, military means such as the Kill-chain and the Korean Air and Missile Defense System (KAMD) have surfaced in South Korea. The budget to deter nuclear threats by North Korea has increased by 23 percent. The government determined that it will complete the Kill-chain system, which detects signs of a nuclear missile launch by North Korea and preemptively deters it, by mid-2020, and will invest 17 trillion KRW more for the KAMD, which can intercept nuclear missiles. Additionally, there are plans to procure the F-35A stealth fighters, Aegis destroyers, Global Hawks (unmanned surveillance vehicle), Apache attack helicopters and new ground-to-ground missiles as early as possible. Some 60 trillion KRW will be allocated to these projects until mid-2020. Furthermore, as North Korea comes closer to the level of combat arrangement that is beyond the possession of nuclear fissionable materials and their delivery systems, the United States and South Korea, in response, conducted an exercise to extend their deterrence capability by transporting mock nuclear weapons from an overseas base during the Key Resolve, Foal Eagle, and UFG exercises.

In reality, it is impossible to remove the DPRK's nuclear threats. Rather, such military responses by the United States and South Korea, employed on the assumption of nuclear threats, will eventually court an exhaustive arms race that justifies the logic of the DPRK's nuclear armament. For North Korea – a step behind American nuclear capabilities and sea-air power – it is quite obvious to accelerate nuclear development in order to overcome such asymmetry of strategic imbalance. Furthermore, if North Korea, with production lines for nuclear materials, takes a step further and produce mini-nukes and diversifies the delivery system for the mobile mid-range missiles, the high-tech deterrence method that requires an astronomical resources, will eventually defeat itself. The businessman who wants to sell leading-edge weapons can take advantage from such situations but they do not overcome the DPRK's nuclear threat. Those kinds of weapons cannot abolish nuclear threats ultimately, and deterrence of DPRK's nuclear is only achievable with countervailing nuclear weapons. Above all, a terrifying nuclear balance is already becoming a reality, as the United States promise to hold up the nuclear umbrella over the ROK as a means of extending deterrence.

We are currently faced with the situation that a true sense of diplomacy remains inoperative. The key element of Obama's policy towards North Korea in the 2008 presidential election was 'firm response and direct dialogue.' But the Obama administration's policy has turned into the twin track of 'dialogue and pressure.' There was no commitment to direct dialogue, and the effects of the sanctions were invisible, in spite of their robustness. The policy of "strategic patience" became obviously counterproductive, but the failure of the February 29 Deal undermined those in favor of negotiating with the DPRK on a realistic basis. Robert Carlin, who served as an officer in the Bureau of Intelligence and Research of the US Department of State, had once warned that "North Korean nuclear issues cannot be resolved from a hostile policy, but acting on the sidelines is the most dangerous." Indeed, strategic patience proved helpless in terms of halting the DPRK's nuclear empowerment, provocations and North-South military confrontations.

As a result of the implosion of the February 29 Deal, President Obama demonstrated moves which are more accurately described as strategic ignorance. As regards the resumption of the Six-Party Talks, his measures were an approach of 'all or nothing.' That is, nothing is possible unless North Korea agrees to abandon its nuclear programs. However, such a measure ignores North Korea and is analogous to simply hope that all problems will eventually fade away, by themselves. But North Korea will never disappear of its own accord. They still possess the nuclear weapons program. Thus, a critical moment when 'strategic patience' or ignorance cannot be tolerated will materialize. In other words, the juncture of doing nothing with having to do something will certainly arrive.

The Double Track of Sanctions and Negotiations

Even though Gallucci clarified that all policies to date toward North Korea have failed, his stance was strong: "diplomatic attempts are still in need, and as for North Korea, it is difficult to abandon nuclear programs, preparing military readiness and sanctions should also be included in the process of negotiations, and we must bring enlightenment in that provocations cannot parallel with negotiations." This stance highlights the fact that negotiations should be initiated as both sanctions and negotiations are required to response to the dual-track policy of North Korea.

Gallucci is a realistic negotiator. He contended that "it will never be possible to destroy DPRK's nuclear weapons until an irreversible situation occurs," and even with this fact he "supported an effort to resume dialogues without any preliminaries." That casts a long shadow in two regards. First of all, it is possible to confirm whether North Korea will put nuclear weapons on the negotiating table. Just like old times, North Korea will abstain from conducting further missile provocations or nuclear tests, at least while the negotiations are ongoing. This is because asserting the theory of uselessness of negotiation – "never reiterate the same words" – will produce a result that empowers DPRK's nuclear threats to become threatening.

With the exception of Gallucci, Stephen Bosworth, the Special Representative for North Korea Policy, Joel Wit, the former US State Department official, and Robert Carlin, the former officer in the Bureau of Intelligence and Research of US Department of State, all demanded that the Obama administration should embark on exploratory negotiations to ascertain the DPRK's will to denuclearize by demonstrating the flexibility of the US. Robert Einhorn, the Special Advisor for Nonproliferation and Arms Control, also shared the same view. He said in July 2014 that "a simple approach of simply managing North Korean issues is a risky strategy, so now is the time to contemplate deliberately on whether an active dialogue with North Korea will be in our interests or not." He particularly emphasized that "it is worthy to verify DPRK's will in restricting nuclear and missile programs in advance of the Six-Party Talks," and added that "the best way of achieving such a goal is to engage in exploratory discussions." Mr. Einhorn was once in the position of generalizing the policy on sanctions against North Korea during the first term of the Obama administration, so his views have particular weight—or should have—in the White House.

Reorganization and Reform of the Guideline of Obama's Policy toward North Korea

In this regard, recent reorganization of implementation of US policies on the Korean Peninsula by the Obama's administration opened up a new possibility in time of the necessity to seek out exploratory discussions.

Most of all, Sydney Seiler, the Korea Policy Chief at the White House National Security Council, was appointed to the Special Envoy for the Six-Party Talks under the Special Representative for North Korea Policy of the US Department of State in September 2014. The Special Envoy for the Six-Party Talks is a position that combines the functions of the Deputy Special Representative for North Korea Policy and that of the Deputy Representative in the Six-Party Talks. As this position had remained vacant for over a year since June 2013, some speculated that there was "no space for North Korea in Obama's consideration." As had been previously mentioned, Seiler made secret visits to North Korea with DeTrani in April and August 2012. In addition, Sung Kim was appointed as the US Ambassador to Seoul on 6 November, succeeding Glenn Davis, the former Special Representative for North Korea Policy for 3 years. Ambassador Sung Kim is an expert on the Korean Peninsula issues and had served as the Director of the Office of Korean Affairs and the Special Envoy for the Six-Party Talks, and served as the US Ambassador to South Korea from 2011 to October 2014. He was also the Deputy Assistant Secretary for Japan and South Korea of the Department of State. With Sung Kim's appointment to the Special Representative for North Korea Policy, the policy team for North Korea had been finally reformed in Obama's final two years. Seiler will be in charge of leading the resumption of the Six-Party Talks with the Special Representative Sung Kim. Allison Hooker, another expert on DPRK's nuclear issue, replaced Seiler on the National Security Council.

The New US Ambassador to Seoul, Mark Lippert, whose first remark was on the DPRK's nuclear issue, was the successor of Sung Kim. At 41 years, Mark Lippert is the youngest US Ambassador to Seoul and he became associated with President Obama as the Secretary on Security and

Foreign Policy since 2005. President Obama and Lippert share a special relationship, as Obama called him a 'brother.' Ambassador Lippert was widely considered as exerting influence over the policymaking process in the Obama administration since he served as the Assistant Secretary of Defense for Asian and Pacific Security Affairs and the Chief of Staff to the Secretary of Defense Chuck Hagel.

The Possibility for Exploratory-Preliminary Discussions

Considering reforms of policies toward North Korea on the occasion of James Clapper's visit to North Korea and the release of three Americans, the possibility of the exploratory-preliminary discussions had been raised.

Director Clapper, who had returned the detained Americans home through his visit to North Korea on November 11, 2014, announced in his interview with CBS on November 16 that "the reason of my appointment to the special envoy was due to the fact that North Korea requested a current officer in the White House NSC. North Korea, however, did not recognize me as President Obama's special envoy." He replied "keep an eye out" to the question on the future of US-DPRK relations. Additionally, he stated that he "hoped that this action taken by North Korea could promote US-DPRK relations."

In response to North Korea's demand on a political deal such as the former President's visit to North Korea in relation to the three American detainees – including Kenneth Bae – the United States resorted to the UN by presenting DPRK's human rights issue. Daniel Russell, the Assistant Secretary of State for East Asian and Pacific Affairs, reemphasized the importance of denuclearization and human rights issue in North Korea during the meeting with the media in New York on September 26. He also stressed that DPRK's nuclear, missile, human rights and the livelihoods of the public are inseparable. The US government brought DPRK's human rights issue in an earnest attempt to respond to the detention of the American citizens. By doing so, US raised the importance of human rights issue to the level of nuclear issues. In this regard, Clapper's visit to North Korea would have positive impacts on easing confrontations and resuming dialogues.

Nonetheless, evaluation from US experts on this outcome was different. During the press conference in the School of Advanced International Studies, Johns Hopkins University, Washington on November 11, 2014, Frank Jannuzi, the President of the Mansfield Foundation, explained the reason behind the DPRK's release of Americans, which was the fact that — besides pressures on human rights from the international society – it contrived a political step forward for the Six-Party Talks. Additionally, he foresaw that the Six-Party Talks could be reopened at the beginning of 2015 if North Korea agrees with the revised preconditions set by the United States. Jannuzi said,

> "The United States can ease preconditions for a resumption of the Six-Party Talks to such an extent in order for North Korea to agree. If North Korea suspends nuclear and missile tests and stops nuclear activities in Yongbyon, including uranium enrichment programs, the United Stateswill agree with the resumption of the Six-Party Talks, which is acceptable to North Korea."

Joel Wit, the former US State Department official on North Korean issues, was skeptical about such opinion. He argued that "an over-optimistic view has been given to the fact that the United States will remedy preconditions for the resumption of the Six-Party Talks and that North Korea will consent to that obediently." In short, even if preliminary discussions initiated, there is still a long way to go.

New Perspective and New Approach

Informed by such viewpoints, it is necessary to look at North Korea in a new way with a new approach. Joel Wit, who was the first secretary of Gallucci, explained the US policy toward North Korea as an approach of 'weak sanction' and 'weak diplomacy' in collaboration with President Lee for the last four years, and criticized it by stating that 'it did not work properly.' Wit also pointed out that "the Obama administration believed that it could control the DPRK's attitude without dialogues, by responding to their provocations with sanctions, but in reality, it not only reinforced DPRK's capability but also worsened the situation."

Wit argues that formulation of a policy is needed to combine 'strong sanction' and 'strong foreign policy.' He explained that since strong sanctions toward North Korea could not resolve the problems, what is urgently needed is direct communications with North Korea. In addition, he exerted that "the period of solving issues with only food and oil aid programs was over, and it is not the right answer. North Korea is seeking a way to resolve an issue concerning its national security. Thus, it is now the time to seriously work on a peace agreement based on what they want, and the abolition of the nuclear weapons program that US aspires to realize, through a direct dialogue."

The Boy and Wolf – Transition of the Perspective on DPRK's Nuclear Issues

The sacrifice of the sheep in Aesop's Fables originates from the shepherd boy's deceit. Even if the shepherd boy's last words were not lies, the village people never did pay attention to his words. In return, the death of a sheep occurred, which was detrimental to the village people, not the boy. Likewise, North Korea has lost their confidence in the international society, or they did not want to accept such a situation. However, the more they behaved in that manner, the more risky the sheep's life became. Just as the last words from the shepherd boy had been true, the story is indicative of the essence of the DPRK's nuclear threats.

Another lesson from Aesop's Fables is that it explains our prejudice. Farley Mowat contended the issue of dichotomy in Aesop's Fables. He is the respected author and environmentalist in Canada, whose book 'Never Cry Wolf' underlines another type of wolf that is quite different from the strange and horrible creature in Aesop's Fables. He had observed wild wolves for a long time, and wild wolves reveal their life styles as being part of nature. Nonetheless, wolves have become extinct due to excessive hunting by humans. The image of wild wolves as described in Aesop's Fables, which have become a common knowledge of the people, had never existed before. An image of a vicious and brutal killer of wolves is a false image. Mowat insists 'that is a shadow of our own.'

Turning the Image of the Wolf Over

Turning the image of the wolf over in Aesop's Fables is helpful in comprehending the North Korean nuclear issues, which signifies equating North Korea with the image of wild wolves and not that of the wolf in Aesop's Fables. In real life, there are no criteria to differentiate a lying shepherd boy from the good village people, and a good sheep from the wicked wolf.

Right after the declaration as a nuclear power state in February 2005, James Laney, the former US Ambassador to Seoul, and Jason Shaplen, a Policy Adviser of KEDO, raised a question on the Bush administration's policy in April 2005.

> "What will be your reaction if the US President takes the following measures against you? First, he designates you an axis of evil (other two are Iraq and Iran). Second, he pursues a preemptive war strategy against you. Third, he removes a leader of Iraq with this strategy, who turns out to have no possession of nuclear weapons. Fourth, if the US deters the European allies' plan to embrace Iran, which has less nuclear capabilities?" The answer will be "as cruel and immoral a man Kim Jong-il may be, he is not stupid. He merely acted as leaders of other countries would have in securing their leadership and the survival of their nations."

This comment from a US diplomat in regard to the North Korean nuclear issues hits the mark. A controversial point of the North Korean nuclear issues stems from the fact that the United States used it to exaggerate the DPRK's security threat, but failed to make an appropriate plan for the predictable outcome. Another diplomat said that "even though a coercive regime change is not an objective, how could providing some security assurance be problematic?" Strictly speaking, threats from the North Korean nuclear issues are based on the confrontation between the second Bush administration's hostile policies, such as the regime change strategy, and North Korea's attempt to procure nuclear weapons and nuclear deterrence in line with the survivor strategy. The dichotomy in differentiating a good sheep from the bad wolf only exists in Aesop's Fables, not in strategic reality.

The Final Round to End Nuclear Negotiations in the Past 20 Years

The word 'end game' in chess refers to the final stage that can finish the game within a few moves. In 2007, North Korean nuclear issues were close to an end game stage. In retrospect, North and South Korea achieved a result of national and global scale in the post-Cold War era with the June 15 Joint Declaration in 2000 and the September 19 2005 Joint Statement. It can be said that at that moment, the Korean Peninsula was close to the final stage in transcending the Cold War era – considering the fact that North and South Korea and its four neighboring counties brought about the October 4 Declaration on denuclearization via the February 13 and the October 3 Agreements in 2007, which stemmed from the September 19 Joint Statement.

A four-way talks or trilateral talks, which would declare the end of war as stipulated in the October 4 Declaration, are political decisions that could lead to the abolition of nuclear programs.

The second stage of denuclearization was of an ambiguous and terminal nature that stood between the third stage and first stage of denuclearization. It allowed North Korea to return to the previous stage if it failed to achieve the second stage. That is, the third stage of denuclearization is an irrevocable stage. Then US decision or assurance that it will abolish its hostile policies toward North Korea should be paralleled with a fulfillment of the third stage. President Roh Moo-hyun and Kim Jong-Il agreed that a declaration to end the war by the United States and China will politically guarantee the aforementioned.

As the United States and the Soviet Union opened a new era by declaring the end of Cold War in 1989, the essence of a declaration to end the war was conceived as a viable step to ushering in a new epoch on the Korean peninsula, as 'North Korea, China, South Korea and the United States are not adversaries to one other.' Since peace on the peninsula is unachievable without denuclearizing North Korea, the denuclearization can be made possible only with the resolution of antagonistic relations between North Korea and the United States, and North and South Korea. Nonetheless, a détente of antagonistic relations cannot be chieved in a single day. A declaration to end the war is both a gate to a new peace regime on the peninsula, as well as a guide to taking North Korea through the process of denuclearization. However, since President Bush enforced a definite advancement for denuclearization and President Lee worsened North Korea-South relations, the possibility of such a declaration has disappeared.

The process of denuclearization since 2008 remained in a parlous state that made the stage of abolishing nuclear programs impossible. Eventually, the issues regarding the North Korean nuclear programs and its verifications weighed down the Six-Party Talks, and the second stage collapsed unto itself.

In March 2009, right after the inauguration of the Obama administration, William Perry, former United States Secretary of Defense, announced that the reason for Stephen Bosworth's appointment to the Special Representative for North Korea Policy by President Obama was to restart negotiations with North Korea. However, the Six-Party Talks have been in a deadlock since the first Obama administration. Stephen Bosworth's visit to North Korea was made only once in December 2009. A chain of events – DPRK's long-range rocket launch and the second nuclear test, the Cheonan incident and Yeonpyeong Island attacks – led to the worst possible North-South relations.

Announcing a full-frontal confrontation, North Korea demanded an either/or decision of a war or peace. Strictly speaking, however, it was an attempt to force a decision to carry out the outcomes of the US-DPRK agreements in the past 20 years. In 2007, North Korea and the United States, plus four other countries in the talks, were already in the end game stage that could move on to the third stage of abolishing North Korea's nuclear program. There is now the need for a final negotiation, one that makes evident that it is the last one of its kind that will finally bring to conclusion the twemty years of fruitless nuclear negotiations. To achieve this, the Six-Party Talks as a venue for exploratory discussions is necessary, and only one chance remains for the Obama administration to achieve it.

PART III

CONCLUSION — KIM DAE JUNG AND BEYONDS

CHAPTER 10

TOWARD A NUCLEAR FREE AND PEACEFUL KOREA AND NORTH EAST ASIA: BEING ON THE RIGHT SIDE OF HISTORY[1]

Gareth Evans

Thank you, Professor Moon Chung-in, Executive Director of the Kim Dae-jung Presidential Library and Museum at Yonsei University, and Madame Lee Hee-ho, Chair of the Kim Dae- jung Peace Centre, for the honour and privilege of being invited to address this conference.

There is no Asian statesman that I, and I believe most of the international community, have held in higher regard, than the late President Kim Dae-jung. There could be no more better way of continuing to honour his legacy than convening this high-level conference series.And there could be no more appropriate topic to discuss than what needs to be done nowto achieve a nuclear-free and peaceful Korean Peninsula and wider North East Asian region.

Most national leaders are quickly forgotten, and rightly so, because most leave no lasting, significant mark on their country, their region or the wider world. Those who are *not* forgotten – who are remembered for decades, for generations – are of two basic kinds: those who are on the

[1] Address by Professor the Hon Gareth Evans AC QC, former Foreign Minister of Australia and President Emeritus of the International Group, to Conference Commemorating the 14th Anniversary of President Kim Dae-jung Winning the Nobel Peace Prize in 2000, Seoul, 10 December 2014.

right side of history and those who are not. The divide is between those who make the right calls at critical, pivotal moments in national or world history, the Lincolns, Gorbachevs and Mandelas – and those who don't, the Hitlers, Stalins, Maos and Milosevics; between the nation builders and the nation wreckers; between the human rights champions and the human rights destroyers; and between those who work to realise the full potential of every member of society and those who crush that potential.

President Kim Dae-jung was one of those unequivocally on the right side of history throughout his long public life: in opposition to Park Chung-hee (and at imminent risk of assassination by his agents); in opposition to Chun Doo-hwan (and under actual sentence of death by his courts); as a fearless supporter of democracy throughout three unsuccessful presidential election campaigns and a fourth triumphant one; and as a real implementer of democracy, of social and economic reform and development, and of political reconciliation with his former persecutors, during his five years in the Blue House. Above all he was on the right side of history as a visionary for peace, in his efforts to achieve a united and peaceful Korea coexisting productively and harmoniously with its North East Asian neighbours – for which he was, along with his democracy achievements, awarded the 2000 Nobel Peace Prize.

The questions I want to address with you now are what does it mean *now* to be on the right side of history in North East Asia generally, and on the Korean Peninsula in particular? What are the steps that can and should be taken by our present generation of political leadersthat will have future generations thinking of them, as do now of Kim Dae-jung, as true visionaries for peace, of builders not wreckers, of affirmers not oppressors of human dignity, of savers rather than destroyers of human life? Will future generations think on the right side of history those who believe that populist, nationalist drum-beating will serve them and their countries as well as a genuine commitment to cooperative security policymaking? Will history count more on the side of the angels those who seek to acquire or retain nuclear weapons, perhaps generally believing they are of real deterrent utility, or those who seek to eliminate them from world's arsenals once and for all?

Let me talk about these issues under three headings: first, the need for a cooperative security approach to the general geopolitics of North East Asia; second, the need to get serious once and for all about nuclear disarmament, and to rid ourselves of the illusion that nuclear weapons buy anyone real security; and third, the need to achieve a nuclear free and sustainably peaceful Korean Peninsula.

The Need for Cooperative Security

The idea of cooperative security has been round for a long time, but it's one of which we constantly need to remind ourselves, because it is the only rational and defensible way of conducting international relations in the contemporary world. It embraces a number distinct elements: the idea of *collective* security, inherent in the UN Charter itself, whereby member states renounce the use of force among themselves but are prepared to come collectively to the aid of any one of them attacked; the idea of *common* security, first articulated by the Palme Commission, that security is best achieved with others, rather than against them; and the idea of *comprehensive* security, that security in the modern age is multidimensional, and there are an ever-growingnumber of non-traditional, transnational threats to both state and human security – like terrorism, climate change, unregulated population flows and health pandemics – that depend on cooperative solutions because they are beyond the capacity of any one state, however big and powerful, to solve for itself.

What cooperative security demands in practice are mind-sets that emphasise consultation rather than confrontation, reassurance more than deterrence, transparency more than secrecy, prevention more than reaction, and interdependence rather than unilateralism. Translated into a North East Asian context, what this means for the various key players is something a little different from the messages that each of them have habitually put out. Getting on the right side of history will require each to do more – and some more than others.

For China, it means more consistent language like that the message elegantly articulated by President Xi Jinping in Australia recently – and behaviour in practice that is more consistent with that language. Xi told the Australian Parliament that he understood that China was seen as the "big guy in the crowd" and that others "may be concerned that the big guy may push them around, stand in their way or even take up their place": he argued that, on the contrary, what China needed most was both a stable domestic and peaceful international environment, that turbulence or war was utterly against its fundamental interests, that it was committed to peacefully addressing territorial and other disputes through dialogue and consultation, and that it wanted win-win progress with all its neighbours.

All fine words, but what President Xi did not explain was how these objectives would be served – to take one key benchmark issue – by China continuing to insist on roughly 80 percent of the South China Sea being its own "historic waters," continuing to resist articulating its claims in any way that make sense under the Law of the Sea Convention, and being utterly unwilling to have competing claims adjudicated in any court of international law. If a state wants to be seen as having a genuine commitment to a rules-based international order, it has to consistently act that way.

For the United States, being on the right side of history means, above all, psychologically adjusting itself to the reality that it is no longer the world's sole superpower, and recognizing that it really does need to give some strategic space to China through mutually accommodating cooperation. The best expression I have ever heard of the mindset required, was a comment I heard former President Bill Clinton make at a private function in Los Angeles in 2002:

> *The U.S. has two choices about how we use the great and overwhelming military and economic power we now possess. We can try to use it to stay top dog on the global block in perpetuity. Or we can use it to try to create a world in which we will be comfortable living when we are no longer top dog on the global block.*

More of that kind of rhetoric in public, with actions to match, rather than the assertions of continued US global and regional leadership, and determination to maintain absolute military dominance, which constantly flow out of Washington – would help a great deal in avoiding the US-China relationship ending in tears, as so many still fear it inevitably will.

For Russia, one can recognize all the sense of national humiliation in the immediate post-Cold War years which Vladimir Putin has been so adept at harvesting, and lament that the West was too triumphalist and insufficiently farsighted in those years in not building, as it should have, a new common security regime embracing rather than excluding Russia. But none of that begins to excuse Moscow throwing its weight around as it has in Ukraine, in defiance of every principle of a rule-based international order. One can only hope that economic pressure from falling oil prices and the eventual impact sanctions will bring it back to its senses, and that Russia will recognize that its interests – to its east and south as well as to its west – are better advanced by cooperation than confrontation.

For both Japan and South Korea, being on the right side of history means, for a start, escaping once and for all being *prisoners* of your history. Japan should long ago have put behind it, as has Germany, any suggestion that it is other than completely apologetic for its war of aggression in Asia and the atrocities that were then committed, but periodic side-stepping or backsliding, including leadership visits to the Yasukuni shrine, keep the issue unhappily alive, with Korea as with China. The Korean comfort women issue should long since have been resolved with Yohei Kono's gracious apology in 1993, but both sides keep scratching away at that scab. The periodically flaring dispute over ownership of the Dokdo/Takeshima islets and their surrounding waters should long ago have been resolved by legal adjudication or joint development negotiation, but it continues to stand in the way of South Korea and Japan having the fully developed alliance relationship they should.

For South Korea and Japan to be on the right side of history in the context of North East Asia security issues generally, and not just in their relations with each other, means I believe developing a degree of healthy independence, and not becoming totally caught up in the US-China power plays which will clearly be the main geostrategic dynamic in the period ahead. That does not for a moment mean relinquishing the alliance relationships with the US, which have been a strongly stabilizing factor in the region, but it does mean making considered, not reflex, judgments about issues as they arise, and working hard to develop deep and multi-layered engagement, both economic and political, with both sides.

It is perfectly appropriate for each country to build the defence capability it needs to be able to deal itself, to the maximum extent possible, with any security threat that may arise, and Japan's moves under Prime Minister Abe to free itself of some constitutional restrictions in this respect should be understood in that light. But should either Japan or South Korea seek to acquire military capability that is manifestly destabilizing, or creates much higher risks than any possible rewards – as would certainly be the case if either went nuclear, and I will come back to this issue – then they would very definitely be on the wrong side of history.

As to what North Korea needs to do put itself on the right side of history, there will be many who would no doubt think that for Pyongyang to embrace the kind of cooperative security approach I have been describing, much more than a change of mindset is required: more likely what is needed is a complete brain transplant! But that said, we have no option but to keep trying to drag North Korea back into the community of civilised and responsible nations, and I will return later to the whole question of the future of the Korean peninsula.

For nearly all the other players I have mentioned there have been a number of encouraging signs that a cooperative security approach is gaining some traction. The joint announcement by Presidents Obama and Xi, in the margins of the November APEC summit on Beijing, on targets for cutting greenhouse-gas emissions, which was then leveraged into a G20 commitment a week later, is a breakthrough that will transform the dynamics of the whole global climate debate. Hopefully this will be a prelude to more thaws in other areas, building on the significant amount of senior-level strategic dialogue between US and China which has in fact been occurring, largely behind the scenes, in recent years.

At the same APEC summit we saw China and Japan take an important step toward rapprochement, or at least defusing some of the acute tension which had been building up over the Senkaku/Diaoyu islands and other longstanding issues. As to China's relations with South Korea, as you will know better than me, these have been rapidly intensifying economically and are currently better politically than they have been for a long time – following the Xi visit here in July, before he visited the North.

As to the remaining key bilateral relationship in this region, between South Korea and Japan, one of the enduring frustrations of your friends is that it is not nearly as close and cooperative as it could and should be. Of course you both have to tiptoe around strongly held nationalist sentiments on the history issues I have mentioned. But it should be clear that the benefits of a full and comprehensive rapprochement would outweigh any possible risks, contribute significantly to the general stability of the region, be helpful in addressing the ongoing North Korean issueand certainly help to advance specific regional projects like President Park Gyeun-hye's proposed Asian EURATOM organization to address civil nuclear energy issues. There have been some small signs in recent months that both sides are willing to work toward that, with next year's 50th anniversary of the establishment of South Korea-Japan relations, but a more sustained and substantial effort in this respect would be very welcome.

The Need to Get Serious About a Nuclear Weapons Free World

There is no single issue about which it is more important to apply the cooperative security approach I have been describing than nuclear arms control. Whatever the nature and intensity of unresolved tensions may prove to be between various major players in North East Asia, it is impossible to believe that greater emphasis on nuclear weapons will improve the situation for anyone. But old habits of thought about nuclear weapons, and nuclear deterrence in particular, die very hard in this region. To be on the right side of history is not be stuck, as a great many policymakers in this region seem to be, in a Cold War time-warp, but to recognize that whatever conceivable stabilizing role nuclear weapons may have played in the past, that time is now over.

The arguments against nuclear weapons start with their human and environmental impact. They are, simply, the most indiscriminately inhumane weapon ever invented, and *any* use of them in any circumstances is a morally indefensible challenge to our common humanity. And they do constitute a threat to life on this planet. Even a relatively small-scale regional nuclear exchange between India and Pakistan – a perfectly imaginable scenario given the continuing volatility of that relationship – has been calculated as likely to cause one billion or more deaths worldwide because of the nuclear winter effect.

But of course the hard-headed policymakers know all that. And some of them go so far as to say the awfulness of nuclear weapons is what makes them so effective as a deterrent. What *they* need to be persuaded about are the *strategic* arguments against nuclear weapons: that in fact they are at best of minimal, and at worst of zero, utility in maintaining stable peace. And that keeping nuclear stockpiles – even if you don't ever intend to use them except by way of retaliation if attacked – is not in fact a risk-free enterprise. They have to be persuaded that the benefits of nuclear weapons are negligible, and far outweighed by the risks involved. The good news for those who care about our children's and our planet's survival, is that there are plenty of good, persuasive arguments to make. They just have to be drummed into the heads of our policymakers.

Let me begin with the risks. Even if there is only a negligible likelihood that nuclear weapons will ever be deliberately and cold-bloodedly used as weapons of attack, no one should think for a moment that there is no risk associated with their possession. So long as any are retained by anyone, the risk really is acutely real of stumbling into a nuclear exchange through accident, miscalculation, system error, or sabotage, and any such exchange would be potentially catastrophic for life on this planet as we know it. Whatever the utility of nuclear deterrence might be thought to be, it has always been an extremely fragile basis for maintaining stable peace.

There is, and always has been, a major risk not only of human error or misjudgement under stress, but of miscommunication (the risks here now compounded by the sophistication of cyber weapons) and of basic system error, with harmless events being read as threatening (as, e.g. in 1995 with Russia's President Boris Yeltsin advised that he should immediately retaliate against an incoming NATO missile, which proved to be a Norwegian scientific rocket launch).

Much archival evidence of the Cold War years – when command and control systems on both sides were thought to be highly sophisticated, and were more so than are some between potential nuclear adversaries today – has now revealed how close to calamity the world regularly came, much more so than was understood at the time. It is not a matter of good policy or good management that the world has avoided a nuclear weapons catastrophe for nearly seventy years: it is sheer dumb luck. These risks are dramatically compounded when nuclear armed states maintain nuclear weapons on dangerously high "launch-on-warning" alert status – as is still the case, more than two decades years after the end of the Cold War, for some 1,800 weapons in the US and Russian arsenals.

Moreover, new technical developments may make old calculations redundant. There is a risk, in particular, that new generation long-range conventional attack weapons, and missile defence systems – of the kind that the US seems determined to develop, and which are genuinely troubling policymakers in Russia and China – will be so sophisticated and powerful as to create real doubts in states' minds about the survivability of their retaliatory, second-strike capability. In an extreme crisis situation this could encourage such states to strike first; and at the very least is likely to encourage them to expand their nuclear armouries, with all the potential that has for setting off new nuclear arms races.

Given the scale of these risks, what is the force of the arguments for nuclear weapons that so many policymakers seem to be persuaded by? The answer is: not very great. None of the main arguments in favour of the utility of nuclear deterrence have, on closer examination, anything like the force they usually seen to possess.

The first and most common argument is that nuclear weapons have deterred, and will continue to deter, war between the major powers – that the balance of nuclear terror between the United States and the Soviet Union maintained peace throughout the Cold War, and has done so since between other potential pairs of belligerents, including India and Pakistan, India and China, and China and the United States.

While nuclear weapons on the other side have always constituted a formidable argument for caution – and fear of their possible use was obviously crucial, for example, in securing the back-downs on both sides that ended the Cuban missile crisis – their impact has been much exaggerated. Certainly, there is simply no evidence that at any stage during the Cold War years either the Soviet Union or the United States ever wanted to cold-bloodedly initiate war, and were only constrained from doing so by the existence of the other's nuclear weapons.

We know that knowledge of the existence on the other side of supremely destructive weapons (as with chemical and biological weapons before 1939) has not stopped war in the past between major powers. Nor has the experience or prospect of massive damage to cities and killing of civilians caused leaders in the past to back down – including after Hiroshima and Nagasaki, where the historical evidence is now very strong that it was not the nuclear attacks which were the key factor in driving Japan to sue for peace, but the Soviet declaration of war later that same week. Although the context there was different – terminating an existing war rather than deterring a new one – the point remains that concern about being on the receiving end of the extreme destructive power of nuclear weapons may not be, in itself, nearly as decisive for decision-makers as usually presumed. Other explanations may be more important.

A plausible *non*-nuclear explanation for the "Long Peace" since 1945 is that what has stopped – and will continue to stop – the great powers from deliberately starting wars each other is, more than anything else, a realization, after the experience of World War II and in the light of all the rapid technological advances that followed it, that the damage that would be inflicted by *any* war would be unbelievably horrific, and far outweighing, in today's economically interdependent world, any conceivable benefit to be derived.

A second familiar argument for the strategic utility of nuclear weapons is that they will deter large-scale conventional attacks. But there is a long list of examples where non-nuclear powers have either directly attacked nuclear powers or have not been deterred by the prospect of their intervention: e.g. the Korea, Vietnam, Yom Kippur, Falklands, two Afghanistan and first Gulf wars. The calculation evidently made in each case was that a nuclear response would be inhibited by the prevailing taboo on the use of such weapons (on which more below), at least in circumstances where the very survival of the state was not at stake.

Of course some smaller states, and North Korea is the most obvious example, do seem to think that a handful of nuclear weapons is their ultimate guarantor against external regime-change-motivated intervention. But that confidence is not well-founded. Weapons that it would be manifestly suicidal to use are not a credible deterrent, nor are weapons that are not backed by the infrastructure (e.g. missile submarines) that would give them a reasonable prospect of surviving to mount a retaliatory attack. In the case of North Korea, its strongest military deterrent remains what it has always been: its capacity to mount a devastating conventional artillery attack on Seoul and its environs.

We are hearing again now plenty of the old argument from pro-nuclear weapons advocates saying that Ukraine would not be in the trouble it is now if it had not given up its nuclear weapons in 1994 on the dissolution of the Soviet Union. But Vladimir Putin knows that if he drives his tanks into Donetsk or even further west, a nuclear-armed Kiev would be no more likely to mount a nuclear strike against it than Washington would. The evidence of history strongly suggests that nuclear weapons simply do not act as stabilizing tools in the real world: simply because the risks associated with their deliberate use are so high, they just do not act as a deterrent to the kind of adventurism we are now seeing in Ukraine. The one thing that Ukrainian nuclear weapons *would* have added to today's mix is another huge layer of potential hazard: from all the risks of system error and human error – miscalculation, misjudgement, mistake – that are associated with the possession of nuclear weapons by anyone, a point I will come back to.

There are also cases where the presence on both sides of nuclear weapons, rather than operating as a constraining factor, has been seen as giving one side the opportunity to launch small military actions without serious fear of nuclear reprisal (because, again, of the extraordinarily high stakes involved in such a response): as with Pakistan in Kargil in 1999, and North Korea in the sinking of the Cheonan and shelling of Yeonpyeong Island in 2010. It may be that – rather than, as the old conservative line would have it, "the absence of nuclear weapons would make the world safe for conventional wars" – it is the *presence* of nuclear weapons that has made the world safer for such wars. There is substantial quantitative, as well as anecdotal, evidence to support what is known in the literature as the "stability/instability paradox" – the notion that what may appear a stable nuclear balance actually encourages more violence under the shelter of the nuclear overhang.

The general point in all of this is that nuclear weapons are inherently *unusable* – and because key players know that, even if so many are reluctant to openly concede it, nuclear deterrence has nothing like the power it is commonly assumed to have. Military commanders have long understood that there are formidable practical obstacles involved in the use (and by extension threatened use) of these weapons at both the tactical and strategic level, not least the damage they can cause to one's own side and to any territory being fought over.

Beyond the practical obstacles, even the most hard-headed policymakers have to take seriously the profound *normative taboo* which unquestionably exists internationally against any use of nuclear weapons, at least in circumstances where the very survival of a state is not at stake. Since the early 1950s – when it began to sink in that their destructive capacity really was infinitely greater than anything previously seen – such deliberate use has been seen as inconceivable by the leaders of any country thinking of itself, as civilized, and wanting to be thought so by others. Presidents Truman, Eisenhower and Kennedy rejected military advice to use nuclear weapons in the Korean War, the Taiwan Straits crisis, and the Cuban missile crisis, and the force of the taboo has if anything since grown. Even John Foster Dulles said that if the United States had used nuclear weapons in Korea, Vietnam or against China over Taiwan, "we'd be finished as far as present-day world opinion was concerned."

So what does it mean for South Korean policymakers to be on the right side of history when it comes to nuclear weapons? And what does it mean for the other major US ally in this region, Japan? It means, for a start, not even beginning to succumb to the temptation to acquire nuclear weapons of your own, despite the continuing enthusiasm of some public figures like Chung Mong-joon for going down that path, and some opinion-poll evidence of greater public support than one would see in Japan, where antinuclear sentiment has been historically much stronger.

Not only would going down this path involve you in tearing up your solemn treaty obligations under the NPT with all the international condemnation that would bring; not only would it involve you spending huge sums of money building weapons systems that would in practice be unusable for all the reasons I have already spelled out, and at the same time carry all the risks I have described; but, so long at least as you enjoy an strong alliance relationship with the United States, and all the security assurances that go with that, there is no conceivable reason for you to do so.

I would make this point just as strongly if the US had no nuclear weapons at all, as I hope one day it will not. What matters for South Korea and Japan, and indeed other US allies in this part of the world, including my own country Australia, and in Europe – who feel, as all of us do, that there are some conceivable military threats we might face in the future that we might not be able to meet entirely on our own – is that we benefit from the *extended deterrence* that the US provides us. And what that means in practice is that we benefit from the US's extraordinarily formidable conventional military capability. What matters to us is not the so called nuclear umbrella but rather that conventional umbrella, which is overwhelmingly capable of dealing with any conceivable threat contingency – be it posed by conventional weapons, by chemical or biological weapons, or even nuclear weapons.

The reality of this conventional protection means that there is something more that we US allies can do to be on the right side of history, making our own contribution to achieving a nuclear weapons free world. I strongly believe that those of us US allies, including my own country, who are presently sheltering – or believing that we are sheltering – under the US nuclear umbrella, should be prepared to make clear our acceptance of a much reduced role for nuclear weapons in our protection.

Of course it is the case that so long as any nuclear weapons continue to exist, in the hands of China, Russia, North Korea or anyone else it is not unreasonable for us to want to be able to rely on US nuclear protection for *nuclear* threat contingencies. Although I personally believe, as I have already indicated, that the arguments for the utility of nuclear deterrence have been grossly exaggerated, I have to acknowledge that there is some psychological comfort involved in being able to retaliate in kind against nuclear attack, and that, for Japan and South Korea particularly, the continued availability of the US nuclear umbrella to defend against nuclear threat contingencies has been politically important in stilling those voices who would like to see each country develop a nuclear weapons capability of its own.

But when it comes to *non*-nuclear threat contingencies, whether they involve chemical or biological or conventional or cyber weapons, surely it is time for us all to step back. We know that, with the US help on which we can all reasonably rely, we have the capacity for the indefinitely foreseeable future to deal with any such contingency, however severe, through the application of *conventional* military force. And we should now all say so, in so many words. Because so long as we continue to insist that the nuclear option be kept open for a variety of non-nuclear threat contingencies, notwithstanding our collective capacity to deal with them by non-nuclear means, we are contributing absolutely nothing but rhetoric to the achievement of a nuclear-free world. Extended deterrence, I repeat, does not have to mean extended *nuclear* deterrence.

The Obama administration has wanted its Asian and European allies to go down the path of accepting a declaration by it that the 'sole purpose' of the US nuclear arsenal is to deter a nuclear attack, not any other kind. This formulation does not go quite as far as a 'No First Use' declaration, but is a long way down that path, and as such would be an extremely important doctrinal shift, and a crucial way-station on the road to nuclear abolition. In the context of the lead-up to its 2010 US Nuclear Posture Review, the then Labor Government in Australia indicated it could live with a 'sole purpose' formulation, and in Japan the then DPJ Foreign Minister Katsuya Okada also dipped at least a toe in that water in a 2009 letter to Secretary of State Hilary Clinton.

But any such move was halted, I'm sorry to say, by the resistance of South Korea, led by its military, and a number of Washington's NATO allies in Central and Eastern Europe. The 2010 NPR ends up saying no more on the subject than that while the United States is 'not prepared at the present time to adopt a universal policy that deterring nuclear attack is the sole purpose of nuclear weapons… [it] will work to establish conditions under which such a policy could be safely adopted.' And nothing has happened since, other than the recent adventurism of Russia in Ukraine no doubt making it harder than ever to persuade Central and Eastern Europeans that they can live comfortably with less nuclear protection, and recent heightened tensions with China and North Korea in this region no doubt having a similar effect here.

A more robust commitment by South Korea and Japan to really leading the way on nuclear disarmament – not just through general rhetoric but by adopting specific path-breaking policies – would I believe pay real dividends. I know it is easier, psychologically and politically, for Australians than others who live in more troublesome neighbourhoods to play a leadership role in this respect. But I really believe that all of us, acting together, could add very considerable momentum to the disarmament cause if we were to come out strongly in favour of the United States adopting a declaration that the "sole purpose" of nuclear weapons was to deter nuclearattack, and better still if we were to argue explicitly for Washington adopting a "No First Use" posture.

For us to continue to be as hypocritical as, frankly, we have been – arguing that everyone else do as we say, but not as we do, when it comes to reliance on nuclear weapons for our security protection – certainly does not help the non-proliferation agenda. And it certainly does not begin to be a recipe for reducing the terrible risks that the world continues to face so long as any nuclear weapons remain anywhere. It's time for us not just to talk, but to act.

The Need For a Nuclear Free and Peaceful Korean Peninsula

In turning now to the specific question of how to achieve a nuclear free and sustainably peaceful Korean Peninsula, we have to disentangle and try to prioritise three distinct policy objectives in relation to North Korea, and the means that are realistically available to advance each of them, recognizing that strategies designed to advance one objective may in practice actually be counterproductive to the achievement of others.

The first is to avoid conflict between North and South, and to create the conditions for peaceful unification; the second is to reverse North Korea's nuclear weapons program and denuclearize the peninsula; and the third is to redress the atrocity crimes and other indefensible human rights violations occurring in the North. There are differing constituencies internationally and domestically, as one would expect, for these different objectives, and when it comes to implementing them, different emphases on the virtues of sticks (sanctions and the like) and carrots (various kinds of engagement strategy).

China strongly supports 'no war, no instability, no nukes,' but is concerned (although probably less now than it used to be) about the strategic implications of unification – and quite unmoved by human rights abuses.

The West would support all three objectives, with human rights violations being a relatively recent addition to the list, being unable any longer to be ignored as a result of the definitive recent report of the UN Commission of Inquiry on Human Rights in the DPRK led by Australian Justice Michael Kirby. Within South Korea there is clearly support for all three objectives, but with considerable differences of emphasis, as to both priorities and means of implementation, being evident over time as between conservative and progressive governments.

It is very difficult in practice to keep the three strands separate, not least when Pyongyang is so dedicated to mixing them up (as when last month it not only threatened another nuclear test but nuclear war in retaliation for the UN General Assembly's human rights committee calling for the Security Council to refer the DPRK to the International Criminal Court). But I agree with the excellent recent Stanford study by Shin, Straub and Lee, which I note has been presented to the National Assembly and received some bipartisan support here, that we should try to de-link nuclear and non-nuclear issues so far as possible.

A Nuclear Free Peninsula

On the question of reversing North Korea's nuclear weapons program, and achieving the denuclearization of the peninsula, I have had some experience of the frustration of these negotiations, having been involved as Australia's Foreign Minister, albeit at some distance, in the negotiation and implementation of the 1994 Agreed Framework. I am less persuaded than some others that all the blame for the breakdown of that first agreement belongs to Pyongyang: our side dragged our feet in building the nuclear reactors and delivering the heavy fuel oil we promised, partly owing to a widespread belief that the regime's collapse was imminent.And when a diplomatic trajectory was re-established a few years later, that was immediately crushed by George W. Bush's "Axis of Evil" declaration in 2002.

The course of events since then has not been encouraging. Since confirming its withdrawal from the NPT in 2003 it has been actively developing and testing nuclear weapons and missile delivery systems, and probably now has up to ten explosive devices in stock which it is getting closer than ever to being able to deliver over long distances. The Six-Party Talks (bringing together North and South Korea with the US, China, Japan and Russia) have been stalled since 2009, and the situation further complicated by Pyongyang's regularly adopting a posture of extreme belligerence with which we are all wearily familiar.

But all that said I don't think that the situation is totally hopeless. I don't think it is naïve to believe that the North Korean regime has no intent to ever aggressively use the nuclear devices it now hasor may build in the future: it is erratic, irresponsible and deeply unpleasant, but it is not completely irrational, and knows that any such use and the South, Japan or the US would be completely suicidal. The reasons for developing them seem to be primarily that they think they will deter attack and bolster the regime's credibility at home and abroad. Pyongyang has used its weapons capability as bargaining chip in the past, and I don't think it impossible that it could enter into a denuclearization bargain in the future if given in return security guarantees in which it can genuinely believe, the normalization of its diplomatic relations, sanctions relief and an appropriately generous economic support package.

The question is how now to get to that bargain, and how long we can wait. The basic posture that the United States has adopted has been described as 'strategic patience' - essentially old-fashioned containment and deterrence. It has been unwilling to negotiate with North Korea in a Six-Party or any other framework, partly because there is no trust that it will deliver on any agreement and partly because it doesn't want to appear to give any ground to its claim to be now a legitimate nuclear weapons state.

But while containment and deterrence are absolutely legitimate strategies in this context, with all the supporting measures like sanctions and the Proliferation Security Initiative that have been accompanying them, they must be accompanied by a serious willingness to leave the door open for negotiations. Letting the situation drag on indefinitely is not risk free. Not only is North Korea improving its capability all the time, but even in the absence of deliberate use, there are all the risks, already discussed, of human and system error, miscalculation and misjudgement associated with any possession of any nuclear weapons anywhere, and particularly in a volatile environment like the Korean Peninsula. The Six-Party Talks remain the best available vehicle for such negotiations, and it is important that united international pressure be maintained for their resumption on an unconditional basis, and that the US fundamentally re-think its position in this respect. To do so would place it on the right side of history.

If talks can be started there are a number of scenarios as to how all the necessary pieces might be brought together. The most comprehensive, and I believe attractive, is that proposed by former senior US official Morton Halperin, which involves a new Treaty on Peace and Security in North East Asia with the following elements: termination of the state of war in Korea; a permanent monitoring council; mutual declaration of no hostile intent; provisions of assistance for nuclear and other energy; and, most ambitiously, establishment of a North East Asia Nuclear Weapons Free Zone, embracing both Koreas and Japan, which all the NPT nuclear-weapon states would agree to abide by. Protection would be given to South Korea and Japan by their having the right within a certain period to withdraw from the Treaty if its denuclearization provisions were not being effectively implemented.

All this is ambitious, but not impossible if the political will is there. And whether there is that political will can only be established if we are prepared to seriously test the ground.

A Peaceful Peninsula

While the key players on the nuclear front will be the United States and the other Six-Party Talks members, the key player in initiating strategies to keep the peninsula peaceful and moving toward ultimate unification is clearly South Korea itself. The most thoughtful and comprehensive proposal I have seen for how this might best be done is the Shin, Straub and Lee Stanford study, which advocates a policy of "tailored engagement."

Their idea is to establish a new high-level policy supremo with overall charge of a policymaking and delivery process which would be built on cross-party domestic consensus, be measured in pace, and focus on developing a number of dimensionsof practical North-South engagement–clearing away obstacles to eventual unification rather than promoting unification as such. The kinds of engagement proposed involve humanitarian activities; educational exchanges; cultural exchanges covering everything from sport to food; economic engagement through trade and investment, even if this might be seen as cutting across some of the international sanctions regimes; and developmental engagement, particularly in building northern infrastructure.

An important and necessary ice-breaking measure to get moving a new and more positive phase in the North-South relationship would be to wind back the May 24th measures of 2010, whereby the administration of President Lee Myung-bak suspended inter-Korean economic cooperation in an understandable and reasonable response to the egregious sinking of the ROKS *Cheonan*. Very far-reaching in their impact, and making it impossible to implement most of the elements of the tailored engagement approach just described, these measures do seem to stand in the way of implementing President Park's own trust-building, or step-by-step confidence building, and it is to be hoped that her administration yields some ground in this respect. To do so would place her on the right side of history.

In the context of the new international focus on North Korea's appalling human rights record – about which Pyongyang is obviously very sensitive, as its mini charm-offensive demonstrated for a few months this year as it tried to hold off an adverse UN vote – there will be those who will argue that any kind of new attempts at engagement by the South will be at odds with the need to keep the North under pressure. I think a better answer is that proposed, again, by Shin, Straub and Lee, when they suggest that South Korea would be better leaving the international running on human rights violations to others (while not hesitating to support appropriate resolutions,) and concentrating internally on providing humanitarian and other targeted assistance to those in most human rights need.

I am well aware that it is not easy either in principle, or in political practice, to reconcile some of the competing imperatives when one is trying simultaneously to pressure North Korea into abandoning its nuclear program, stopping its appalling record of human rights abuse, and at the same time trying to create a constructive environment, and a web of engaged economic and other relationships, which will build trust and confidence to the point that peaceful unification will ultimately be achievable. And there is always the risk that whatever progress is felt to be made, it may be undone overnight by some new egregious Northern provocation.

But ultimately these objectives do converge, in a sense that a North Korea which has a confident, trusting and mutually beneficial set of economic and other relationships with the South will be much less inclined to think it needs nuclear weapons for its protection, or hopefully, that it needs to oppress its own people.

This was the vision that we know drove the late President Kim Dae-jung, He did more than any other leader before or after him to bridge the division of North and South. His dream of reunification is one we can all share. He was a true visionary for peace in every sense of that phrase. But he was nobody's pushover. His idealism and his optimism was not in any way a product of naivete. His "sunshine" policy was a pragmatic blend of incentivisation and engagement that recognised the critical importance of direct contact between the governmentsand peoples of North and South.

He understood and applied the basic principles of cooperative security. He understood all too well that peace-making is a messy process and that we must deal with the facts as they are, and not as we would like them to be. But he didn't just drift along, waiting for something to happen. He made things happen, and he was prepared to take the risks necessary to produce the rewards. He was a man who in everything he said and did was on the right side of history.

Kim Dae-jung's approach has never been more needed than now, and I express my thanks and gratitude once again for being given this opportunity to honour the memory of this great Korean, and great international, statesman.

Biography

Chung-in Moon

Professor Chung-in Moon is an executive director of Kim Dae-Jung Presidential Library and Museum and a professor of political Science of Yonsei University. He is an academic and political analyst with an unrivalled breadth of experience in contemporary Korean politics and international relations. He is also a former chairman of the Presidential Committee on the Northeast Asian Cooperation Initiative, a cabinet-level post, and has served as Ambassador for International Security Affairs at the South Korean Ministry of Foreign Affairs and Trade. He has published more than 40 books and 230 articles in edited volumes and scholarly journals, and is a recipient of the Public Policy Scholar Award from the Woodrow Wilson International Center, the Lixian Scholar Award from Peking University, and the Pacific Leadership Fellowship from UCSD.

Peter Hayes

Professor Peter Hayes has been an environment, energy and security consultant working for international and American government agencies in more than twenty countries since 1975. Hayes creates and applies near-term solutions to the nexus of global security, environment and energy policy problems, with an emphasis on innovative cooperative engagement strategies in North Korea, East Asia, Australia, and South Asia. He covers scientific, technical, institutional, and geopolitical aspects of energy security, global nuclear insecurity (including risks of nuclear proliferation and nuclear next-use), and inter-city collaboration for urban climate change adaptation. He has visited North Korea seven times.

Choon-geun Lee

Dr. Choon-geun Lee is currently a Senior Researcher at Science and Technology Policy Institute, Technical Expert at the Presidential Committee for Unification Preparation, Policy Consultant for the Ministry of Unification, and Consultant for The National Unification Advisory Council. Previously, he was a visiting fellow at Asia-Pacific Research Center, Peking University Science and Society Research Center, and Institute of Policy and Management, Chinese Academy of Sciences. He received a Ph. D in Engineering from Seoul National University and a Ph. D in Education from the Beijing University of Education. His main publications include Science and Technology of North Korea, Reading North Korean Nuclear Power with Science and Technology, and Understanding the North Korean System (Science and Technology).

Han Hua

Professor Han Hua is Associate Professor and Director of the Center for Arms Control and Disarmament at the School of International Studies (SIS), Peking University, China. She teaches courses in International Relations in South Asia, International Arms Control, Disarmament and Nonproliferation, and US Politics and Foreign Policy. Her research interests cover South Asia and arms control and nonproliferation.Han Hua has been a visiting researcher at School of International Affairs, Georgia Institute of Technology, USA, The Stockholm International Peace Research Institute (SIPRI), Sweden, The Stimson Center and Monterey Center for Nonproliferation in Washington D.C. and Monterey, The Victoria University, Canada, and the Peace and Conflict Institute, Uppsala University, Sweden. She has also written extensively on Arms Control, nonproliferation and South Asia for journals and newspapers in China and abroad.

Won-young Yang Lee

Ms. Won-young Yang Lee is an environmental activist of Korea. She is in charge of energy policy and denuclearization policy at the Korea Federation for Environmental Movements. Her activities have focused on informing the public that it is the most economic policy to stop the nuclear reactors while they are still safe and that Korea will be better off without them. She has a B.A. in Biology and M.A. in Public Policy and Management. Her main publications include Denuclearization in One Book (Korean) and Talbaggeum—A World that Changes and Dreams through

Denuclearization (Korean).

Hiromichi Umebayashi

Director Hiromich Umebayashi is the founder and the President of the Peace Depot, a non-profit organization based in Yokohama, Japan and has Ph. D. in applied physics. He also serves as the International Coordinator of the Pacific Campaign for Disarmament and Security (PCDS), a Pacific regional network for disarmament, the Editor-in-Chief of Nuclear Weapon and Nuclear Test Monitor, a bi-weekly Japanese publication which covers regional security and nuclear issues, a member of the Middle Powers Initiative (MPI) International Steering Committee, and the East Asian Coordinator of the Parliamentarian Network for Nuclear Disarmament (PNND). He is known as one of the key leaders of the well-known 1972 massive civil movement in Japan to resist the transportation of the U.S. Army tanks from the U.S. Army Sagami Depot, Japan to the Vietnam War field. He is the author of many books, including "The Aim of the US Forces Realignment," "The US Forces Japan," and is the co-author of "Nuclear Disarmament in 21st Century", "Regional Security in Northeast Asia - From the Rule of US Forces to Rule of Law", "A Northeast Asia Nuclear-Weapon-Free-Zone," and a frequent contributor to major progressive Japanese periodicals, including "Sekai," "Gunshuku," and "Ronza."

Yoon-won Park

Professor Yoon-won Park is a professor of Nuclear Power and Quantum Electronics at KAIST. Since 2015, he has been appointed as the International Consultant for FANR (Federal Authority for Nuclear Regulation) for UAE. Previously, he has served as the Head of the Department of Safety Policy, Head of International Cooperation Division and as the President of KINS (Korea Institute of Nuclear Safety). While working at KINS, he had served as an international leader in the area of nuclear safety on various occasions as the Chair of ANSN (Asia Nuclear Safety Network), Chair of RCF (Regulatory Cooperation Forum), and Vice Chair for OECD/NEA Committee on Nuclear Regulatory Activities. He received his B.A. in Mechanical Design from Seoul National University and his Ph. D from *Ecole Centralle Paris*, France.

Wooksik Cheong

Director Wooksik Cheong is the director of Peace Network, Korea. He is also an editor of Pressian, and a head of operation of Civil Peace Forum. He received his B.A. in Political Science in Korea University and M.A. in the North Korean Studies from the University of North Korean Studies. His key publications include Real Face of Missile Defense (Korean), World History of Nuclear Power (Korean), Global Armageddon (Korean), and The Direction of 21C Korea-US Alliance (Korean).

Taeho Kang

Mr. TaehoKang is a senior reporter on inter-Korean relations. After receiving his M.A. in Economics from Seoul National University, he has dealt with topics on the Korean Peninsula including inter-Korean relations for twenty years at the Hankyorae as the head of Unification Department. His key works include translations for America's Global Strategy and Korea Endgame and authoring Inquiring about Corvette Cheonan (Korean), Northern Route Report (Korean), as well as various contributions to Changbi Publishers.

Gareth Evans

Professor Gareth Evans is Chancellor of the Australian National University. He was a Cabinet Minister in the Hawke and Keating Labor Governments and Foreign Minister. During his 21 years in Australian politics he was Leader of the Government in the Senate (1993-96) and Deputy Leader of the Opposition in the House of Representatives (1996-98). From 2000 to 2009 he was President and CEO of the Brussels-based International Crisis Group, the independent global conflict prevention and resolution organisation. He has participated in the publication of 12 books - including Nuclear Weapons: The State of Play 2015(co-author), Inside the Hawke-Keating Government: A Cabinet Diary (2014), and The Responsibility to

Protect: Ending Mass Atrocity Crimes Once and for All (2008); has published many newspaper articles and over 100 journal articles and chapters on foreign relations, human rights and legal and constitutional reform; has honorary doctorates from Melbourne, Sydney, Carleton and Queen's Universities; and has lectured at many universities around the world, including Oxford, Cambridge, Princeton, Yale, Stanford and the Central European University.

REFERENCES

Albright, David, and Corey Hinderstein. "Cooperative Verified Dismantlement of Nuclear Programs: An Eye Toward North Korea." Paper presented at the Institute for Nuclear Materials Management Annual Conference, June 1, 2003, http://isis-online.org/conferences/detail/cooperative-verified-dismantlement-of-nuclear-programs-an-eye-toward-north-/10.

_____, and Serena Kelleher-Vergantini. "Yongbyon: Centrifuge Enrichment Plant Expands while 5 MWe Reactor is Possibly Shut Down." *ISIS Imagery Brief*, October 3, 2014.

Blechman, Barry, and Russel Rumbaugh. "Bombs Away: The Case for Phasing Out U.S. Tactical Nukes in Europe." *Foreign Affairs* July/August (2014).

Bracken, Paul. *The Command and Control of Nuclear Forces*. New Haven:Yale University Press, 1983.

Buys, Andre. "Proliferation Risk Assessment of Former Nuclear Explosives/Weapons Program Personnel: South African Case Study." *NASPNet Special Report*, July 14, 2011, http://www.nautilus.org/publications/essays/napsnet/reports/Buys-research-report-final.pdf.

_____. "Tracking nuclear capable individuals." NAPSNet Special Report, April 19, 2011, http://nautilus.wpengine.netdna-cdn.com/wp-content/uploads/2011/12/Tracking_Nuclear_Individuals_Buys.pdf.

Cavazos, Roger. "Mind the Gap Between Rhetoric and Reality." *NAPSNet Special Reports*, June 26, 2012.

Cheon, Seongwhun. "The Limited Nuclear Weapon Free Zone in Northeast Asia: Is It Feasible?" *The Mongolian Journal of International Affairs* 14 (2007): 115, http://www.mongoliajol.info/index.php/MJIA/article/viewFile/31/31/.

_____, and Tatsujiro Suzuki. "The Tripartite Nuclear-Weapon-Free Zone in Northeast Asia: A Long-term Objective of the Six-Party Talks." *International Journal of Korean Unification Studies* 12:2 (2003).

Cheong, Wooksik. "The Future Development of the Six-Party Talks in order to denucleari-zation of Korean Peninsula and establishment of Peace Regime." (in Korean) Presented at Foreign Affairs and Unification Committee, National Assembly of South Korea, December, 2013.

Cho, G.J. "South Korea's Nuclear Armament for Self-Defense: Secret Story of Israel's Clandestine Nuclear Weapons Development." *Monthly Chosun*, February 2011.

Choi, Seung-eun."Basic content of Japan's basic energy plan (full text)."*World Energy Issue Insight* 13:4, December 2013.

_____. "Gist of Japan's basic energy plan revision (draft)." *World Energy Market Insight* 13:45, December 13, 2014.

Cochran, Thomas B., William M. Arkin, and Milton M. Hoenig. *US Nuclear Forces and Capabilities, Nuclear Weapons Databook*. Ballinger: Cambridge, 1984.

Colby, Elbridge. "Choose Geopolitics Over Nonproliferation." *The National Interest*, February 28, 2014.

Consulate General of the ROK in Fukuoka. October 29, 2014, http://goo.gl/CDLEUF.

Crawford, Timothy W. "The Endurance of Extended Deterrence, Continuity, Change, and Complexity in Theory and Policy." In *Complex Deterrence, Strategy in the Global Age*, edited by T.V. Paul, P. Morgan, and J. Wirtz. University of Chicago Press, 2009.

Cushman, John H. *Organization and Operational Employment of Air/Land Forces*. Pennsylvania: U.S. Army War College, Carlisle Barracks, 1984.

_____. "Military Options in Korea's End Game." *NAPSNet Policy Forum*, May 23, 1994.

Dhanapala,Jayantha. "NWFZS and Extended Nuclear Deterrence: Squaring the Circle?" *NAPSNet Special Report*, May 1, 2012, http://nautilus.org/napsnet/napsnet-special-reports/nwfzs-and-extended-nuclear-deterrence-squaring-the-circle/.

Dutton, Peter. *Scouting, Signaling, and Gatekeeping, Chinese Naval Operations in Japanese Waters and the International Law Implications*. Rhode Island, Naval War College Press, https://www.usnwc.edu/Research---Gaming/China-Maritime-Studies-Institute/Publications/documents/CMS2_Dutton.aspx/.

Editorial. *Chosun Ilbo*, February 13, 2013; February 20, 2013.

Endicott, John E. "Limited nuclear-weapon-free zones: the time has come." *Korean Journal of Defense Analysis* 20:1(2008): 17, doi:10.1080/10163270802006305.

_____, and Alan G. Gorowitz. "Track II Cooperative Regional Security Efforts: Lessons from the Limited Nuclear-Weapon-Free-Zone for Northeast Asia." *Pacific Review* 11:3 (1999).

Enkhsaikhan, J. Statement at the ceremony of signing of the P5 and Mongolian declarations regarding the latter's nuclear-weapon-free status, September 17, 2012.

Foreign Ministry Statement of the DPRK. "DPRK Foreign Ministry Vehemently Refutes UNSC's Presidential Statement." *Korea Central News Agency*, April 14, 2009.

Gregory, Shaun. "The command and control of British tactical nuclear weapons." *Defense Analysis* 4:1 (1988): 39-51. http://dx.doi.org/10.1080/07430178808405328.

Halperin, Morton H. "A Proposal for a Nuclear Weapons-Free Zone in Northeast Asia." *Global Asia* 6:4 (2011).

_____. "The Role of A NE Asia NWFZ In Eliminating Nuclear Weapons From The Korean Peninsular." Paper presented at the East Asia Nuclear Security Workshop, cosponsored by Nautilus Institute, Mansfield Foundation, and Asia-Pacific Leadership Network for Nuclear Non-proliferation and Disarmament, Tokyo, Japan, November 11, 2011.

_____. "A New Approach to Security in Northeast Asia: Breaking the Gridlock." *The Asia Pacific Journal* 10:34 (2012).

_____. "A comprehensive agreement for security in Northeast Asia." *NAPSNet Policy Forum*, March 16, 2015.

Hamel-Green, Michael. "Implementing a Korea–Japan Nuclear-Weapon-Free Zone: Precedents, Legal Forms, Governance, Scope, Domain, Verification, Compliance and Regional Benefits." *Pacific Focus* 26:1 (2011): 97-8, doi:10.1111/j.1976-5118.2011.01057.x.

_____. "Regions That Say No: Precedents and Precursors for Denuclearizing Northeast Asia." Paper presented at the East Asia Nuclear Security Workshop, Tokyo, Japan, November 11, 2011, http://goo.gl/zmvuj4/.

Hayes, Peter. *Pacific Powderkeg, American Nuclear Dilemmas in Korea.* Lexington Press, 1990.

_____, and and Scott Bruce. "North Korean Nuclear Nationalism and the Threat of Nuclear War in Korea." *Pacific Focus* 26:1 (2011): 65–89, doi:10.1111/j.1976-5118.2011.01056.x.

_____, and Jeffrey Lewis. "The DPRK and the Warsaw Clause: An Unnoticed Change in US Nuclear Policy." *NAPSNet Policy Forum*, July 28, 2011, http://nautilus.org/napsnet/napsnet-policy-forum/the-dprk-and-the-warsaw-clause-an-unnoticed-change-in-us-nuclear-policy/.

_____, and Richard Tanter. "Key Elements of Northeast Asia Nuclear-Weapons Free Zone (NEA-NWFZ)." September 26, 2012, http://goo.gl/fMcKEe.

_____, and Richard Tanter."Key Elements of Northeast Asia Nuclear-Weapons Free Zone (NEA-NWFZ)." *NAPSNet Policy Forum*, November 13, 2012, http://nautilus.org/napsnet/napsnet-policy-forum/key-elements-of-northeast-asia-nuclear-weapons-free-zone-nea-nwfz.

_____, Richard Tanter, and Joan Diamond. "General Assessment of the DPRK Nuclear Situation." Paper presented at A Comprehensive Approach to a NEA-NWFZ, Nagasaki, Japan, December 7, 2012.

_____. "A Breakthrough Six-Party Summit in 2013? Why Not?" *Global Asia* 7:4 (2012).

_____, Richard Tanter and Joan Diamond."General Assessment of the DPRK Nuclear Situation." December 7, 2012, http://goo.gl/2HUHMB.

_____, and Roger Cavazos. "North Korean and US Nuclear Threats:Discerning Signals from Noise." *The Asia-Pacific Journal*, 11:14:2, April 8, 2013, http://japanfocus.org/-Roger-Cavazos/3924#/.

_____. ""Mutual Probable Destruction": Nuclear Next-Use in a Nuclear-Armed East Asia?" *NAPSNet Policy Forum*, May 14, 2014.

Hecker, Siegfried S. "Redefining denuclearization in North Korea." *Bulletin of the Atomic Scientists,* December 20, 2010.

Hippel, David von, and Peter Hayes. "Engaging the DPRK Enrichment and Small LWR Program." *Nautilus Institute Special Report*, December 23, 2010.

Hwang, Jihwan. "North Korea's Foreign Policy Strategy in Kim Jong-un Era: The Parrllel Line Continuation and Change." *Korean and World Politics* 84 (2014).

International Atomic Energy Agency (IAEA) Power Reactor Information System (PRIS). "The Database on Nuclear Power Reactors." http://www.iaea.org/PRIS/home.aspx.

International Energy Agency (IEA). "World Energy Outlook 2014." http://www.worldenergyoutlook.org/publications/weo-2014/

Jack, Bryan, Marcella Agmon, Steven L. Head, David McGarvey, Beverly Rown, and Henry S. Rowen. *The South Korean Case: A Nuclear Weapons Program Embedded in an Environment of Great Power Concerns, volume II, Regional Rivalries and Nuclear Responses*, Panheuristics Final Report to US Defense Nuclear Agency, DNA 001-77-C-0052, February 28, 1978.

Kampmark, Binoy, Peter Hayes, and Richard Tanter. "Summary Report: A New Approach to Security in Northeast Asia: Breaking the Gridlock." Paper presented at the Breaking the Gridlock Workshop, Woodrow Wilson International Center for Scholars, Washington, D.C., October 9-10, 2012.

Kaneko, Kumao. "Japan Needs No Umbrella." *Bulletin of Atomic Scientists* March/April, 1996.

Kang, Jungmin. "Denuclearization of North Korea." Paper presented at CSIS-EAI Con-ference on Korean Unification, Washington D.C., December 10, 2014, unpublished.

_____, Peter Hayes, Li Bin, Tatsujiro Suzuki, and Richard Tanter. "South Korea's Nuclear Surprise." *Bulletin of the Atomic Scientists* January-February (2005): 40-9.

Kim, D.J. "S. Korea needs to consider acquiring nuclear weapons." *Chosun Ilbo*, July 10, 2012.

Kim, Jong-seon."China's nuclear safety policy and implication." (in Korean), *STEPI Insight* 96 (2012).

Koch, Susan. *The Presidential Nuclear Initiatives of 1991-1992.* NDU Press: Washington, D.C., October 1, 2012, http://wmdcenter.dodlive.mil/files/2012/10/CSWMD-Case-Study-5-for-web.pdf.

Korea Central News Agency. "Joint communique between DPRK and USA." *KCNA*, October 12, 2000.

_____. "FM Spokesman on Right to Bolster Nuclear Deterrent." *KCNA*, May 26, 2010, http://www.kcna.co.jp/item/2010/201005/news24/20100524-15ee.html.

_____. "U.S. Can Never Evade Blame for Blocking Solution to Nuclear Issue: Rodong Sinmun." *KCNA,* October 21, 2014, http://www.kcna.co.jp/item/2014/201410/news21/20141021-11ee.html.

Korea Energy Economic Insitutue. *World Energy Market Insight* 15:7, February 2015.

Korea Institute of Science and Technology Information. "Global Brief." December 12, 2014, http://mirian.kisti.re.kr/futuremonitor/view.jsp?record_no=254051&cont_cd=GT.

Korea-Japan Foundation's Japan Economic Research. "Japan's basic energy plan [abstract]." 2014.

Kwon, K. J. "Under Threat, South Koreans mull nuclear weapons." *CNN*, March 18, 2013.

Larson, Christina. "Xi Jinping Gives the Nod To China's Expansion of Nuclear Energy." *Bloomberg Businessweek*, June 17, 2014.

Lee, Choon-geun, and Jong-seon Kim. "North Korea's Nuclear and Rocket Technology Development and Outlook." (in Korean) *STEPI Insight* 22 (2009).

"Nuclear Armament: An Interpretation from International Political Perspective." *Bukhan (North Korea)* 417 (2011).

_____. "Resurgent Voices urging South Korean Nuclear Armament, Lee Choon-geun, 'American Nuclear Umbrella Cannot Guarantee South Korea's Security.'" *Newsis*, April 18, 2013.

_____. "Assessing North Korea's Nuclear Weapons Capability." *NAPSNet Special Reports*, May 11, 2015.

Lewis, Paul, Heather Williams, Benoit Pelopidas, and Sasan Aghlani. "Chatham House Report: Too Close for Comfort: Cases of Near Nuclear Use and Options for Policy." April 28, 2014, https://goo.gl/DLKsSn.

Li, Zhidong. "China's nuclear development condition and policy trends." June 2011.

Lieber, Kier A.,and Daryl G. Press. *Coercive Nuclear Campaigns in the 21st Century: Understanding Adversary Incentives and Options for Nuclear Escalation.* PASCC, Naval Postgraduate School, 2013.

Lim, Jong Hyeok. "The Investigation for radioactive mineral in North Korea by Japanese research institutes at Japanese colonial era." KAST Symposium, July 2007.

Mack, Andrew. "A Northeast Asia Nuclear-Free Zone: Problems and Prospects." In *Nuclear Policies in Northeast Asia*, UMDIRI95I16, United Nations, 1995.

Mabhongo, Xolisa. Statement at the First PrepCom for the 2015 Review Conference of NPT, May 3, 2012.

Ministry of Foreign Affairs. "Approval on new project of building Nuclear Power Plan of Chna."March 25, 2015, http://goo.gl/tDRQ3S.

Morgan, Patrick. *Deterrence: a conceptual analysis.* Sage Publications, 1977.

_____. "Deterrence and System Management: The Case of North Korea." *Conflict Management and Peace Science* 23:2 (2006): 121-138.

_____. "Considerations Bearing on a Possible Retraction of The American Nuclear Umbrella Over the ROK." Prepared for Nautilus Institute, June 21, 2009 and published by National Committee on North Korea, Washington D.C., October 2009, http://goo.gl/PW9gcg.

Nautilus Institute. "Korea-Japan Nuclear Weapon Free Zone (KJNWFZ) Concept Paper." May 6, 2010.

Nebehay, Stephanie. "Exclusive: North Korea envoy says door is open on nuclear issues, rights, abductees." *Reuters*, October 2, 2014.

New York Times. "BUSH'S ARMS PLAN; Remarks by President Bush on Reducing U.S. and Soviet Nuclear Weapons." *New York Times*, September 28, 1991.

Nichols, Tom. "The Case for Conventional Deterrence." *The National Interest*, April 20, 2014.

Okonogi, Masao. "Exploring Major Powers' Policy on North Korea under Kim Jong Un's Leadership - A Japanese perspective." Paper presented at the International Conference on the Peace of the Korean Peninsular, Seoul, Korea, March 12, 2012.

Pak, Chi-Young. *The Korean Straits.* Martinis Nijhoff, *1988: 79-81.*

Pak, Kil Yon. Statement at the high level meeting on nuclear disarmament of the 68th UN General Assembly, New York, September 26, 2013.

Park, Chang Kwoun, and Victor A. Utgoff. "On Strengthening Extended Deterrence for the ROK-US Alliance." *Joint Forces Quarterly* 68:1(2013): 84-90.

Park, Yoon-won. "Securing Nuclear Safety in Northeast Asia: ROK Proposal on Northeast Asia Nuclear Safety Mechanism." *NAPSNet Special Reports*, May 04, 2015, http://nautilus.org/napsnet/napsnet-special-reports/securing-nuclear-safety-in-northeast-asia-rok-proposal-on-northeast-asia-nuclear-safety-mechanism.

Roehrig, Terence."The Case for a Nuclear-free South." *JoongAng Daily*, June 19, 2014.

Santaro, David. "Will America's Asian Allies Go Nuclear?" *The National Interest*, January 30, 2014.

Schneider, Mycle, Antony Froggatt, Yurika Ayukawa, Shaun Burnie, Raffaele Piria, Steve Thomas, and Julie Hazeman. "The World Nuclear Industry Status Report 2014." http://www.worldnuclearreport.org/IMG/pdf/201408msc-worldnuclearreport2014-lr-v4.pdf

Schmitt, Eric. "Bush's Arm Plan; Cheney Orders Bombers Off Alert, Starting Sharp Nuclear Pullback."*New York Times*, September 29, 1991, http://goo.gl/rIRxaN.

Ser, Myo-ja. "U.S. arms control chief backs nuke redeployment,Says placing tactical atomic arms in South would be symbolic gesture." *Korea Joongang Daily*, March 1, 2011.

Suh, Ho-won. *The Great Leader Kim Il-sung Comrade's Science Technology Guidance.* National Science Institute, 2002.

Suh, Jaejung. "Wither the Korean Peninsula? – The U.S., Korea and Northeast Asia at a Critical Juncture." Paper presented at The Fourth Busan International Symposium, November 20, 2008.

The Brookings Institution."50 facts about nuclear weapons today."April 28, 2014.

Tsakhia, Elbegdorj. Statement at the High-level Meeting of The United Nations General Assembly on Nuclear Disarmament, September 26, 2013.

Umebayashi, Hiromichi. "A Northeast Asia NWFZ: A Realistic and Attainable Goal." Paper presented at the INESAP Conference, Gothenburg, Sweden, May 30-June 2, 1996.

_____. "A Northeast Asia NWFZ: A Realistic and Attainable Goal An Asia-Pacific Approach to the Nuclear Weapon Free Word." *INESAP Bulletin*10 August, 1996, http://www.inesap.org/sites/default/files/inesap_old/bulletin10/bul10art03.htm.

_____. *Nuclear Weapon Free Zone – A Pathway to the World Without Nuclear Weapons (Hi-kakuheikichitai – Kakunaki Sekai eno Michisuji.)* Iwanami-Shoten, 2011.

_____. "A Northeast Asia Nuclear-Weapon-Free Zone with a Three Plus Three Arrangement." Paper presented at the East Asia Nuclear Security Workshop, Tokyo, Japan, November 11, 2011, http://goo.gl/XOVkMF.

_____. "A Northeast Asia Nuclear Weapon Free Zone with a three-plus- three Arrangement." March 13, 2012, http://goo.gl/zv2xzS.

United Nations. 2010 Review Conference of the Parties to the Treaty on the Non-Proliferation of Nuclear Weapons Final Document Volume 1 Part 1, NPT/CONF.2010/50 (Vol. I).

United Nations Disarmament Commission. "Establishment of nuclear-weapon-free zones on the basis of arrangements freely arrived at among the States of the region concerned." Report of the Disarmament Commission, Annex I, General Assembly Official Records, Fifty-fourth session Supplement No.42 (A/54/42), 1999.

United Nations General Assembly. "Comprehensive Study Of The Question Of Nuclear-Weapon-Free Zones In All Its Aspects, Special report of the Conference of the Committee on Diarment (A/100027/Add.1)." October 8, 1975, http://www.un.org/disarmament/HomePage/ODAPublications/DisarmamentStudySeries/PDF/A-10027-Add1.pdf.

_____. "Work of the Advisory Board on Disarmament Matters – Report of the Secretary General (A/68/206)." July 26, 2013.

_____. "Report of the Open-ended Working Group to develop proposals to take forward multilateral nuclear disarmament negotiations for the achievement and maintenance of a world without nuclear weapons (A/68/514)." October 9, 2013.

United Nations NPT PrepCom. "Transparency of nuclear weapons: the Non-Proliferation and Disarmament Initiative (NPT/CONF.2015/PC.I/WP.12)." April 20, 2012.

United Nations Secretary General Department for Disarmament Affaris. "Chapter 4. Doctrines and Strategies Concerning Nuclear Weapons." In *Nuclear Weapons: A Comprehensive Study*, 41-56. New York, United Nations, 1991.

United Nations Security Council Resolution 2087. 2013; S/RES/2087. 2013.

US Pacific Command.Command History, 1991, Office of the Historian Volume 1, released under US FOIA to Nautilus institute.

Vignard, Kerstin, and Michael Hamel-Green, Noel Stott, Jan Prawitz, Nabil Fahmy, and Patricia Lewis, and Chen Kane. *Disarmament Forum* 2: *Nuclear Weapons Free Zones.* Geneva:UNDIR, 2011, http://www.unidir.org/files/publications/pdfs/nuclear-weapon-free-zones-en-314.pdf/

Wong, John On-Fat Wong. "Security Requirements In Northeast Asia." PhD diss., University of Wisconsin, 1982.

. "Security Requirements in Northeast Asia." *NAPSNet Special Reports*, May 13, 2014.

World Nuclear Association. "World Nuclear Power Reactors & Uranium Requirements." http://www.world-nuclear.org/info/Facts-and-Figures/World-Nuclear-Power-Reactors-and-Uranium-Requirements/.

Yoo, Ho-yeol. "Northeast Asia under New Leaderships: Foreign and North Korean Policy of the Park Geun-hye Government." Presented at the 72nd Monthy Discussion at Hankuk Seonjinhwa Forum, February 28, 2013.

. "Is It Right Time to Propose a Dialogue with North Korea?" *JTBC*, April 18, 2013.

Yu, Hee-gon. *The Kyunghyang Shinmun*, October 13, 2014.

Yu, Keun-young. "The bright and dark side of China Nuclear Power Plant."January 29, 2015, http://goo.gl/SERbbs.

INDEX